War Powers

WAR POWERS

The President, the Congress, and the Question of War

Donald L. Westerfield

Foreword by Donald H. Rumsfeld

Westport, Connecticut
London

Library of Congress Cataloging-in-Publication Data

Westerfield, Donald L.
    War powers : the president, the Congress, and the question of war
/ Donald L. Westerfield ; foreword by Donald H. Rumsfeld.
        p.   cm.
    Includes bibliographical references and index.
    ISBN 0–275–94701–7 (alk. paper)
    1. War and emergency powers—United States.   2. Executive power—
United States.   3. Separation of powers—United States.   I. Title.
    KF5060.W457   1996
    342.73'062—dc20
    [347.30262]   95–43774

British Library Cataloguing in Publication Data is available.

Library of Congress Catalog Card Number: 95–43774
ISBN: 0–275–94701–7

First published in 1996

Praeger Publishers, 88 Post Road West, Westport, CT 06881
An imprint of Greenwood Publishing Group, Inc.

Printed in the United States of America

The paper used in this book complies with the
Permanent Paper Standard issued by the National
Information Standards Organization (Z39.48–1984).

10 9 8 7 6 5 4 3 2 1

With affection, to
Mary
and to
Ronald and Douglas
and
Susan, Ashley, and Errin

As I made clear to congressional leaders at the outset, my request for congressional support did not, and my signing this resolution does not, constitute any change in the longstanding positions of the executive branch on either the President's constitutional authority to use the Armed Forces to defend vital U.S. interests or the constitutionality of the War Powers Resolution.

President George Bush, The White House
January 14, 1991, in "Statement on Signing the
Resolution Authorizing the Use of Military Force
Against Iraq"

Contents

	Exhibits	xiii
	Foreword *by Donald H. Rumsfeld*	xv
	Preface	xvii
Chapter 1	Introduction	1
	Vietnam: Unrepresentative Period	1
	Vietnam Buildup: Gulf of Tonkin	2
	War Powers Resolution: A Protest Vote	3
	Vietnam Syndrome	4
	War Powers in New Context	5
Part I	**Constitutional Authority for War Powers**	11
Chapter 2	The War Powers Conflict	13
	National Commitments Resolution	13
	Executive Branch	15
	Single Executive with "Executive Power"	16
	Taft's View of President's War Powers	17
	First Constitutional Convention	18
	Legislative Branch	19
	Constitution: Article I, Section 8 War Powers	20
	Cuban Missile Crisis	21

	Chief Justice of Supreme Court View	22
	Undeclared War	23
	President Thomas Jefferson's View	23
	Judicial Branch	25

Chapter 3   Aggregate Powers of the Presidency — 31
    Aggregation through Roles of the President — 32
    Manager of Economic Welfare and Growth — 35
    Emergency Executive Power — 36
    Aggregation Argument — 38

Part II   **Powers through Treaties and Other Agreements** — 43

Chapter 4   Treaties and Executive Agreements — 45
    Constitutional Authority — 45
    Advice and Consent: Executive View — 47
    Executive Agreements — 49
    Executive Agreements as Quasitreaties — 52

Chapter 5   United Nations Obligations — 63
    Dumbarton Oaks Proposals — 63
    United Nations Treaty Obligations on Member Nations — 64
    United Nations Chapter VII Action — 66
    Authority to Call Armed Forces — 68

Part III   **Congress and War Powers** — 77

Chapter 6   The War Powers Resolution — 79
    SEATO and the Gulf of Tonkin — 80
    Constitutional Impediments of Section 5(b) — 90
    Concurrent Resolution in Section 5(c) — 91

Chapter 7   Prior Consultation and Reporting — 101
    Consultation with Congress — 102
    Consultation on the *Mayaguez* Incident — 105
    Congress Requests State Department Answers — 106

Part IV   **Executive War Powers**   117

Chapter 8   Desert Shield, the President, the United Nations   119

Desert Shield   120

Response to the Invasion of Kuwait   121

President Bush Declares National Emergency   121

Troops Deployed to Saudi Arabia   125

Shipping to Iraq Blockaded   128

Civilians Used as "Human Shields"   130

Bush Signs Accord with Gorbachev at Helsinki   132

United Nations Orders "All Necessary Means"   136

Congressional and United Nations Resolutions   137

Congressional and Presidential Consultation   141

Chapter 9   Use of "All Necessary Means"   147

United Nations Security Council Resolution
678   148

President Requests Congressional Support   151

Declaration of War or Assistance   154

Authorization for Use of Military Force   155

Operation Desert Storm   159

Desert Storm: Presidential Consultation   161

Part V   **Necessity of Declaration of War and War Powers
Resolution**   165

Chapter 10 The Question of War   167

Concept of Declaration of War   168

Somalia and Bosnia-Herzegovina   169

War Power or Political Power   171

Repealing the War Powers Resolution   174

Appendix A U.S. Presidents and Their Terms of Office   181

Appendix B United Nations Security Council Resolutions
Issued for Desert Shield and Desert Storm   183

Appendix C Two Hundred and Eight Instances of
           United States "Use of Force" Abroad without
           a Declaration of War, 1798–1989   197
Appendix D Five Declared Wars between 1787 and 1993   207
Appendix E Excerpts from the United Nations Charter   209
           Bibliography   215
           Index   237

Exhibits

Exhibit 4.1 Constitutional Authority for Treaties and Executive Agreements   46

Exhibit 4.2 Selected Executive Agreements—Nontreaty Commitments   50

Exhibit 4.3 Gulf of Tonkin Resolution—S.J. Res. 189   53

Exhibit 6.1 Letter from President Lyndon Johnson to Congress—August 5, 1964   80

Exhibit 6.2 Gulf of Tonkin Resolution—S.J. Res. 189   82

Exhibit 6.3 The War Powers Resolution—P.L. 93–148   85

Exhibit 8.1 United Nations Security Council Resolution 660   122

Exhibit 8.2 President Bush Declares National Emergency   123

Exhibit 8.3 United Nations Security Council Resolution 662 (Excerpts)   126

Exhibit 8.4 United Nations Security Council Resolution 664 (Excerpts)   129

Exhibit 8.5 President Bush's Letter Mobilizing U.S. Reserves   130

Exhibit 8.6 United Nations Security Council Resolution 665 (Excerpts)   131

Exhibit 8.7 United Nations Security Council Resolution 666 (Excerpts)   134

Exhibit 8.8   United Nations Security Council Resolution 667
                 (Excerpts)   135

Exhibit 8.9   United Nations Security Council Resolution 670
                 (Excerpts)   136

Exhibit 8.10   Senate Concurrent Resolution 147—October 2,
                 1990   138

Exhibit 9.1   Letter from President Bush to Congress—Troop
                 Deployment   147

Exhibit 9.2   United Nations Security Council Resolution 678   149

Exhibit 9.3   Letter from President Bush to Congressional
                 Leaders   152

Exhibit 9.4   H.J. Res. 77—Authorization for Use of Military
                 Force against Iraq   156

Exhibit 9.5   President Bush's Statement on Signing H.J. Res. 77   158

Exhibit 9.6   Letter from President Bush to Congress Regarding
                 H.J. Res. 77   160

Exhibit 9.7   Press Secretary's Statement on Kuwaiti Liberation   160

Foreword

Donald H. Rumsfeld

The war powers controversy is as old as our Constitution and as recent as the most recent use of U.S. armed forces in a conflict abroad. The division of power between the legislative and the executive branches of our government was not perfectly spelled out in the Constitution. Wisely, perhaps, our Founding Fathers left it up to Congress and the executive to work out any differences between the "spirit and the letter of the law."

This work by Dr. Donald Westerfield has provided a balanced and scholarly perspective on the war powers controversy. His presentation and analysis of debates among the Founding Fathers, congressional and United Nations resolutions, communications between the executive and Congress, and issues surrounding the use of military force in foreign conflicts are both interesting and insightful. Scholars, historians, and students of law and the Constitution will benefit from this work.

My own experience in the U.S. Congress and service with three presidents in a variety of posts, including NATO, the White House, and the Department of Defense, allowed me to observe, in the most intimate manner, how the president, his staff, and cabinet officers consult with Congress on the use of armed forces in foreign conflict situations. These experiences have led me to appreciate how Congress feels a need for closer communication with the president *before* troops and military resources are deployed in a foreign conflict. Equally, I appreciate how and why the president feels that, as chief executive and as commander in chief of the armed forces, he must act quickly and decisively to protect U.S. national interests.

Dr. Westerfield rightly points out that the War Powers Resolution grew out of a perception by Congress that the powers delegated to President

Lyndon Johnson through the Gulf of Tonkin Resolution had given authority without defining responsibility. National and congressional frustration with the Vietnam conflict found a focal point—a resolution that would curb the powers of the president to use U.S. armed forces in foreign conflicts.

Ironically, even though the War Powers Resolution was passed over President Richard Nixon's veto, members of Congress were divided over the question of whether the War Powers Resolution was an encroachment on the prerogatives of the president as commander in chief and as chief executive. This book analyzes the major issues surrounding this long-standing controversy and provides a sharp focus to the forces underlying the congressional and executive perspectives.

Having been personally involved in hearings before Congress and in communications with members of Congress regarding the war powers controversy, I recognize that there are merits to the constitutional and legal concerns on both sides of the issue. With regard to war making, the roles of Congress and the president are intertwined in such a manner that a clear division of power and responsibility is virtually impossible.

The lessons of Vietnam have made indelible impressions in the minds of those who had any part in the Vietnam experience. Almost a quarter of a century has passed since the passage of the War Powers Resolution. During that period, the president has responded to resolutions calling for armed forces assistance by NATO and the United Nations in situations such as the Desert Shield/Desert Storm operation and a number of other operations. In each of those situations, members of Congress have raised the question of whether the particular situation should trigger the War Powers Resolution.

The pattern and nature of U.S. armed forces intervention in foreign conflicts have clearly changed since Vietnam. This book suggests that perhaps the usefulness of and the need for the War Powers Resolution have changed also. I agree. For myself, I urge repeal of the War Powers Resolution. However, regardless of one's conviction on this matter, Dr. Westerfield's study provides useful insights.

NOTE

The Honorable Donald H. Rumsfeld served four terms in Congress, was counselor to President Richard Nixon, was U.S. ambassador to NATO, was White House chief of staff to President Gerald Ford, and was the thirteenth secretary of defense. He was awarded the Presidential Medal of Freedom in 1977.

Preface

The U.S. Constitution is remarkable in so many ways. Scholars have studied it for over 200 years and will continue to do so, finding new meanings with each study. While the Founding Fathers provided enough of a foundation to guide the nation in a general direction, they left many of the powers and responsibilities of the Congress and the executive inextricably intermingled. These overlapping areas still confound constitutional and legal scholars.

Even before the drafting of our Constitution was completed, recurring questions on the scope of power of Congress versus the president as chief executive and commander in chief were the basis for seemingly endless debate. Documents in this book indicate that this debate continues with the same emotion and intensity as in those early days of the drafting of our Constitution. My own interest of many years in the Constitution and in the questions underlying this issue became almost overwhelming while I was conducting research for my second book, *Congressional Intent*, which I coauthored with the late Congressman Thomas Curtis. At that time Congress was concerned about whether the president should seek its approval before sending U.S. armed forces to help Kuwait against a possible attack by Iraq.

For the next few months, almost on a daily basis, members of Congress, the news media, and members of the president's staff and cabinet were embroiled in the issues associated with the powers of the president as commander in chief and whether or not any action taken by the president would be covered by the War Powers Resolution. It was obvious from the discussions in the news media by the "experts" from Congress and from the White House that there were serious disagreements among them regarding the subtle nuances of the constitutional foundation for these issues. Almost without exception, they could not explain (1) the War Powers Resolution itself, (2) the force of the United Nations resolutions, or (3) the scope of constitutional and legal issues surrounding use of U.S. military force in nations with which we have mutual defense treaties or executive agreements. This book attempts to accomplish what they did not and to place the war powers controversy in the proper constitutional, political, and military context.

Many committee members and committee staff from the U.S. Senate and the U.S. House of Representatives have provided material and comments for this book. The Senate Armed Services Committee and the House of Representatives Foreign Affairs Committee and Ways and Means Committee provided invaluable committee reports and transcripts of hearings relating to the War Powers Resolution and current military operations. The U.S. Department of State also kindly provided material relating to United Nations resolutions. For their personal comments and/or material, I would like to thank the following:

Senator Robert Dole (R-Kans.)

Senator (now Vice President) Albert Gore (D-Tenn.)

Speaker of the House Newt Gingrich (R-Ga.)

Senator Strom Thurmond (R-S.C.)

Senator Sam Nunn (D-Ga.)

Representative Dante Fascell (D-Fla.)

Representative David Funderburk (R-N.C.)

Representative Richard Gephardt (D-Mo.)

Representative Henry Hyde (R-Ill.)

Senator Edward Kennedy (D-Mass.)

Senator John McCain (R-Ariz.)

Throughout this project, the Honorable Senator Thomas Eagleton, one of the architects of the original version of the War Powers Resolution, spent time with me and gave me personal advice and encouragement. I sincerely thank him. The Honorable Donald Rumsfeld, author of the Foreword, was kind enough to meet with me several times to discuss some of the topics in this book. I am sincerely grateful for his counsel and encouragement.

A number of scholars have offered valuable comments or material that have been included in this book. To them I am truly grateful. I should also mention that Dr. James Brasfield has carefully followed the progress of the book and has offered many suggestions for revision and addition. I am especially grateful for his concern and friendship.

James Dunton, publisher at Praeger Publishers, has helped me in every phase of the publication of my previous three books and this one. He has my warmest expression of gratitude. I am also grateful to Desirée Bermani, Production Editor, and to Bayard Van Hecke, Copyeditor, for their respective contributions to the production of this book.

War Powers

Chapter 1

Introduction

Resolved, That the Committee initiate an inquiry into the division of constitutional authority between the Congress and the President respecting military operations amounting to an exercise of the power of the United States to make war.[1]

This resolution was adopted by the Committee on Foreign Relations of the U.S. Senate on May 11, 1970, and reflects the major thrust of this book; that is, this book is concerned with an in-depth inquiry into the division of constitutional authority between Congress and the president and the impact on congressional and presidential action when the United States is called upon for armed forces assistance through treaties, mutual defense agreements, executive agreements, and the like.

VIETNAM: UNREPRESENTATIVE PERIOD

Recent works have discussed the war powers issue primarily in the context of the Vietnam conflict and issues surrounding that period through the drafting of the War Powers Resolution.[2] That period, however, was an anomaly by any standard of history. No previous war or foreign conflict had been so universally rejected by both the civilians and military as the Vietnam conflict. There also had never been such a flagrant disregard for the constitutional division of powers and such a misuse of executive power as the extension of the war into Laos and the bombing in Cambodia.[3]

The Korean conflict was a different matter with regard to the war powers controversy. Beginning, during, and after the Korean conflict, the public, the Congress, and the military, with few exceptions, supported President Truman's actions to defend South Korea, especially in the light of the authorizations by the United Nations Security Council.[4] The purpose was clear, people generally believed that military intervention was necessary, and there was a general feeling of pride to serve in the military. Even the draft was not seriously opposed, although some dissatisfaction regarding the strategy of the war was beginning to be evident among some leading politicians.

Whether the strong anti-Communist sentiment played an overwhelming emotional role in mustering support for the action or whether pride in the military coming out of World War II still dominated our public conscience, the Korean conflict and its aftermath were in sharp contrast to the Vietnam conflict. An era of public skepticism and of an extremely aggressive, adversarial press was emerging with the increasing tempo of activity in Southeast Asia.

VIETNAM BUILDUP: GULF OF TONKIN

President Harry Truman and President Dwight Eisenhower played peripheral roles in providing military advisors and moral support to South Vietnam.[5] As the number of American military advisors began to build up under President John Kennedy, however, conflict intensified both in Southeast Asia, on American campuses, and among military enlisted men and officers. After President Kennedy's assassination and just prior to the August 2, 1964, Gulf of Tonkin episode (under the new Lyndon Johnson administration) there were about 16,000 troops working in South Vietnam as military advisors.[6]

The Gulf of Tonkin episode is described in the U.S. House of Representatives Committee on Foreign Affairs document as follows:[7]

On August 2, 1964, the U.S. Department of Defense reported that three North Vietnamese PT boats had fired at the U.S. destroyer *Maddox* while it was on a routine patrol 30 miles off North Vietnam. Three days later it announced that another engagement had been fought between the Maddox, the destroyer *C. Turner Joy* and North Vietnamese vessels, again in international waters. Both attacks had occurred in the Gulf of Tonkin.

After the second attack, President Johnson asked for and received the support of Congress in the Vietnam conflict. The congressional approval was expressed in what is generally referred to as the Gulf of Tonkin Resolution and more formally as "A Joint Resolution to Promote the Maintenance of International Peace and Security in Southeast Asia."[8] On August 7, 1964, the U.S. House of Representatives approved the resolution with a vote of 416 to 0. On the same day, the U.S. Senate approved the resolution with a vote of 88 to 2. President Johnson signed the resolution on August 10, 1964.

This would be the last time that a president would be given the full support to "take all necessary steps, including the use of armed force" without an effective expiration date or time constraint. Even though Senator Richard Russell added Section 3 to the resolution to include a constraint on the president by concurrent resolution of the Congress, the language was so broadly interpreted that it would haunt Congress throughout the Vietnam campaign.[9] Section 3 stated,[10]

This resolution shall expire when the President shall determine that the peace and security of the area is reasonably assured by international conditions created by action of the United Nations or otherwise, except that it may be terminated earlier by concurrent resolution of the Congress.

It seemed to Congress at the time that it would be a simple matter to pass a concurrent resolution, which incidentally does not require a presidential signature and is not subject to a veto, to end the conflict. They would find that granting authority is much easier than taking it back! Almost from the time that President Johnson was granted this blanket approval to use armed force, Congress began to have second thoughts about it.[11]

WAR POWERS RESOLUTION: A PROTEST VOTE

It took an almost ten-year struggle with President Johnson and subsequently President Richard Nixon before a hostile Congress passed the War Powers Resolution—the vote was 75 to 20 in the Senate and 283 to 123 in the House of Representatives.[12] President Richard Nixon vetoed the War Powers Resolution on October 24, 1973, but his veto was overridden by the House of Representatives on November 7, 1973, by a vote of 284 to 135.[13] Later, on that same day, the Senate voted to override the presidential veto with a vote of 78 to 18.[14]

There were many reasons why the Vietnam era was so unrepresentative of any period of American history, before or since: (1) it was a war in which television was on the forward edge of the battle area; (2) it was a war directed almost entirely by politicians in Washington, D.C., instead of by the commanders in the field—even President Johnson would spend hours in the Situation Room identifying targets for bombing raids; (3) it was a war in which daily televised "body counts" and public briefings brought almost every detail of the war into our living rooms; (4) finally, it was a war in which the drug culture, the protest culture, a national suspicion of the motives of those directing the war from Washington, an inability to distinguish between the Vietnamese enemies and allies, and a White House caught up on a torrent of controversy converged to produce a national mood of distrust, anger, and anxiety.[15]

VIETNAM SYNDROME

The Vietnam experience permanently traumatized the world and left a psychological scar that is visible every time a president goes before the American people to brief them on planned or current foreign intervention with American troops. Vietnam has also produced a permanent collective skepticism associated with almost any armed intervention in foreign affairs. The common mantra is "We don't want to get into another Vietnam," or "We don't want this to turn into another Vietnam."

A good example of the caution in the minds of political and military leaders caused by the Vietnam experience is given by Bob Woodward when he recounts the briefing of President George Bush by the then secretary of defense, Dick Cheney, regarding General Norman Schwarzkopf's deployment of troops in the Iraqi invasion of Kuwait:[16]

By now Cheney had come to realize what an impact the Vietnam War had had on Bush. The President had internalized the lessons—send enough force to do the job and don't tie the hands of the Commanders.

That era and that experience stand out apart from the rest of history as a sociological, psychological, and political mutant. Any debate regarding the war powers of Congress versus the president placed in that setting cannot appropriately account for what we have learned since that era. It will be evident as one examines the evidence in this book that the War Powers Resolution, though renounced as unnecessary and unconstitutional by all presidents from Richard Nixon through Bill Clinton, has been, to a significant degree, effective in forcing Congress and the president to accommodate each other when it is necessary to use American armed forces in foreign conflict.

Even though all presidents have objected to the War Powers Resolution (P.L. 93–148) as unconstitutional and an encroachment upon the authority and responsibilities of the president as commander in chief of the armed forces of America, they have nevertheless been almost meticulous in complying with the reporting requirements of Section 4 of that resolution. In that respect, the post-Vietnam era under the War Powers Resolution has been significantly different from all history before it. That difference is the major focus of this book.

In the following chapters, we consider the impact on the war powers controversy of the ways in which time has changed the nature of warfare from largely conventional warfare to electronic warfare and from major movement of ground forces to swift air strikes and troop deployment and air mobility. The major tactics, effective response times, logistics of troop deployment, and political-military coalitions have radically changed since Vietnam. Lessons learned from that era have been indelibly etched in the minds of the public, Congress, the executive, and the military. The role of the United Nations Security Council and the makeup of its members have changed significantly also since both Vietnam and the dismantling of the Berlin Wall.

WAR POWERS IN NEW CONTEXT

Examination of the war powers of the president and Congress in the times of overall world peace, but with sporadic regional conflicts, is especially relevant. Most scholars believe that these conditions will continue for the foreseeable future and that they will also provide a new context in which to study the struggle between Congress and the executive over limits and constraints of "war-making and war-conducting" powers.

This book places the Vietnam experience in context and concentrates on what one might call the "invisible handshake" between the Congress and the executive to "agree to disagree" regarding the role that the War Powers Resolution plays during actual and contemplated deployment of troops on foreign soil. Whether the troops are introduced[17]

(1) into hostilities or into situations where imminent involvement in hostilities is clearly indicated by the circumstances;

(2) into the territory, airspace or waters of a foreign nation, while equipped for combat, except for deployments which relate solely to supply, replacement, repair, or training of such forces;

(3) in numbers which substantially enlarge United States Armed Forces equipped for combat already in a foreign nation

has been viewed by all commanders in chief as more within the prerogatives of the executive than of Congress, that is, more a strictly military call rather than a political call. Where the line is crossed so that the president feels morally, if not constitutionally, obligated to notify Congress, as called for in Section 4 of the War Powers Resolution, is where we find the conflict between Congress and the executive.

The evidence in this book will prove that there is considerably more consultation between Congress and the executive than most of the literature admits. For this reason, Chapters 8 and 9 give step-by-step accounts of the communications among the executive, the Congress, and the United Nations Security Council. By presenting (verbatim, as often as possible) communications between the executive and members of Congress, Security Council resolutions, and related testimony before congressional committees, the book enables scholars from all disciplines, strategists, and those individuals interested in the issues underlying the war powers controversy to decide for themselves the effectiveness of the War Powers Resolution and whether there is a need for amending it to place additional constraints on the president as commander in chief.

Chapters 2 and 3 of Part I present the constitutional basis for the powers and authority of the executive, legislative, and judicial branches of the government, but with special attention to the aggregate powers of the presidency. By examining the attitudes and arguments of the early founders and leaders, both the letter of the law and the spirit of the law are placed in a constitutional context. Both the scholar and the general reader will be struck by the passion for individual and collective freedom and the insights that the early drafters of the Constitution crafted into the ultimate document. They will also be fascinated to observe the manner in which, almost from the inauguration of the first president, the chief executive acquired extraordinary enumerated, accumulated, and delegated war and foreign affairs power.

Part II presents an interesting mixture of passages from treaties, executive agreements, and United Nations documents. Special attention is given to the development of the sections of the United Nations Charter that are directly related to the use of force by member nations and to sanctions against violators of the provisions of the United Nations Charter. Presentation of these documents and issues is of paramount importance in light of the fact that, for the last two decades, the pattern of U.S. armed forces intervention into foreign conflict has typically been preceded by United Nations resolutions calling for assistance in solving regional conflicts. Chapter VII of the United Nations Charter is particularly applicable to the intervention by the United States in the Iraqi-Kuwaiti conflict.

In Part III we turn our attention to the authority of both the president and Congress in both treaties and the Constitution to determine whether the president should be more constrained and consultative in his relationship with Congress. What are the impediments of the sixty-day reporting period set out in Section 5(b) of the War Powers Resolution? Section 5(c) of the War Powers Resolution states; [18]

at any time that United States Armed Forces are engaged in hostilities outside the territory of the United States, its possessions and territories without a declaration of war or specific statutory authorization, such forces shall be removed by the President if the Congress so directs by concurrent resolution.

Is the president bound by the concurrent resolution mentioned above? This issue is analyzed in Chapter 6.

The most unique part of the book, Part IV, goes into rather meticulous detail in revealing the communications among the executive, the Congress, and the United Nations in the Iraqi-Kuwaiti conflict. The style of this part is deliberate. It seemed that the only way to objectively reveal the level and nature of consultation between the Congress and the president was to show verbatim messages between them while concurrently interweaving the United Nations resolutions which were bases for the Desert Shield and Desert Storm "use of force" responses by President George Bush to the Iraqi invasion and its aftermath. Finally, Part V examines the issues of declared and undeclared war as they are related to the War Powers Resolution.

NOTES

1. Jacob Javits before the U.S. Senate. Committee on Foreign Relations, *Documents Relating to the War Power of Congress, the President's Authority as Commander-in-Chief and the War in Indochina,* 91st Cong., 2nd Sess. (Washington, D.C.: U.S. Government Printing Office, 1970), p. III. Hereafter in this chapter, this document will be referred to as *Documents Relating to the War Power.*

2. Larry Berman, *Lyndon Johnson's War: The Road to Stalemate in Vietnam* (New York: Norton, 1989); Gregory Palmer, *The McNamara Strategy and the Vietnam War* (Westport, Conn.: Greenwood Press, 1978); Larry Cable, *Conflict of Myths: The Development of American Counterinsurgency Doctrine and the Vietnam War* (New York: New York University Press, 1986); William Westmoreland, "Vietnam in Perspective," *Military Review* 59 (January 1979): 34–43; Bruce Palmer, Jr., *The 25-Year War: America's Role in Vietnam* (Lexington: University of Kentucky Press, 1984); John Ely, *On Taking Up Arms and Taking Responsibility: Constitutional Lessons of Vietnam and its Aftermath* (Princeton, N.J.: Princeton University Press, 1993); Barry Blechman, *The Politics of National Defense: Congress and U.S. Defense Policy from Vietnam to the Persian Gulf* (Oxford: Oxford University Press, 1990); Richard M. Nixon, "Veto of War Powers Bill," *Congressional Quarterly Almanac, 1973* 29 (1974): 90–A–91–A; Francis Wormouth, *The Vietnam War: The President versus the Constitution* (Santa Barbara, Calif.: Center for the Study of Democratic Institutions, 1968).

3. Mark Clodfelter, *The Limits of Airpower: The American Bombing of North Vietnam* (New York: Free Press, 1989); see also Harry Summers, Jr., *On Strategy: A Critical Analysis of the Vietnam War* (Novato, Calif.: Presidio Press, 1982), and

Dave Palmer, *Summons of the Trumpet: U.S.-Vietnam in Perspective* (San Rafael, Calif.: Presidio Press, 1978); Larry Cable, *Conflict of Myths: The Development of American Counterinsurgency Doctrine and the Vietnam War* (New York: New York University Press, 1986).

4. Compare Robert Donovan, *Tumultuous Years: The Presidency of Harry S. Truman* (New York: Norton, 1982); Glen Paige, *The Korean Decision, June 24–30, 1950* (New York: Free Press, 1968); Burton Kaufman, *The Korean War: Challenges in Crisis, Credibility, and Command* (New York: Knopf, 1986); Joseph Dawson, *Commanders in Chief: Presidential Leadership in Modern Wars* (Lawrence: University Press of Kansas, 1993); Harry S. Truman, *Years of Trial and Hope, 1946–1952* (New York: New American Library, 1956); Margaret Truman, *Harry S. Truman* (New York: William Morrow, 1973).

5. Edgar Robinson et al., *Powers of the President in Foreign Affairs* (San Francisco: Commonwealth Club, 1966); Ernest May, ed., *The Ultimate Decision: The President as Commander in Chief* (New York: George Braziller, 1960); Richard Neustadt, *Presidential Power: The Politics of Leadership from FDR to Carter*, rev. ed. (New York: John Wiley, 1980); Dwight D. Eisenhower, *Mandate for Change, 1953–56* (New York: New American Library, 1963); Dwight D. Eisenhower, *Waging Peace* (Garden City, N.Y.: Doubleday, 1965); Harry S. Truman, *Years of Trial and Hope, 1946–1952* (New York: New American Library, 1956).

6. *New York Times*, July 28, 1964, p. 1; Frank Vandiver, "Lyndon Johnson: A Reluctant Hawk," in Joseph Dawson, *Commanders in Chief: Presidential Leadership in Modern Wars* (Lawrence: University Press of Kansas, 1993): 127–143; John Ely, *On Taking Up Arms and Taking Responsibility: Constitutional Lessons of Vietnam and Its Aftermath* (Princeton, N.J.: Princeton University Press, 1993), p. 13; William D. Rogers, "The Constitutionality of the Cambodian Incursion," *American Journal of International Law* 65 (January 1971): 26–37; Arthur Schlesinger, Jr., *A Thousand Days: John F. Kennedy in the White House* (Boston: Houghton Mifflin, 1965).

7. U.S. House of Representatives Committee on Foreign Affairs, *The War Powers Resolution: A Special Study of the Committee on Foreign Affairs* (Committee Print) (Washington, D.C.: U.S. Government Printing Office, 1989).

8. A text of the Gulf of Tonkin Resolution may be found in ibid., pp. 2–3; U.S. Senate Foreign Relations Committee, "Hearings on the Southeast Asia Collective Defense Treaty," 83rd Cong., 2nd Sess., November 11 (Washington, D.C.: U.S. Government Printing Office, 1954); U.S. Senate Foreign Relations Committee, "Hearings on U.S. Commitments to Foreign Powers," 90th Cong., 1st Sess., August 16–September 19 (Washington, D.C.: U.S. Government Printing Office, 1967).

9. President Lyndon Johnson would, in an August 18, 1967, press conference defiantly hold that his administration never did believe that the resolution was necessary to authorize his activities in Indochina. See "Weekly Compilation of Presidential Documents," August 21, 1967. This argument was a precursor to the

same position held by subsequent presidents regarding the War Powers Resolution. See also Robert Scigliano, "The War Powers Resolution and the War Powers," in Joseph Bessette, and Jeffery Tullis, eds., *The Presidency in the Constitutional Order* (Baton Rouge: Louisiana State University Press, 1981); Francis Wormuth, *The Vietnam War: The President versus the Constitution* (Santa Barbara, Calif.: Center for the Study of Democratic Institutions, 1968); Frances Wormuth, and Edwin Firmage, *To Chain the Dog of War: The War Power of Congress in History and Law*, 2nd ed. (Urbana: University of Illinois Press, 1989).

10. U.S. House of Representatives, *The War Powers Resolution: A Special Study of the Committee on Foreign Affairs* (Washington, D.C.: U.S. Government Printing Office, 1989), pp. 2–3.

11. Ibid., pp. 7–10; See also U.S. Senate, *Documents Relating to the War Powers of Congress: The President's Authority as Commander-in-Chief and the War in Indochina*, Committee on Foreign Relations, 91st Cong., 2nd Sess. (Washington, D.C.: U.S. Government Printing Office, 1970); Robert Turner, *The War Powers Resolution: Its Implementation in Theory and Practice* (Philadelphia: Philadelphia Foreign Policy Research Institute, 1983); Robert Turner, "The War Powers Resolution: Unconstitutional, Unnecessary and Unhelpful," *Loyola of Los Angeles Law Review* 17 (1984): 683; U.S. House of Representatives, *Congress, the President, and the War Powers Hearings before the House Subcommittee on National Security Policy and Scientific Developments of the Committee on Foreign Affairs*, 91st Cong., 2nd Sess. (Washington, D.C.: U.S. Government Printing Office, 1970); U.S. House of Representatives, *Committee on Foreign Affairs War Powers Legislation: Hearings*, 93rd Cong., 1st Sess., March 7–8, 13–15, 20 (Washington, D.C.: U.S. Government Printing Office, 1973); U.S. Senate Foreign Relations Committee, "National Commitments," *Senate Report No. 797*, 90th Cong., 1st Sess., November 20 (Washington, D.C.: U.S. Government Printing Office, 1967); U.S. Senate, *War Powers*, S. Rept. 93–220, 93rd Cong., 1 Sess. (Washington, D.C.: U.S. Government Printing Office, 1973).

12. U.S. House of Representatives, *The War Powers Resolution: A Special Study of the Committee on Foreign Affairs* (Washington, D.C.: U.S. Government Printing Office, 1989), pp. 153–154.

13. Ibid., p. 163.

14. Ibid., p. 165.

15. Richard M. Nixon, *The Memoirs of Richard Nixon* (New York: Grosset & Dunlap, 1978); Richard M. Nixon, *Six Crises* (New York: Pyramid Books, 1968); Henry Kissinger, *White House Years* (Boston: Little, Brown, 1979); Henry Kissinger, *Years of Upheaval* (Boston: Little, Brown, 1982); U. S. G. Sharp, *Strategy for Defeat: Vietnam in Retrospect* (Novato, Calif.: Presidio Press, 1978); Peter Braestrup, *Big Story: How the American Press and Television Reported and Interpreted the Crisis of Tet 1968*, 2 vols. (Boulder, Colo.: Westview, 1977); "Congress, the President, and the Power to Commit Forces to Combat," note, *Harvard Law Review* 81 (June 1968): 1771–1805; Thomas Eagleton, "Congress and War Powers," *Missouri Law Review* 37 (Winter 1972): 1–32; Thomas Eagle-

ton, "The August 15 Compromise and the War Powers of Congress," *St. Louis University Law Journal* 18 (Fall 1973): 1–11; Thomas Eagleton, *War and Presidential Power: A Chronicle of Congressional Surrender* (New York: Liveright, 1974); Thomas Eagleton, "Whose Power Is War Power?" *Foreign Policy* 8 (Fall 1972): 23–32.

16. Bob Woodward, *The Commanders* (New York: Simon & Schuster, 1991), pp. 306–307.

17. Public Law 93–148, 93rd Cong., H.J. Res. 542, Sec. 4.(a)(1)–4.(a)(3), November 7, 1973, "Joint Resolution Concerning the War Powers of Congress and the President," in U.S. House of Representatives, *The War Powers Resolution: A Special Study of the Committee on Foreign Affairs* (Washington, D.C.: U.S. Government Printing Office, 1989), pp. 278–292; Thomas Franck, and Faiza Patel, "UN Police Action in Lieu of War: 'The Old Order Changeth,'" *American Journal of International Law* 81:1 (January 1991): 63–74; Michael Glennon, "The Constitution and Chapter VII of the United Nations Charter," *American Journal of International Law* 85:1 (January 1991): 74–88; Michael Glennon, "The Gulf War and the Constitution," *Foreign Affairs* (Spring 1991): 84–101; Michael Kinsley, "The War Powers War," *The New Republic* (December 31, 1990): 4; Michael Kinsley, "War and Powers," *The New Republic* (November 8, 1993): 6; Richard Lacayo, "A Reluctant Go-Ahead: As Hopes for Peace Fade, a Divided Congress Authorizes the President to Lead the United States into Battle," *Time* (January 21, 1991): 32–33; Richard Lacayo, "On the Fence: The President Says He Can Take America to War without Asking Congress. The Lawmakers Disagree—But Most Would Rather Not Take a Public Stand At All," *Time* (January 14, 1991): 12–14.

18. U.S. House of Representatives, *The War Powers Resolution: A Special Study of the Committee on Foreign Affairs*, Section 5(c) (Washington, D.C.: U.S. Government Printing Office, 1989).

PART I

Constitutional Authority for War Powers

Chapter 2

The War Powers Conflict

In this chapter the focus is on the specific clauses in the Constitution and resolutions by the U.S. House of Representatives and the U.S. Senate that provide the foundation for, and some constraints on, the powers of Congress, the powers of the president, and those shared between them. Enough of the original sources are quoted verbatim so that it is possible to establish the true context of subsequent constitutional arguments and debates and the manner in which the divergent views of the original drafters of the Constitution are woven together to establish the concurrent and autonomous powers of both the Congress and the executive with regard to war and the deployment of armed forces into a foreign conflict.

After more than 200 years—since September 17, 1787—the war powers of the president and Congress, as provided or implied by the U.S. Constitution, have not been settled. Curiously enough, some quarter of a century after the passage of the War Powers Resolution, the question of the limits of the war powers of Congress and the president increasingly confront the president, the Congress, and those foreign powers who look to the United States for military assistance during their own national and international crises.[1]

NATIONAL COMMITMENTS RESOLUTION

In Senate Resolution 85, 91st Congress, 2nd Session, the U.S. Senate sought to further clarify the obligation of Congress to commit armed forces to help foreign powers by the following "sense of the Senate" resolution, commonly referred to as the National Commitments Resolution:[2]

THE NATIONAL COMMITMENTS RESOLUTION

Whereas accurate definition of the term "national commitment" in recent years has become obscured: Now, therefore, be it

Resolved, That (1) a national commitment for the purpose of this resolution means the use of the Armed Forces of the United States on foreign territory, or a promise to assist a foreign country, government, or people by the use of the Armed Forces or financial resources of the United States, either immediately or upon the happening of certain events, and (2) it is the sense of the Senate that a national commitment by the United States results only from affirmative action taken by the executive and legislative branches of the United States Government by means of a treaty, statute, or concurrent resolution of both Houses of Congress specifically providing for such commitment.

It is interesting to note that, in the National Commitments Resolution, the executive's powers as commander in chief are not mentioned, nor is any of the president's authority under the "take care" clause mentioned. The resolution does seek to explicitly circumscribe the executive war power to be limited to joint action by Congress and the executive in

1. Treaties
2. Statutes
3. Concurrent resolution of both houses of Congress

This is but one illustration of the interminable struggle between the executive and the Congress to delineate responsibility in foreign affairs. The phrases of the second clause of the resolution just cited providing the basis for the conflict are the phrases beginning "results only from" and "by means of," implying that only concurrent action by the executive and legislative branches define a national commitment. This restrictive language was immediately repudiated by Nicholas Katzenbach, then undersecretary of state, as the first witness before the Committee on Foreign Relations of the U.S. Senate, which was holding hearings on the war power of Congress and the president in the war in Indochina.[3] He concluded, near the end of the formal statement in his testimony, as follows:[4]

As I have said, the Constitution relies not on express delineation to set the powers of the Executive and the Congress in this field, but depends instead on the practical interaction between the two branches. Today, these considerations require that the President fill the preeminent role:

He alone has the support of the administrative machinery required to deal with the sheer volume of our foreign affairs problems.

He alone is the focus of diplomatic communications, intelligence sources and other information that are the tools for the conduct of foreign affairs.

He alone can act, when necessary, with speed and decisiveness required to protect our national security.

These two opposing views, the one stated in the National Commitments Resolution and the other just stated above by Nicholas Katzenbach, are specific examples of the tug-of-war conflict between the executive and the Congress regarding the war powers. The foundation of this conflict is challenged by asking, (1) What are the limits of executive authority regarding involvement in foreign armed conflict when Congress remains relatively silent regarding executive action taken or planned? (2) What are the limits of authority of the executive and of Congress when they disagree regarding involvement in foreign armed conflict? (3) "How does the allocation of authority between the executive and Congress change when an international institution such as the United Nations or NATO, or a foreign head of state, requests military assistance in an armed conflict? (4) Can legislation alter the allocation of war powers, expressed or implied by the Constitution, between the executive and Congress?

In order to begin to analyze the thrusts and nuances of these questions and the opposing views regarding the use of force in discharging a real or perceived national commitment, it is necessary to turn to the U.S. Constitution and see what is formally stated regarding the authority of the executive, the legislative, and the judicial branches of our government.

EXECUTIVE BRANCH

As we examine the language of the Constitution, it should be obvious that there are vagaries of the language regarding prerogatives, competing grants of authority to the executive and Congress, and outright omissions. Even the debates surrounding the drafting of the Constitution were clouded with conflicts, gaps in the process of recording the opposing arguments, and a perspective that was colored by the culture and events surrounding the 1787 era.[5]

The powers and authority of the president of the United States, relating to foreign affairs and war, are presented in Article II of the U.S. Constitution as follows:[6]

Article. II. Section. 1. The executive Power shall be vested in a President of the United States of America. . . .

Section. 2. The President shall be Commander in Chief of the Army and Navy of the United States, and of the Militia of the several States, when called into the actual Service of the United States; . . . He shall have Power, by and with the Advice and Consent of the Senate, to make Treaties, provided two thirds of the Senators present concur; and he shall nominate, by and with the Advice and Consent of the Senate, shall appoint Ambassadors, other public Ministers and Consuls, . . .

Section. 3. . . . he shall receive Ambassadors and other public Ministers; he shall take Care that the Laws be faithfully executed, . . .

There is an additional measure of responsibility inherent in the oath of office that is required of the president before he takes over the presidency. That oath, presented below, is found in the U.S. Constitution:[7]

Before he enter on the Execution of his Office, he shall take the following Oath or Affirmation:—"I do solemnly swear (or affirm) that I will faithfully execute the Office of President of the United States, and will to the best of my Ability, preserve, protect and defend the Constitution of the United States."

One must conclude from the language of Article II, Sections 1 and 2, of the Constitution that some of the executive powers are autonomous with respect to Congress and some are shared with Congress.

SINGLE EXECUTIVE WITH "EXECUTIVE POWER"

There is no question, however, that the intent of the framers of the Constitution was to have one executive with executive powers concentrated in that single entity, the presidency. The language which served as a model for that in the U.S. Constitution was found in the various state constitutions. Professor Edward Corwin contrasts two views of the scope of executive powers in the Virginia and Pennsylvania constitutions. Corwin states,[8]

In the Virginia constitution of 1776 it was stipulated, as out of abundant caution, that "the executive powers of government" were to be exercised "according to the laws" of the commonwealth, and that no power or prerogative was ever to be claimed "by virtue of any law, statute, or custom of England." "Executive power," in short, was left to legislative definition and was cut off entirely from the resources of the common law and of English constitutional usage.

. . . In the famous report of the Pennsylvania Council of Censors of 1784 the Pennsylvania constitution of 1776 is interpreted as entrusting all power not otherwise specifically provided for either to "the legislative or the executive according to its nature"; and, as is pointed out by Hamilton in The Federalist, the New York constitution of 1777 suggested not a few of the outstanding features of the presidency. The New York governor was not a creature of the legislature but was directly elective by the people; his term was three years and he was indefinitely re-electable; except in the matter of appointments and vetoes he was untroubled by a council; he bore the designation of "Commander-in-Chief," possessed the pardoning power, and was charged with the duty of "taking care that the laws are faithfully executed to the best of his ability."

We can see that many of these duties and responsibilities of the New York governor were carried over directly into Article II, Section 1, of the U.S. Constitution. Corwin also points out that the designation "president" appeared in several of the state constitutions in the same period of approximately 1776 through 1784.

The Article II, Section 2 and Section 3, powers of the president which are not shared with the Congress are (1) to be commander in chief of the army and navy; (2) to be commander in chief of the state militia, when called into the service of the United States; (3) to receive ambassadors and other public ministers and consuls; and (4) to take care that the laws be faithfully executed (Section 3).

The Article II, Section 2, powers shared with the Congress are (1) to make treaties and (2) to appoint ambassadors and other public ministers and consuls.

It is interesting to note that these powers do not include any power to either "declare" war or to "make" war. Is either of these powers implied by the nature or substance of powers specifically outlined above? This is the kernel of the conflict between the legislative branch and the executive branch over the so-called war powers.

TAFT'S VIEW OF PRESIDENT'S WAR POWERS

William Howard Taft, twenty-seventh president of the United States, gives us his personal insight into a president's perception of his war powers under the "commander in chief" clause, when he argues as follows:[9]

Under the Constitution, only Congress has the power to declare war, but with the army and the navy, the President can take action such as to involve the country in war and to leave Congress no option but to declare it or to recognize its existence. This was the charge made against President Polk in beginning the Mexican War. War as a legal fact, it was decided by the Supreme Court in the Prize Cases, can exist by invasion of this country by a foreign enemy or by such an insurrection as occurred during the Civil War, without any declaration of war by Congress at all, and it is only in the case of a war of our aggression against a foreign country that the power of Congress must be affirmatively asserted to establish its legal existence.

President Taft's perception of the war powers of the president would conflict with that of a majority of constitutional scholars, especially his notion that "it is only in the case of a war of our aggression against a foreign country that the power of Congress must be affirmatively asserted." This perception does not preclude "use of force" action by the president as commander in chief in response to a treaty obligation such as that which may arise from the United Nations, NATO, or SEATO. In such cases,

1. The action almost always involves safety or welfare of U.S. personnel or property or a compelling national interest through treaty or international agreements.
2. The action usually does not have a clearly defined beginning.
3. The United States has typically been a part of a multinational coalition.
4. The level of public debate and the amount and type of information passed between the executive and Congress tacitly amount to "consultation with Congress."
5. Through congressional authorization and allocation of funding, that very process is viewed as a form of tacit approval for such action.

FIRST CONSTITUTIONAL CONVENTION

The ability of the commander in chief to respond quickly and with flexibility to attacks against the nation or its vital interests was a consideration of the first Constitutional Convention when, after the first full draft of the Constitution, as a report by the Committee of Detail on August 6, 1787, the question of whether to let the national legislature "make war" was debated. On Friday, August 17, 1787, James Madison's notes recorded the following debate among Mr. Charles Pinkney, Mr. Pierce Butler, Mr. James Madison, Mr. Roger Sherman, Mr. Elbridge Gerry, Mr. Oliver Elseworth, and Mr. George Mason:[10]

"To make war"

Mr. PINKNEY opposed the vesting power in the Legislature. Its proceedings were too slow. It wd meet but once a year. The Hs of Reps would be too numerous for such deliberations. The Senate would be the best depositary, being more acquainted with foreign affairs, and most capable of proper resolutions. If the States are equally represented in Senate, so as to give no advantage to large States, the power will notwithstanding be safe, as the small have their all at stake in such cases as well as the large States. It would be singular for one authority to make war, and another peace.

Mr. BUTLER. The objections agst the Legislature lie in great degree agst the Senate. He was for vesting the power in the President, who will have all the requisite qualities, and will not make war but when the Nation will support it.

Mr. MADISON and Mr. Gerry moved to insert "declare," striking out "make" war; leaving to the Executive the power to repel sudden attacks.

Mr. SHARMAN thought it stood very well. The Executive shd be able to repel and not to commence war. "Make" better than "declare" the latter narrowing the power too much.

Mr. GERRY never expected to hear in a republic a motion to empower the Executive alone to declare war.

Mr. ELSWORTH. there is a material difference between the cases of making war and making peace. It shd be more easy to get out of war, than into it. War also is a simple and overt declaration. peace attended with intricate & secret negociations.

Mr. MASON was agst giving the power of war to the Executive, because not safely to be trusted with it; or to the Senate, because not so constructed as to be entitled to it. He was for clogging rather than facilitating war; but for facilitating peace. He preferred "declare" to "make."

On the motion to insert declare—in place of make, it was agreed to.

Going back to these original notes by James Madison, one clearly sees that there was a distinction in the minds of the framers of the Constitution between the power/authority to "make war" and the power/authority to "declare war." The original draft of the Constitution as presented to the Constitutional Convention by Mr. John Rutledge on Monday, August 6, 1787, listed the power "to make war" as Article VII, Section 1, Clause 13 of the report to the Committee of Detail.[11] The same phrase was listed as a power of Congress in Article I, Section 8, Clause 11, of the Wednesday, September 12, 1787, version:[12] "To declare war, grant letters of marque and reprisal, and make rules concerning captures on land and water."

The original August 6, 1787, draft of the Constitution enumerated the executive powers in Article X, Sections 1 and 2. There is an overlapping in the powers of the executive and legislative branches, but the methods of discharging their respecive responsibilities differs. The Constitution did, however, make most of the authority and responsibilities of the executive explicitly delineated.

LEGISLATIVE BRANCH

It has already been established that the conflict over the allocation of war powers in the Constitution between the executive and Congress is often more real than apparent. An excerpt from the report of the Foreign Relations

Committee on Senate Resolution 85, April 16, 1969, emphasizes the radical difference between the perception of war powers as viewed from the eyes of a past president—William Howard Taft, cited above—and by the Senate Foreign Relations Committee. Under the section entitled "The Intent of the Framers," we find the following argument:[13]

It should be remembered as well that the Congress was not expected to be in session for more than 1 month a year and that it was thought that it would be dangerous to leave the country defenseless during the long adjournment. Were the matter being considered now, in our age of long congressional sessions, rapid transportation, and instantaneous communication, *one may wonder whether it would be thought necessary to concede the Executive any authority at all in this field* [emphasis added]. In any case it was authority to repel sudden attacks—that and nothing more—that the framers conceded to the President.

The testimony just cited is also in sharp contrast to the view of executive power as pronounced by President Roosevelt in his "Notes for a Possible Autobiography," discussed by President Taft in his book. Taft quotes Roosevelt as having said,[14]

I declined to adopt this view that what was imperatively necessary for the Nation could not be done by the President, unless he could find some specific authorization to do it. My belief was that it was not only his right but his duty to do anything that the needs of the Nation demanded unless such action was forbidden by the Constitution or by the laws.

CONSTITUTION: ARTICLE I, SECTION 8 WAR POWERS

Having indicated what the executive may have as a perception of its war powers, let us now examine the wording of congressional war powers as listed in the Constitution in Article I, Section 8, Clauses 11, 12, 13, 14, and 18:[15]

Section. 8. The Congress shall have Power . . .

To *declare War*, grant Letters of Marque and Reprisal, and make Rules concerning Captures on Land and Water; [Emphasis added]

To raise and support Armies, but no Appropriation of Money to that Use shall be for a longer Term than two Years;

To provide and maintain a Navy;

To make Rules for the Government and Regulation of the land and naval Forces;

To make all Laws which shall be necessary and proper for carrying into Execution the foregoing Powers and all other Powers vested by this Constitution in the Government of the United States, or in any Department or Officer thereof.

The authority of Congress to "declare war" is held to be a quite narrow authority.[16] A literal reading of congressional authority would bring Congress into the question of war in only those cases for which it is necessary or where there is a compelling national interest to "declare" war—strictly a formal and symbolic power. What about the action leading up to a formal declaration of war? What about armed conflict where there never has been or will be a formal declaration of war? Should the commander in chief of the United States wait for a declaration of war before assisting other governments when obligated to provide security by treaty?

CUBAN MISSILE CRISIS

The Cuban missile crisis in 1962 was the result of intelligence information indicating that the Soviet Union was accumulating missiles capable of striking targets in the United States. There had been no armed conflict between the United States and Cuba. Cuba, however, was a puppet government of the Soviet Union. There was no "sudden attack" to repel, only the threat that Cuba would now have a striking capability. Should President John Kennedy have taken any action at all? The Report gives an account of the interaction between the Congress and the Kennedy administration:[17]

In September 1962 Congress adopted a joint resolution pertaining to Cuba. The Kennedy administration favored a concurrent resolution expressing the sense of Congress that the President "possesses all necessary authority" to prevent Cuba, "by whatever means may be necessary, including the use of arms," from "exporting aggressive purposes" in the hemisphere, to prevent the establishment of a foreign, i.e., Soviet, military base in Cuba, and to support Cuban aspirations for self-determination. Senator Russell opposed the concurrent resolution favored by the administration. "I do not believe," he said, "that the Armed Services Committee is going to make a constitutional assertion that the President of the United States has the right to declare war, and that is what this does." The Cuban missile crisis occurred 1 month later.

President Kennedy did provide a military blockade against the missiles on board the ships inbound to Cuba. On October 22, 1962, Kennedy met with congressional leaders to discuss with them his plans and decision for the Cuban missile blockade. Some two hours later, President Kennedy appeared on national television to announce the "quarantine" on shipments of offensive Soviet missiles.[18] In light of the view of Congress regarding the president's war power, would it have been possible for Congress to make a decision regarding the intelligence reports quickly enough and with enough unanimity to prevent the missiles from reaching Cuba?

According to the second clause of the National Commitments Resolution, cited earlier in this chapter, President Kennedy did not have the proper authority to commit our armed forces to the threat of the Cuban missiles. The argument that "a national commitment by the United States results only from affirmative action taken by the executive and legislative branches of the United States Government by means of a treaty, statute, or concurrent resolution of both Houses of Congress specifically providing for such commitment" would have precluded the swift action to blockade the missiles from Cuba. There was actually no "attack" on the United States to "repel."

CHIEF JUSTICE OF SUPREME COURT VIEW

The extent of prerequisite congressional approval required of the executive where national interest is concerned is discussed in a paper initially delivered by William H. Rehnquist before the Society of International Law, June 16, 1970, and entered into the record of the U.S. Senate Committee on Foreign Relations. Rehnquist, who now is the chief justice of the U.S. Supreme Court, argues as follows:[19]

I think there are at least three propositions that may be deduced from the Nation's nine score years of operation under this constitutional mandate. The first is that the notion that the United States may lawfully engage in armed hostilities with a foreign power only if Congress has formally declared war is wrong. Our constitutional history is directly to the contrary. It has been recognized from the earliest days of the Republic by the President, by the Congress, and by the Supreme Court that the United States may lawfully engage in armed hostilities without any formal declaration by Congress. Our history is replete with instances of "undeclared wars," from the war with France in 1798 through 1800, to the Vietnamese War. The Fifth Congress passed a law contained in the first book of the Statutes at Large, authorizing President Adams to "instruct the commanders of the public armed vessels which are, or which shall be employed in the service of the United States, to subdue, seize and take any armed French vessel, which shall be found within the jurisdictional limits of the United States, or elsewhere, on the high seas." The Supreme Court in a case arising out of this undeclared war, recognized the difference between what is called "solemn war," which required a declaration by Congress, and "imperfect" war, which did not, in The Eliza, 4 Dall. 37.

The Chief Justice of the Supreme Court does not mince words in indicating that the president does have power to conduct "use of force" operations without a formal "declaration of war" by Congress. The implication that the president can "make war" but cannot "declare war" would seem to reduce the war powers of Congress to those few situations for which Congress felt the need to formally declare war.

UNDECLARED WAR

Abraham Sofaer draws an altogether different conclusion from the motion by Madison and Gerry in the 1787 Constitutional Convention, discussed above, to grant to Congress the power to "declare war." Notice from the argument given below that he believes the Congress should have not only the power to "declare war" but also, presumably, the power over the conduct of a war. He suggests that[20]

they therefore appear to have intended the clause to authorize the President to defend the United States from attack without consulting the legislature, at least where the attack is so "sudden" that consultation might jeopardize the nation. But nothing in the change signifies an intent to allow the President a general authority to "make" war in the absence of a declaration; indeed, granting the exceptional power suggests that the general power over war was left in the legislative branch.

Sofaer's case seems, on its face, to be much weaker than that of Chief Justice William Rehnquist, especially in the light of the historical background, both in the "undeclared wars" that Rehnquist cited, and in the court cases cited by Rehnquist.

PRESIDENT THOMAS JEFFERSON'S VIEW

Another encounter with the "undeclared war" question is illustrated in the events surrounding the blockade of Tripoli in 1802 and the Moroccan emperor's permission to let the Tripolitan ambassador take wheat from Morocco to Tripoli. American naval commanders refused to grant passports to the emperor's vessels, and the emperor of Morocco ordered the American consul, James Simpson, from Morocco. Upon learning of Simpson's being ordered from Morocco, President Thomas Jefferson asked his secretary of the treasury, Albert Gallatin, for advice regarding the disposition of frigates in the Mediterranean. In response to this request, on August 16, 1802, Gallatin advised Jefferson as follows:[21]

The executive cannot declare war, but if war is made, whether declared by Congress or by the enemy, the conduct must be the same, to protect our vessels, and to fight, take, and destroy the armed vessels of that enemy. The only case which admits of doubt is whether, in case of such war actually existing, we should confine our hostilities to their armed vessels or extend them by capture or blockage to the trade.

The subsequent details of the Moroccan conflict proved to be a turning point in the scope of war powers as President Jefferson began to assume, with little challenge, more of the war powers. Jefferson also demonstrated the principle that "knowledge is power" in his deliberate evasion and his concealment from Congress of information that would have allowed Congress leverage in delimiting executive war powers. Jefferson's tactic was to cast a conflict in terms of an "emergency" so that the Congress was placed in an "after the fact" posture in the national crises.[22]

Norman J. Small, in a doctoral dissertation submitted to Johns Hopkins University in 1930 and twice published—in 1932 by Johns Hopkins University and in 1970 by the Da Capo Press—suggests that Jefferson acquiesced to Congress more than Hamilton in the matter of war powers. Small writes as follows:[23]

The Executive, when obliged to employ the armed forces for the national defense, can point specifically to the Acts of 1795 and 1807 for a definite authorization of his commands. Strictly construed, these acts empower the President to adopt such measures as are necessary to "repel" an invasion or to suppress an insurrection; but a more practical interpretation of their content would seem to permit him to anticipate such dangers and to eradicate them at their source. Authorities may be cited who are of the opinion that this additional power is recognized in dicta contained in the Prize Cases; and, in practice, only one Executive, Jefferson, has considered himself limited, in the absence of a declaration of war, to repelling attacks only as they are made.

Small suggests two things in the passage cited above: (1) that the executive may take "use of force" measures to foreign countries if they are the "source" of an invasion or insurrection, and (2) the Prize Cases contain dicta directly relating to the scope of war powers of the executive. He also cites the argument that the role of Congress was narrowed when the wording was changed from "making" war to "declaring" war. He underscores this point by arguing that "the Executive was to be intrusted, not only with the prosecution of war, but with the adoption of all necessary measures of defense prior to the action of the Legislature."[24]

The Prize Cases just mentioned suggest that the judicial branch has a stake in the conflict between Congress and the executive regarding war powers. Let us see what authority the judiciary has over such matters.

JUDICIAL BRANCH

The judiciary has taken a "backseat" in the matter of war powers. It has been reluctant to tender rulings in favor of either Congress or the president. The separation of powers issues and the feeling by the Supreme Court that the "turf battles" are better viewed when they have "ripened" have caused the Court to be virtually silent, and perhaps appropriately so, in the war powers controversy. The judicial restraint in disputes between the executive and Congress has quite appropriately forced them to work out some method of accommodating each other. This attitude by the Court has helped to avert several potential "constitutional crises."

Article III, Sections 1 and 2, of the U.S. Constitution outline the powers of the judiciary as follows:

Article. III.

Section. 1. The judicial Power of the United States, shall be vested in one supreme Court, and in such inferior Courts as the Congress may from time to time ordain and establish. . . .

Section. 2. The judicial Power shall extend to all Cases, in Law and Equity, arising under this Constitution, the Laws of the United States, and Treaties made, or which shall be made under their Authority;—to all Cases affecting Ambassadors, other public ministries and Consuls;—to all Cases of admiralty and maritime Jurisdiction;—to Controversies to which the United States shall be a Party; . . .

In all Cases affecting Ambassadors, other Public Ministers and Consuls, and those in which a State shall be Party, the supreme Court shall have original Jurisdiction. . . .

It would seem that the Supreme Court would have a full docket of cases relating to the ongoing conflict between Congress and the president regarding their respective war powers. The contrary is the case. The Supreme Court really did not get materially involved in the conflict until the Bey of Tripoli incident, referred to earlier, resulted in *Talbot v. Seeman*, 1 Cr. (5 U.S.), 1,28 (1801) and 2 Stat. 129,130 (1802), regarding whether a state of war already exists when another nation makes war upon the United States, and whether a declaration of war is needed.[25]

The judiciary made a significant and landmark imprint on the debate regarding war powers when it decided the celebrated Prize Cases in 1863.

In U.S. Senate Document No. 92–82 we have an explanation of what might have been referred to in that day as a "constitutional crisis" involving President Abraham Lincoln's blockade of our Southern ports:[26]

Sixty years later the Supreme Court sustained the blockade of the Southern ports instituted by Lincoln in April 1861 at a time when the Congress was not in session. Congress had subsequently ratified Lincoln's action, so that it was unnecessary for the Court to consider the constitutional basis of the President's action in the absence of congressional authorization, but the Court nonetheless approved, five-to-four, the blockade order as an exercise of Presidential power alone, on the ground that a state of war was a fact. "The President was bound to meet it in the shape it presented itself, without waiting for Congress to baptize it with a name; and no name given to it by him or them could change the fact."

The Prize Cases illustrate the willingness of the Court to try to resolve any dispute in such a manner that there is no appearance of a reallocation of powers which may be thought to be vested in either Congress or the president by the Constitution. Having settled the question of whether a state of war could exist without formal declaration by Congress, the Prize Cases represent one of the major excursions of the judiciary into the war powers question.

Typically the Supreme Court has been steadfastly reluctant to enter into issues regarding whether the president is empowered to commit armed forces abroad to protect national interests when there is no evidence of an attack and in the absence of a declaration of war or specific congressional authorization short of a declaration of war. It is true also that lower courts are reluctant to adjudicate questions involving the constitutional authority of Congress versus that of the president on "political question" grounds. We will go into this matter more deeply in Chapter 3.

The following chapter considers the issue of aggregate powers of the executive. This notion that war power is an aggregate of the various powers granted by Article I, Section 8, of the Constitution got its roots from Alexander Hamilton and his writings in *The Federalist*.

NOTES

1. Jacob Javits before the U.S. Senate. Committee on Foreign Relations, *Documents Relating to the War Power of Congress, the President's Authority as Commander-in-Chief and the War in Indochina*, 91st Cong., 2nd Sess. (Washington, D.C.: U.S. Government Printing Office, 1970), p. III (hereafter in this chapter, this document will be referred to as *Documents Relating to the War Power)*; Charles Lefgren, "War-Making under the Constitution: The Original Under-

standing," *Yale Law Journal* 81 (March 1972): 672–702; Pat Holt, *The War Powers Resolution: The Role of Congress in U.S. Armed Intervention* (Washington, D.C.: American Enterprise Institute, 1978); Norman Graebner, "The President as Commander in Chief: A Study in Power," *Journal of Military History* 57:1 (January 1993): 111–132.

2. "The National Commitments Resolution," S. Res. 85, 91st Cong., 1st Sess. This is essentially a restatement of S. Res. 151, the object of debates in U.S. Senate hearings before the Committee on Foreign Relations, 90th Cong., 2nd Sess., 1967. U.S. Senate, *Documents Relating to the War Power*, p. vi.

3. U.S. Senate, *Documents Relating to the War Power*, pp. 1–7; Anthony Austin, *The President's War: The Story of the Tonkin Gulf Resolution and How the Nation Was Trapped in Vietnam* (Philadelphia: J. B. Lippincott, 1971); George Ball. "Top Secret: The Prophecy the President Rejected," *Atlantic Monthly* 230 (July 1972): 35–49; Larry Berman, *Lyndon Johnson's War: The Road to Stalemate in Vietnam* (New York: Norton, 1989).

4. Nicholas Katzenbach before the U.S. Senate Committee on Foreign Relations, *Documents Relating to the War Power*, p. 6. See also the strong statement of Senator Gale McGee before the same committee, pp. 35–40, and especially the following statement (p. 37): "Because Senate Resolution 85 implies that the President and the Congress *together* would be the exclusive means by which the Government of the United States in the future could enter into commitments with a foreign power, it runs counter to constitutional intent [emphasis added]."

5. Gaillard Hunt, ed., *The Writings of James Madison* (New York: Putnam, 1900–1910); Max Farrand, ed., *The Records of the Federal Convention of 1787*, 4 vols. (New Haven, Conn.: Yale University Press, 1937); Paul Ford, *The Works of Thomas Jefferson* (federal edition), 12 vols. (New York: G. P. Putnam's Sons, 1904–1905); Henry Cabot Lodge, *The Works of Alexander Hamilton*, 2nd ed., 12 vols. (New York: G. P. Putnam's Sons, 1903); Catherine Bowen, *Miracle at Philadelphia* (Boston: Little, Brown, 1966); Julian Boyd, ed., *The Papers of Thomas Jefferson*, 17 vols. (Princeton, N.J.: Princeton University Press, 1950–1965); Irving Brant, *James Madison: Father of the Constitution, 1787–1800* (Indianapolis: Bobbs-Merrill, 1950).

6. See Bernard Schwartz, *A Commentary on the Constitution of the United States*, Part 1: *The Powers of Government*, Vol. 2: *Powers of the President* (New York: Macmillan, 1936); Joseph Bessette, and Jeffery Tullis, eds., *The Presidency in the Constitutional Order* (Baton Rouge: Louisiana State University Press, 1981); Edmund Muskie, et al., eds., *The President, Congress, and Foreign Policy* (Lanham, Md.: University Press of America, 1986).

7. The Constitution of the United States of America, Article II, Section 1.

8. Edward Corwin, *The President: Office and Powers 1787–1957* (New York: New York University Press, 1957), pp. 6–7. See also Edmund Burnett, ed., *Letters of Members of the Continental Congress, 1774–1789*, 8 vols. (Washington, D.C.: Carnegie Institution of Washington, 1921–1936); Charles Adams, ed., *The Works of John Adams*, 10 vols. (Boston: Little, Brown, 1850–1856); Catherine

Bowen, *Miracle at Philadelphia* (Boston: Little, Brown, 1966); Jacob Cook, ed., *The Federalist* (Middletown, Conn.: Wesleyan University Press, 1961).

9. William Taft, *The President and His Powers* (New York: Columbia University Press, 1967; originally published in 1916 under the title *Our Chief Magistrate and His Powers*), pp. 94–95; See also Demetrios Caraley, ed., *The President's War Powers: From the Federalists to Reagan* (New York: Academy of Political Science, 1984); Louis Fisher, *The Politics of Shared Power: Congress and the Executive* (Washington, D.C.: Congressional Quarterly Press, 1981); Louis Fisher, *The President and Congress: Power and Policy* (New York: The Free Press, 1972).

10. James Madison, *Notes of Debates in the Federal Convention of 1787 Reported by James Madison* (Athens: Ohio University Press, 1966), pp. 475–476. Reprint of House Document No. 398, *Documents Illustrative of the Formation of the Union of the American States* (Washington, D.C.: Government Printing Office, 1927). The names of Elseworth and Sherman were misspelled in the original notes by James Madison on this date as "Elsworth" and "Sharman." Additionally, the abbreviations used by James Madison are reflected in this quotation. Thomas Jefferson's account of this early foundation issue is addressed in the superb work by Paul Ford, *The Works of Thomas Jefferson* (federal edition), 12 vols. (New York: G. P. Putnam's Sons, 1904–1905).

11. James Madison, *Notes of Debates in the Federal Convention of 1787 Reported by James Madison* (Athens: Ohio University Press, 1966), p. 389.

12. Ibid., p. 620.

13. "Foreign Relations Committee Comments on the National Commitments Resolution" included in U.S. Senate, *Documents Relating to the War Power*, pp. 11–12. Other good analyses of the issue are Louis Fisher, *Constitutional Conflicts between Congress and the President*, 3rd ed. (Lawrence: University Press of Kansas, 1991); Kenneth Holland, "The War Powers Resolution: An Infringement on the President's Constitutional and Prerogative Powers," in Gordon Hoxie, ed., *The Presidency and National Security Policy* (New York: Center for the Study of the Presidency, 1984), pp. 378–400.

14. William Taft, *The President and His Powers* (New York: Columbia University Press, 1967), p. 143.

15. Contrast Gaillard Hunt, ed., *The Writings of James Madison* (New York: Putnam, 1900–1910) and William Hutchison, and William Rachal, eds., *The Papers of James Madison*, 6 vols. (Chicago: University of Chicago Press, 1962–1969) with the following: Harold Syrett, ed., *The Papers of Alexander Hamilton* 15 vols. (New York: Columbia University Press, 1961–1969); Broadus Mitchell, *Alexander Hamilton* (New York: Macmillan, 1962); Norman Small, *Some Presidential Interpretations of the Presidency* (Baltimore: Johns Hopkins Press, 1932).

16. See Henry Cabot Lodge, *The Works of Alexander Hamilton*, 2nd ed., 12 vols. (New York: G. P. Putnam's Sons, 1903); *The Prize Cases*, 67 U.S. (2 Black) 635 (1863); "Congress, the President, and the Power to Commit Forces to Combat," *Notes Harvard Law Review* 81 (June 1968): 1771–1805. See also William

Rehnquist, "Statement by William H. Rehnquist, Assistant Attorney General Office of Legal Counsel, on the President's Constitutional Authority to Order the Attack on the Cambodian Sanctuaries," in U.S. Senate, *Documents Relating to the War Power of Congress, The President's Authority as Commander-in-Chief and the War in Indochina,* 91st Cong., 2nd Sess. (Washington, D.C.: U.S. Government Printing Office, 1970).

17. U.S. Senate, *Documents Relating to the War Power,* p. 21, and "Situation in Cuba," *Hearings before the Senate Foreign Relations and Armed Services Committees,* U.S. Senate, 87th Cong., 2nd Sess., September 1962 (Washington, D.C.: U.S. Government Printing Office, 1962), p. 72; Dan Caldwell, "A Research Note on the Quarantine of Cuba, October 1962," *International Studies Quarterly* XXII (December 1978): 625–633; David Detzer, *The Brink: Cuban Missile Crisis, 1962* (New York: Thomas Y. Crowell, 1979); Elie Abel, *The Cuban Missile Crisis* (Philadelphia: J. B. Lippincott, 1966).

18. It is also interesting to see the description of this episode in Theodore Sorensen, *Kennedy* (New York: Harper & Row, 1965), and Arthur Schlesinger, Jr., *A Thousand Days: John F. Kennedy in the White House* (Boston: Houghton Mifflin, 1965).

19. William Rehnquist, "Statement by William H. Rehnquist, Assistant Attorney General Office of Legal Counsel, on the President's Constitutional Authority to Order the Attack on the Cambodian Sanctuaries," in U.S. Senate, *Documents Relating to the War Power,* pp. 182–185.

20. Abraham Sofaer, *War, Foreign Affairs and Constitutional Power: The Origins* (Cambridge, Mass.: Ballinger Publishing Company, 1976), pp. 31–32. See also Edmund Burnett, ed., *Letters of Members of the Continental Congress, 1774–1789,* 8 vols. (Washington, D.C.: Carnegie Institution of Washington, 1921–1936); Jonathan Elliot, ed., *The Debates in the Several State Conventions, on the Adoption of the Federal Constitution,* 5 vols. (Washington, D.C.: Carnegie Institution of Washington, 1836–1845); Max Farrand, ed., *The Records of the Federal Convention of 1787,* 4 vols. (New Haven, Conn.: Yale University Press, 1937).

21. Abraham Sofaer, *War, Foreign Affairs and Constitutional Power: The Origins* (Cambridge, Mass.: Ballinger Publishing Company 1976), p. 222.

22. Edward Corwin, *The President: Office and Powers 1787–1957* (New York: New York University Press, 1957); Julian Boyd, ed., *The Papers of Thomas Jefferson,* 17 vols. (Princeton, N.J.: Princeton University Press, 1950–1965); Paul Ford, *The Works of Thomas Jefferson* (federal edition), 12 vols. (New York: G. P. Putnam's Sons, 1904–1905); Merlo Pusey, *The Way We Go to War* (Boston: Houghton Mifflin Company, 1969).

23. Norman Small, *Some Presidential Interpretations of the Presidency* (Baltimore: Johns Hopkins Press, 1932), p. 89. For the acts of 1795 and 1807 see 1 Stat. L. 424 and 2 Stat. L. 443. See also Edmund Burnett, ed., *Letters of Members of the Continental Congress, 1774–1789,* 8 vols. (Washington, D.C.: Carnegie Institution of Washington, 1921–1936); Julian Boyd, ed., *The Papers of Thomas Jeffer-*

son, 17 vols. (Princeton, N.J.: Princeton University Press, 1950–1965); Paul Ford, *The Works of Thomas Jefferson* (federal edition), 12 vols. (New York: G. P. Putnam's Sons, 1904–1905); Harold Syrett, ed., *The Papers of Alexander Hamilton*, 15 vols. (New York: Columbia University Press, 1961–1969); Broadus Mitchell, *Alexander Hamilton* (New York: Macmillan, 1962).

24. Ludwell John III, "Abraham Lincoln and the Development of Presidential War-Making Powers: Prize Cases," *Civil War History* (September 1989): 208–224; Norman Small, *Some Presidential Interpretations of the Presidency* (Baltimore: John Hopkins Press, 1932), p. 89; Abraham Sofaer, *War, Foreign Affairs and Constitutional Power: The Origins* (Cambridge, Mass.: Ballinger Publishing Company, 1976); Charles Lofgren, "War-Making under the Constitution: The Original Understanding," *Yale Law Journal* 81 (March 1972): 672–702.

25. U.S. Department of State, Historical Studies Division, *Armed Actions Taken by the United States without a Declaration of War, 1789–1967*, Res. Proj. No. 806A (Washington, D.C.: U.S. Government Printing Office, 1967); Morton Halperin, "Lawful Wars," *Foreign Policy* 72 (Fall 1988): 173–195; Robert Turner, "The War Powers Resolution: Unconstitutional, Unnecessary and Unhelpful," *Loyola of Los Angeles Law Review* 17 (1984): 683. See some of the early arguments in Max Farrand, ed., *The Records of the Federal Convention of 1787*, 4 vols. (New Haven: Yale University Press, 1937), pp. 318–319; Gaillard Hunt, ed., *The Writings of James Madison* (New York: Putnam, 1900–1910); Henry Cabot Lodge, *The Works of Alexander Hamilton*, 2nd ed., 12 vols. (New York: G. P. Putnam's Sons, 1903).

26. U.S. Senate, *The Constitution of the United States of America: Analysis and Interpretations*, 92nd Cong., 2nd Sess., Document No. 92–82 (Washington, D.C.: U.S. Government Printing Office, 1973), p. 327. The statement at the end of the cited passage was presented in the Prize Cases, 2 Bl. (67 U.S.) 635, 669 (1863); Ludwell John III, "Abraham Lindoln and the Development of Presidential War-Making Powers: Prize Cases," *Civil War History* (September 1989): 208–224.

Chapter 3

Aggregate Powers of the Presidency

Thirty-year-old Alexander Hamilton, with thirty-six-year-old James Madison and forty-two-year-old John Jay, penned perhaps the most important work on the Constitution up to this time.[1] In the collection of eighty five-papers, representing what we refer to as *The Federalist*, these three young men eloquently discuss and lay the foundation for the major issues that face and often confound scholars of our own day. Hamilton, Madison, and Jay were imminently qualified to carry on their remarkable exposition of the Constitution in the Federalist Papers. Writing under the pseudonym "Publius," the three men tried to put precept before personality and advocated a republican government based on the representative principle. Their aim was to lay out an architecture of a government with enough centralization to provide coherent and consistent direction but enough autonomy among the various departments to be able to respond to the evolution of the needs of a nonhomogeneous constituency. Their task was enormous in the light of a lack of years of orderly precedent in law and federal governance (as we now enjoy) and the excruciating slowness of mass communication of that day.

Even in their time, these men of vision recognized that the president must rise to many different occasions and shoulder many different types of responsibilities. Although they could not document as extensively as now, with precedent and anecdote, the many facets of the aggregate powers of the president, they provided arguments for an aggregate profile of the president that appealed to reason, even though it was not explicitly outlined in the Constitution.

AGGREGATION THROUGH ROLES OF THE PRESIDENT

Almost immediately after the Constitutional Convention, the office and person of the president began to gain power and prestige through an aggregation of many different roles required by the demands and needs of the people, the Congress, and the necessities of war and diplomacy. Perhaps the roles which have provided the greatest justification to the claim of aggregate powers of the presidency are those listed below. Some are explicitly or implicitly derived from the Constitution of the United States, while others are derived from custom, precedent, and necessity. Those roles are

1. Chief executive
2. Commander in chief
3. Chief diplomat
4. Chief of state
5. Chief legislator
6. Voice of the people
7. Chief of his political party
8. Manager of economic welfare and growth
9. Guardian of peace
10. World leader

To a greater measure than in any of the other roles listed above, the authority and responsibilities of the president in his capacities as commander in chief, chief executive, and chief diplomat overlap and intermingle in national emergencies. In these situations, the president acts on the basis of his "aggregate" powers—expressed, implied, bestowed, and even usurped (in the opinions of some). As commander in chief, he was, in the words of the Supreme Court, vested with "such supreme and undivided command as would be necessary to the prosecution of a successful war."[2] As chief executive, he is obliged to "take care that the laws be faithfully executed."[3] As chief diplomat, he "alone has the power to speak or listen as a representative of the Nation."[4] A complex of roles is suggested by Senate Document No. 92–82, which argues as follows:[5]

"Ambassadors and other public ministers" embraces not only "all possible diplomatic agents which any foreign power may accredit to the United States," but also, as a practical construction of the Constitution, all foreign consular agents, who therefore may not exercise their functions in the United States without an exequatur from the President. The power to "receive" ambassadors, et cetera, includes, moreover, the right to refuse to receive them, to request their recall, to dismiss them, and to determine their eligibility under our laws. Furthermore, this power makes the President the sole mouthpiece of the nation in its dealings with other nations.

As another indication of how the power and authority of Commander in chief and chief diplomat become mixed, during the period between 1882 and 1896 the outlaw or marauding Indians were seeking refuge back and forth between Mexico and the United States. Under his authority as commander in chief, the president, without the advice and consent of the Senate, entered into a series of agreements with Mexico to permit the hot pursuit of the Indians into each other's territory. The Supreme Court in *Tucker v. Alexandroff*, commented as follows:[6]

While no act of Congress authorizes the executive department to permit the introduction of foreign troops, the power to give such permission without legislative assent was probably assumed to exist from the authority of the President as Commander-in-Chief of the military and naval forces of the United States.

We observe that this situation involved the exchange of agreements with a foreign nation without a formal exchange of ratifications necessary for treaties between nations. Which role of the president was predominant? In *Watts v. United States*, such action was thought to be a convention which adheres to every national government where "executive power is vested."[7]

As chief of state, the president performs duties appropriate to offices that range from ceremonial king to goodwill ambassador to city mayor. He ceremonially receives heads of state and visiting dignitaries, lays wreaths on the Tomb of the Unknown Soldier, and speaks at every conceivable type of convention—political, charitable, military, benevolent, industrial, and so on. It is in this role that the president comes into personal and physical contact with the people and becomes the embodiment of pomp and ceremony that the common man or woman envisions as surrounding a "personal" leader.

In his role as chief legislator, the president provides leadership in obtaining legislation that he perceives as "mandated from the people." His State of the Union address to the nation is a vehicle for steering the nation's course through congressional initiatives. He is looked upon as the means of setting goals and limits on constitutional, political, and social welfare activity. He is supposed to be able to both reflect and affect the mood and sense of Congress through his own party and through coalitions with the opposition party in responding to the legislative needs and desires of the nation.

Radio and television have expanded and compounded the role of the president as the voice of the people. No person is able to move the whole nation in such a manner as the president. His leadership in formulating and responding to public opinion and public sentiment is second to none in the nation. Foreign governments and people listen to the president as though he were the collective and unified voice of the our nation—from common laborer to corporate executive, from those with the most meager education to the scholar—his is the voice heard above the sea of voices of the large and small.

The president is both titular and actual head of his political party while he is incumbent. He usually is either one or the other or both during the presidency of the opposition party. The president plays a dominant role in choosing the head of the Republican or Democratic National Committee and is also dominant in the selection of key national committee and party men and women of his political party. When a candidate for Congress or the office of governor is a member of the president's party and desperately needs support, a "photo op" with the president or a member of his cabinet is usually expected by the candidate. It is common belief that at least some part of each day is spent by the president attending to his role as chief of his political party.

The president's roles as guardian of peace and as world leader are interwoven with his roles as chief executive and commander in chief. When Iraq invaded Kuwait in the summer of 1990, President George Bush took the initiative in Operation Desert Shield and Operation Desert Storm to form a coalition of major peace keeping nations to fight the Iraqi invasion. His roles as guardian of peace and as world leader were prominent in the eyes of the rest of the world. In August 1990, he sent U.S. troops to Saudi Arabia and countries which bordered Kuwait and Iraq. His justifications were manifold:

1. Foremost, maintaining the national sovereignty of both Kuwait and Saudi Arabia
2. Maintaining internal security and political stability throughout the Middle East, but especially in Kuwait and Saudi Arabia and neighboring territories
3. Deterrence of the Iraqi invasion and aggression
4. Security and protection of American citizens, property, and interests in Kuwait and Saudi Arabia
5. Preservation of national interests in access to Middle Eastern oil.

President Bush autonomously sent U.S. troops to Saudi Arabia without formal, explicit approval of Congress. Two legal challenges to his deployment of troops to Saudi Arabia sought to have the War Powers Resolution effective—*Ange v. Bush* and *Dellums v. Bush*. These both failed; the former failed because the Court held that it was a political question inappropriate for adjudication by the Court and the latter failed because the Court held that the case was not "ripe" for judicial determination.[8] External to the United States, the Desert Storm operation was an example of the president's role as guardian of the peace and world leader, but internal to the United States, it was a mixture of the roles just mentioned plus that of chief executive and especially that of commander in chief of our armed forces.

MANAGER OF ECONOMIC WELFARE AND GROWTH

The role that the president plays as manager of economic welfare and growth is worthy of special attention. It is an admixture of several roles, but the impact of this particular role in the whole aggregation of presidential power is significant. One of the first truly dramatic illustrations of the president as a major player in determination of economic policy occurred during World War II when President Roosevelt delivered a speech to Congress, September 7, 1942. Roosevelt had been concerned that some of the provisions of the Emergency Price Control Act were impeding economic growth after the Great Depression. In that speech before Congress he sought to have Congress repeal some of the provisions of the Emergency Price Control Act that he felt were contrary to economic growth and full employment. Excerpts of that speech indicate his perceptions of his authority during such a national emergency:

I ask the Congress to take this action by the first of October. Inaction on your part by that date will leave me with an inescapable responsibility to the people of this country to see to it that the war effort is no longer imperiled by threat of economic chaos. In the event that the Congress should fail to act, and act adequately, I shall accept the responsibility, and I will act. At the same time that farm prices are stabilized, wages can and will be stabilized also. This I will do. The President has powers, under the Constitution and under Congressional acts, to take measures necessary to avert a disaster which would interfere with the winning of the war. The American people can be sure that I will use my powers with a full sense of my responsibility to the Constitution and to my country.

It is interesting to note here the references by President Roosevelt to his powers "under the Constitution and under Congressional acts." His was a concept of aggregation of powers whether expressed or implied. This argument must have had an impact on President Truman when Truman had his bout with the steel industry.

During approximately the same time span of the years after the Great Depression and during World War II, businesspeople, scholars, legislators, and public officials were also concerned with full employment and economic growth. John Maynard Keynes's and his macroeconomics theories were being debated as germane to the nation's economic solutions.

By 1946, the Congress was ready to make a national commitment to the concept of full employment (in the economic sense) and a dominant role for the federal government in monetary policy. The Full Employment Act was therefore passed in 1946 and was hailed by most economists as a major or perhaps "the major" piece of social welfare legislation of recent times. Gerhart Colm quotes President Harry Truman as remarking on the Full Employment Act of 1946: "[There was] almost no other piece of domestic legislation enacted while I was President to which I would attach equal significance."[9] Why Truman said this can be inferred from the declaration of policy introducing the clauses implementing the act, which contained the following language:[10]

it is the responsibility of the Federal Government to pursue such consistent and openly arrived at economic policies and programs as will stimulate and encourage the highest feasible levels of employment opportunities through private and other non-Federal investment and expenditure; (e) To the extent that continuing full employment cannot otherwise be achieved, it is the further responsibility of the Federal Government to provide such volume of Federal investment and expenditure as may be needed to assure continuing full employment.

President Truman was acting as chief executive, commander in chief, and manager of economic welfare and growth primarily when he seized control of the steel industry to avert a nationwide strike and prevent loss of steel production during a time of national emergency. The action requiring the secretary of commerce, Charles S. Sawyer, to take possession of the mills in the name of the federal government is judged by many scholars as bizarre, but the arguments used by President Truman to justify his action in the context of a "national emergency" are important to the notion that the roles of the president are often simultaneously justified by the Constitution, custom, and the need for immediate and decisive action. The following section illustrates just this point.

EMERGENCY EXECUTIVE POWER

The arguments of Hamilton, Madison, and Jay before, during, and shortly after the Constitutional Convention become an integral part of any justification for authority based on an array of aggregate "implied powers" under the Constitution. It is remarkable to observe their arguments almost exactly duplicated in arguments before district courts and the Supreme Court of the United States about 180 years later.

Alexander Hamilton versus James Madison is replayed in *Youngstown Sheet & Tube Co. v. Sawyer* and *United States v. Curtiss-Wright Export Corporation.*[11] The treatment by Westin of the Youngstown case is particularly insightful since it presents portions of transcripts of the hearings in the district court, appeals court, and Supreme Court to place the arguments for the executive's "aggregate powers" in context. Specifically, the arguments of Holmes Baldridge, assistant attorney general, and of Charles Sawyer, secretary of commerce, in trying to present the executive powers under the Constitution indicate the manner in which the executive claims and views its powers under Article II of the Constitution.

In federal district court before Judge David Pine, April 24, 1952, Baldridge makes several attempts to explain the executive powers during a national emergency. He responds in various places to Judge Pine's queries as follows:[12]

MR. BALDRIDGE. Well, Your Honor, we base the President's power on Sections 1, 2, and 3 of Article II of the Constitution, and whatever inherent, implied or residual powers may flow therefrom. . . .

THE COURT. If the emergency is great, it is unlimited, is it?

MR. BALDRIDGE. I suppose if you carry it to its logical conclusion, that is true. But I do want to point out there are two limitations on the Executive power. One is the ballot box and the other is impeachment. . . .

THE COURT. Have you read the case of McCullough v. Maryland lately?

MR BALDRIDGE. I have, Your Honor. Section 1, Article II, of the Constitution reposes all of the executive power in the Chief Executive. I think that the distinction that the Constitution itself makes between the powers of the Executive and the powers of the legislative branch of Government are significant and important. In so far as the Executive is concerned, all executive power is vested in the President. In so far as legislative powers are concerned, the Congress has only those powers that are specifically delegated to it, plus the implied power to carry out the powers specifically enumerated.

THE COURT. So, when the sovereign people adopted the Constitution, it enumerated the powers set up in the Constitution . . . limited the powers of the Congress and limited the powers of the judiciary, but it did not limit the powers of the Executive.

MR. BALDRIDGE. That is the way we read Article II of the Constitution.

Point II, Section E, of a joint brief filed by Youngstown, Republic, Armco, Bethlehem, Jones and Laughlin, U.S. Steel, and E. J. Lavino Companies, is entitled "E. The Seizure Cannot be Justified by Any Claim of an 'Aggregate of Powers' or by Isolated Instances of Past Executive Action Which Were Never Legally Challenged." This section contains the kind of arguments typically argued by James Madison—that the powers of the executive are narrowly defined. Regarding this point, Westin comments,[13] "The argument proceeds by necessary implication, upon the nebulous theory of a 'broad residuum of powers' in the President and of his 'aggregate' powers."

Although the Supreme Court affirmed the judgment of the district court in favor of the company, the case is instructive as an illustration of the manner in which the president sought to apply broad specified and unspecified powers to emergencies. Incidentally, it is only fair to point out here that the Department of Defense sincerely did believe that a steel strike during the Korean conflict had grave national defense implications.

AGGREGATION ARGUMENT

Constitutional scholars recognize that there are "aggregate powers" which are both implied and explicit in the exercise of the responsibilities of the president. Both Congress and the courts are reluctant to have a constitutional "showdown" with the president regarding his aggregate powers. Courts have been especially reluctant to involve themselves with what they consider to be essentially political arguments between the Congress and the president. Not only does this provide the executive with leverage in taking autonomous action in international disagreements, but it also makes Congress more reactive than proactive when the public perceives military action to be important.

The emerging pattern has been for the United Nations to request some "humanitarian" assistance from the United States. This often involves U.S. troops to deliver the food, medical supplies, and the logistic infrastructure to distribute the aid. Congress observes a small contingent of troops accompanying the aid, but typically is not inclined to require the president to account for his offer of aid, due to public opinion. When the delivery of aid becomes a small skirmish, Congress still takes a "wait and see" attitude, preferring to determine the projected scale of any hostilities. By this time, American troops, or at least American interests, are in harm's way and acceleration of hostilities make opposition to the president's action look like the United States is backing away from its commitments. President Lyndon Johnson delivered a message to Congress on May 4, 1965, that contained just such a veiled threat for members of Congress not to back away from their commitments in Vietnam. He remarked, in part, [14] "To deny and to delay this means to deny and delay the fullest support of the American people and the American Congress to those brave men who are risking their lives for freedom in Vietnam."

If we freeze the scenario at this point, it should be obvious that the constitutional obligations of the president and the Congress cannot be easily separated. In the following chapter, we shall examine some of the major international instruments that make such a scenario, as outlined above, develop.

NOTES

1. Alexander Hamilton, John Jay, and James Madison, *The Federalist: A Commentary on THE CONSTITUTION OF THE UNITED STATES Being a Collection of Essays Written in Support of the Constitution Agreed Upon September 17, 1787, by the Federal Convention* (Washington, D.C.: Robert B. Luce, Inc., 1976), referred to hereafter in this chapter as *The Federalist*. See also Irving Brant, *James Madison: Father of the Constitution, 1787–1800* (Indianapolis: Bobbs-Merrill, 1950); Edmund Burnett, ed., *Letters of Members of the Continental Congress, 1774–1789*, 8 vols. (Washington, D.C.: Carnegie Institution of Washington, 1921–1936); Jacob Cook, ed., *The Federalist* (Middletown, Conn.: Wesleyan University Press, 1961); Jonathan Elliot, ed., *The Debates in the Several State Conventions, on the Adoption of the Federal Constitution*, 5 vols. (Washington, D.C.: Carnegie Institution of Washington, 1836–1845).

2. *United States v. Sweeny*, 157 U.S. (1895) 281, 284; *Talbot v. Seeman*, 5 U.S. (1 Cr.) 1 (1801); *Martin v. Mott*, 25 U.S. (12 Wheat.) 19 (1827); *Bas v. Tingy*, 4 U.S. (4 Dall.) 36 (1800). See also Thomas Jefferson's views in Paul Ford, *The Works of Thomas Jefferson* (federal edition), 12 vols. (New York: G. P. Putnam's Sons, 1904–1905); Gaillard Hunt, ed., *The Writings of James Madison* (New York: Putnam, 1900–1910); William Hutchison, and William Rachal, eds., *The Papers of James Madison*, 6 vols. (Chicago: University of Chicago Press, 1962–1969).

3. See the arguments in *Myers v. United States*, 272 U.S. 52 (1926); also the section on the "take care" clause in Lester Jayson, et al., eds., *The Constitution of the United States of America: Analysis and Interpretation*, U.S. Senate Doc. No. 92–82 (Washington, D.C.: U.S. Government Printing Office, 1973), pp. 431–437.

4. The development of arguments for the president's powers as chief diplomat is compelling in *United States v. Curtiss-Wright Corp.*, et al., 299 U.S. 304 (1936); *Myers v. United States*, 272 U.S. 52 (1926). See also Nicholas Katzenbach, "Comparative Roles of the President and the Congress in Foreign Affairs," *Department of State Bulletin* 47 (September 11, 1967): 333–336; Harold Koh, "Why the President (Almost) Always Wins in Foreign Affairs: Lessons of the

Iran-Contra Affair," *Yale Law Journal* 97 (June 1988): 1292–1297; John Lehman, *The Executive, Congress, and Foreign Policy: Studies of the Nixon Administration* (New York: Praeger, 1976); Charles Lofgren, *"United States v. Curtiss-Wright Export Corporation*: An Historical Reassessment," *Yale Law Journal* 83 (November 1973): 21–32; Thomas Mann, ed., *A Question of Balance: The President, the Congress, and Foreign Policy* (Washington, D.C.: The Brookings Institution, 1990); Edmund Muskie, et al., eds., *The President, Congress, and Foreign Policy* (Lanham, Md.: University Press of America, 1986); Harold Syrett, ed., *The Papers of Alexander Hamilton*, 15 vols. (New York: Columbia University Press, 1961–1969).

5. U.S. Senate, *The Constitution of the United States of America: Analysis and Interpretations*, 92nd Cong., 2nd Sess., Document No. 92–82 (Washington, D.C.: U.S. Government Printing Office, 1973): 537; Rexford Tugwell, *The Enlargement of the Presidency* (New York: Doubleday, 1960); Aaron Wildavsky, ed., *Perspectives on the Presidency* (Boston: Little, Brown, 1975); Aaron Wildavsky, ed., *The Presidency* (Boston: Little, Brown, 1969).

6. *Tucker v. Alexandroff*, 183 U.S. 424 (1902); Demetrios Caraley, ed., *The President's War Powers: From the Federalists to Reagan* (New York: Academy of Political Science, 1984); Thomas Eagleton, *War and Presidential Power: A Chronicle of Congressional Surrender* (New York: Liveright, 1974); Thomas Eagleton, "Whose Power Is War Power?" *Foreign Policy* 8 (Fall 1972): 23–32; Ronald Elving, "America's Most Frequent Fight Has Been the Undeclared War," *Congressional Quarterly Weekly Report* 49:1 (January 5, 1991): 37–39; Norman Graebner, "The President as Commander in Chief: A Study in Power," *Journal of Military History* 57:1 (January 1993): 111–132.

7. *Watts v. United States*, 1 Wash. Terr. 288 (1870); Robert Goldwin, and Robert Licht, *Foreign Policy and the Constitution* (Washington, D.C.: American Enterprise Institute for Public Policy Research, 1990); Taylor Reveley III, "Prepared Statement," in *The War Power after 200 Years: Congress and the President at a Constitutional Impasse*, Hearings before the Special Subcommittee on War Powers of the Senate Committee on Foreign Relations, 100th Cong., 2nd Sess. (Washington, D.C.: U.S. Government Printing Office, 1989); John Murphy, "Treaties and International Agreements Other Than Treaties: Constitutional Allocation of Power and Responsibility among the President, the House of Representatives, and the Senate," *University of Kansas Kaw Review* 23 (1975): 221. Myres McDougal, and Asher Lans, "Treaties and Congressional-Execuitive or Presidential Agreements: Interchangeable Instruments of National Policy," *Yale Law Journal* 54 (1945): 181, 534.

8. The "ripeness" determination by the Court in *Dellums v. Bush* was the cause for considerable controversy by legal scholars. See the arguments presented by eleven law professors in an amicus curiae brief and discussed in "Law Professors Demand War-Making Limits," *New York Times*, November 27, 1990, p. A17; William Carpenter, "The Separation of Powers in the Eighteenth Century," *American Political Science Review* 22 (1928): 32; Michael Glennon, "The Use of

Custom in Resolving Separation of Powers Disputes," *Boston University Law Review* 64 (1984): 109; William Bondy, "The Separation of Governmental Powers in History, in Theory, and in Constitution," *Studies in History, Economics, and Public Law* 5: 2 (Columbia University, 1896).

9. Gerhart Colm, "The Executive Office and Fiscal and Economic Policy," *Law and Contemporary Problems* (Autumn 1956): 715. This article is particularly interesting for its rich description of Truman's analyses of his tenure as president. See also Harry S. Truman, *Memoirs*, Vol. 2 (Garden City, N.Y.: Doubleday, 1956); Harry S. Truman, *Year of Decisions, 1945* (New York: New American Library, 1955); Harry S. Truman, *Years of Trial and Hope, 1946–1952* (New York: New American Library, 1956); Robert Donovan, *Conflict and Crisis: The Presidency of Harry S. Truman, 1945–1948* (New York: Praeger, 1977); Robert Donovan, *Tumultuous Years: The Presidency of Harry S. Truman, 1949–1953* (New York: W. W. Norton, 1982).

10. Stephen Bailey, *Congress Makes a Law* (New York: Columbia University Press, 1950), p. 243. This work is a comprehensive analysis of the economic setting surrounding the Full Employment Act of 1946.

11. Especially good analyses are found in Alan Westin, *The Anatomy of a Constitutional Law Case: Youngstown Sheet and Tube Co. v. Sawyer* (New York: Macmillan, 1958); Charles Lofgren, *"United States v. Curtiss-Wright Export Corporation:* An Historical Reassessment," *Yale Law Journal* 83 (November 1973): 21–32. See also the arguments in the court actions *Regan v. Wald*, 468 U.S. 222, 243 (1948); *Haig v. Agee*, 453 U.S. 280, 291 (1981); *Dames and Moore v. Regan*, 453 U.S. 654, 661 (1981).

12. Alan Westin, *The Anatomy of a Constitutional Law Case: Youngstown Sheet and Tube Co. v. Dawyer* (New York: Macmillan, 1958), pp. 62, 64; also *New York Times Co. v. United States,* 403 U.S. 713 (1971) with Justice Stewart concurring at 727, 728–730 and Justice Harlan dissenting at 752, 756–759; and U.S. Senate, *Executive Orders in Times of War and National Emergency,* Senate Special Committee on National Emergencies and Delegated Powers, 93rd Cong., 2nd Sess., Committee Print (Washington: U.S. Government Printing Office, June 1974); William Hebe, "Executive Orders and the Development of Presidential Power," *Villanova Law Review* 17 (1972): 688.

13. Alan Westin, *The Anatomy of a Constitutional Law Case: Youngstown Sheet and Tube Co. v. Sawyer* (New York: Macmillan, 1958), pp. 97–98; James Madison, *Notes of Debates in the Federal Convention of 1787 Reported by James Madison* (Athens: Ohio University Press, 1966) reprint of House Document No. 398, *Documents Illustrative of the Formation of the Union of the American States* (Washington, D.C.: U.S. Government Printing Office, 1927); Louis Fisher devotes several chapters to the discussion of presidential powers in his *Constitutional Conflicts between Congress and the President,* 3rd ed. (Lawrence: University Press of Kansas, 1991) and his *The Constitution between Friends: Congress, the President, and the Law* (New York: St. Martin's Press, 1978). Supporting views are given in Norman Small, *Some Presidential Interpretations*

of the Presidency (Baltimore: Johns Hopkins Press, 1932); Eugene Rostow, "President, Prime Minister or Constitutional Monarch?" *American Journal of International Law* 83:4 (October 1989): 740–749.

14. Speech to Congress on May 4, 1965, in *Congressional Record* 111 (1965): 9284; Lyndon Johnson, *The Vantage Point: Perspectives on the Presidency, 1963–1969* (New York: Holt, Rinehart & Winston, 1971); Larry Berman, *Lyndon Johnson's War: The Road to Stalemate in Vietnam* (New York: Norton, 1989); Richard Evans, and Robert Novak, *Lyndon B. Johnson: The Exercise of Power* (New York: The New American Liberty, 1966).

PART II

Powers through Treaties and Other Agreements

Chapter 4

Treaties and Executive Agreements

There are compelling reasons why the United States intervenes in disputes between or among other nations when the United States is not a direct party to the dispute. Perhaps the most compelling reason is that the definition of "U.S. interests" has been increasingly expanding, primarily (by sheer numbers of them) through executive agreements and secondarily through treaties. The Constitution provides a basis for both, but constitutional scholars have not been able to determine the legal constraints appropriate for either entity. In order to provide a setting for subsequent analyses, the language from the Constitution germane to treaties and executive agreements is examined in the following section.

CONSTITUTIONAL AUTHORITY

The role of the president as diplomat was discussed in the previous chapter. We observed from that discussion that the penumbra of a treaty may be extended through executive agreements. As we review excerpts from the Constitution of the United States of America relevant to the authority for treaties and executive agreements it is instructive to keep in mind that the president may make a treaty with the "advice and consent" of the Senate. The House of Representatives does not play a direct role in the treaty process. This has been a source of contention in the House of Representatives and, as we will see in examples throughout later chapters, it has played a prominent role in the arguments for requiring the president to consult with Congress prior to and during any use of U.S. armed forces in foreign conflicts.

What makes the authority of the president to make treaties of so much interest to the Congress is the fact that one of the major arguments for using American armed forces in foreign conflicts is to protect American interests and to fulfill our commitment under any treaty with the foreign government requesting our assistance. How much authority does the president have in his dual roles as chief executive and commander in chief under the Constitution with regard to treaties and executive agreements? Let us go to the Constitution itself for some guidance.

Exhibit 4.1
Constitutional Authority for Treaties and Executive Agreements

---

Article. I.

Section. 10. No State shall enter into any Treaty, Alliance, or Confederation; grant Letters of Marque and Reprisal; . . .

No State shall, without the Consent of Congress, . . . enter into any Agreement or Compact with another State, or with a foreign Power, or engage in War, unless actually invaded, or in such imminent Danger as will not admit of delay.

Article. II.

Section. 1. The executive Power shall be vested in a President of the United States of America. Before he enter on the Execution of his Office, he shall take the following Oath or Affirmation:—"I do solemnly swear (or affirm) that I will faithfully execute the Office of President of the United States, and will to the best of my Ability, preserve, protect and defend the Constitution of the United States."

Section. 2. The President shall be Commander in Chief of the Army and Navy of the United States, . . . He shall have Power, by and with the Advice and Consent of the Senate, to make Treaties, provided two thirds of the Senators present concur; and he shall nominate, and by and with the Advice and Consent of the Senate, shall appoint Ambassadors, other public Ministers and Consuls, . . .

Section. 3. He shall from time to time give to the Congress Information on the State of the Union, and recommend to their Consideration such Measures as he shall judge necessary and expedient; . . . he shall take Care that the Laws be faithfully executed, . . .

Article. VI.

This Constitution, and the Laws of the United States which shall be made in Pursuance thereof; and all Treaties made, or which shall be made, under the Authority of the United States shall be the supreme Law of the Land; and the Judges in every State shall be bound thereby, any Thing in the Constitution or Laws of any State to the Contrary notwithstanding.

These passages from the Constitution lay the foundation for the divergent opinions regarding the authority for a president to engage United States resources in foreign disputes. Notice that the president and the Congress have their separate constitutional responsibilities, but that they also have joint responsibilities.[1] The language is sufficiently general and vague that an overlapping of authority and responsibility can be inferred. Without question the president and the Senate have a joint responsibility in the treaty-making process. When the Constitution was being drafted, however, the Senate was first thought to have the power to make treaties and appoint ambassadors.[2] This notion gave way to the current language in the Constitution giving that authority and responsibility to the chief executive with the advice and consent of the Senate.

ADVICE AND CONSENT: EXECUTIVE VIEW

One of the central constitutional questions regarding the Senate's role in treaties is what is considered "advice and consent." Scholars have suggested that the Senate's role in the treaty process is largely legislative, while the president's role is primarily that of negotiator. In the broadest sense, the Senate has several alternatives for expressing its advice and consent: (1) it may offer its consent unconditionally; (2) it may refuse its consent without further consideration; (3) it may offer its consent, provided certain conditions be added to the treaty as amendments, which, if accepted by the president and the other parties, become binding on all parties to the treaty; or (4) it may offer its consent, provided certain conditions be accepted as reservations which limit the obligations of the United States only.[3] Since the Senate's participation in the treaty is that of advice and consent only, the president may accept any conditions or reservations or he may not accept them and choose, instead, to abandon that treaty altogether.

President George Washington got involved in the struggle for power with the U.S. Senate when he was trying to work out a treaty with the Chickasaw, Choctaw, and Creek Indians. He was a participant in the early discussions centering around the power of the president to enter into a treaty by and with the advice of the Senate, as cited above. Emotions regarding the stability of relations with the Indians were inflamed, and the atmosphere regarding the Indians was volatile, to say the least. Recognizing the benefits of engendering peaceful relations with the Indians, Washington sincerely sought both the advice and consent of the Senate in a treaty that he had devised with his secretary of war and their advisors.

Louis Fisher describes Washington's encounter with the Senate in the Indian treaty affair as follows:[4]

The Constitution empowers the President, "by and with the advice of the Senate, to make treaties, provided two-thirds of the Senators present concur. . . . " It was assumed that the President and the Senate would work jointly on both stages of treaty-making, on negotiation as well as ratification. When Washington met with Senators in August 1789 to secure their advice and consent on an Indian treaty, they refused to commit the Senate to any agreement in his presence. Moreover, they disliked having to rely solely on information supplied by his Secretary of War. Although Washington agreed to return two days later, and the Senate gave its advice and consent to the treaty, the experience convinced him that personal consultation with the Senate was ill-advised.

William Maclay's account of the confrontation of President Washington with the Senate gives much greater detail.[5] Specifically, Washington went to the Senate in person on August 22, 1789, with his secretary of war, General Knox, to sincerely seek the advice and consent of the Senate on the treaty with the Indians. Maclay called for a reading of the treaties and other documents. Senator Morris moved to have the papers communicated to a committee of five in the Senate by the president for consideration by the following Monday (August 22 was a Saturday). Washington did return on Monday (August 24) to the Senate to witness hours of debate regarding terms and conditions of the treaty. The Senate adjourned after the president left the Senate chamber. It ultimately did approve the treaty, but it left a scar on the relationship between Washington and the Senate that subsequent presidents remembered. They would not again go personally before the Senate to obtain the Senate's "advice and consent."

Constitutional scholars are mixed regarding the degree and timing of participation of the Senate in the treaty-making process. Some believe that the negotiations stage is more properly left to the executive and the Department of State with only peripheral participation, at most, by the Senate. This view would have the Senate vote "up or down" on a treaty that had been largely formulated, negotiated, and drafted by the executive with informational reports provided to the Senate. The justification for such an argument is that the executive and the Department of State are in a better position to obtain the proper information and more or less live with a given problem through all the stages and with the parties involved until the scope and substance of it can be reduced to a document that the parties can live with.

The Senate is distracted from long, drawn-out negotiations by the sheer volume of different issues presented to it. Additionally, the senators must always contend with the purely political side of their job by having to continually prepare for the next election. Treaty negotiators in the State Department are typically career staff who provide continuity irrespective of political parties. This does not diminish the value of the Senate as a representative body of the people to reflect the needs and voice of the people on any relationship contained within the terms of the treaty.

EXECUTIVE AGREEMENTS

As we have already noted in greater detail, the sections of the Constitution which provide the basis for the authority of the president to make executive agreements are as follows:

1. Article II, Sections 1 and 2: the president has executive power and authority as commander in chief.
2. Article II, Section 2: the president as commander in chief is authorized to make treaties.
3. Article II, Section 2: the president has the authority to appoint ambassadors, other public ministers, and consuls.
4. Article II, Section 3: the president has the duty to "take care that the laws be faithfully executed."

In addition to the authority mentioned above, the president usually cites his "implied powers" and "aggregate powers" derived from the various sources outlined and discussed earlier in this book. The main difference between a treaty and an executive agreement is that an executive agreement does not require Senate approval, as mentioned in Article II, Section 2, of the U.S. Constitution.

In one of his earlier works, Louis Fisher contrasts the growth in treaties with that of executive agreements between 1789 and 1970.[6] His Table 1 indicates that there were 60 treaties and 27 executive agreements in the period 1789–1839. By contrast, in the period 1940–1970, the number of treaties was 310, but the number of executive agreements was 5,653. For the whole period from 1789 through 1970, of 7,944 treaties and executive agreements, there were 1,109 treaties as compared to 6,839 executive agreements.

To be sure, many of the executive agreements are refinements of treaties already made or actions which have been authorized by Congress in one manner or another. This is especially true in times of war, when the president must, on his own initiative, enter into temporary alliances when swift action is called for. Jayson et al. clarify this point by observing as follows:[7]

Many types of executive agreements comprise the ordinary daily grist of the diplomatic mill. Among these are such as apply to minor territorial adjustments, boundary rectifications, the policing of boundaries, the regulation of fishing rights, private pecuniary claims against another government or its nationals, in Story's words, "the mere private rights of sovereignty."

Executive agreements become of constitutional significance when they constitute a determinative factor of future foreign policy and hence of the country's destiny."

Congress has viewed with dismay the degree to which the president has made use of the executive agreement in lieu of the treaty, which must be approved by the Senate. The Senate has no effective power to prohibit the president from making them, but it does have the power to take action against them once they have been made by the president. Since the president must work with Congress in so many different ways and on so many different issues, the prudent president recognizes the political expediency of seeking the approval of Congress on executive agreements involving major national interests. Best examples of agreements for which the president will seek prior and continuing Senate approval are arms limitations agreements, major bilateral trade agreements, control of strategic facilities in foreign territories, and the like. Some of the important executive agreements (nontreaty commitments) by early and recent presidents are presented below in Exhibit 4.2.

Exhibit 4.2
Selected Executive Agreements—Nontreaty Commitments

1. Seventh annual message of President Monroe to Congress (the "Monroe Doctrine"), December 2, 1983.
2. The Ogdensburg Agreement: joint statement by President Roosevelt and Prime Minister Mackenzie King of Canada, August 18, 1940.
3. President Truman's message to Congress (the "Truman Doctrine"), March 12, 1947.
4. Joint resolution regarding Formosa, Pescadores, and related territories ("Formosa Straits Resolution"), January 29, 1955.
5. Joint resolution to promote peace and stability in the Middle East (the "Eisenhower Doctrine"), March 9, 1957.
6. Multilateral declaration respecting the Baghdad Pact, July 28, 1958.
7. Joint communiqué, President Kennedy and the Shah of Iran, Washington, D.C., April 13, 1962.

8. Statement on Jordan and Saudi Arabia by Secretary of State Dean Rusk, March 8, 1963.

9. Joint resolution on maintenance of international peace and security in Southeast Asia ("Tonkin Gulf Resolution"), August 10, 1964.

10. Senate joint resolution regarding authorization for use of military force against Iraq (S.J. Res. 2, H.J. Res. 77), January 12, 1991.

When the United States is called upon to provide military assistance or support to a foreign government, an interchange of "protocols" among the members of any coalition of nations involved precedes any movement of military troops, weapons, and so on. As mentioned earlier, between 1882 and 1896 the president, in his role as commander in chief, entered into a series of agreements with Mexico to allow the troops of each nation to pursue hostile Indians across the U.S.–Mexican border.

The executive agreements are often first introduced to the U.S. public as presidential statements of support and assistance to a foreign government. The verbal and written forms of these declarations are viewed by the parties involved as formal obligations of the U.S. Some examples of these were brought out in the United States Senate Foreign Relations Committee hearings on the National Commitments Resolution. The reader may recall from Chapter 2 that these hearings were scheduled by the Committee on Foreign Relations to debate the constitutional questions involving the war powers of the president and Congress raised by the presence of U.S. armed forces in Cambodia and the presence of American armed forces in Vietnam. Presented below are some excerpts from that testimony:

Consider, for example, the widely held view that the United States is committed to the defense of Israel even though we have no security treaty with that country. The course of this alleged commitment is in fact nothing more than a long series of executive policy declarations, including: President Truman's declaration of support for the independence of Israel in 1948; the British-French-American tripartite declaration of 1950 pledging opposition to the violation of frontiers or armistice lines in the Middle East; President Eisenhower's statement of January 1957 that the United States regarded the Gulf of Aquaba as an international waterway; President Kennedy's press conference of March 1963 pledging American opposition to any act of aggression in the Middle East; and President Johnson's statement of February 1964 indicating American support for the territorial integrity and political independence of all Middle Eastern countries.[8]

The denigration of treaties goes back at least to President Franklin Roosevelt's destroyer deal of 1940, referred to in section 3 above.[9]

The destroyer deal was followed by a long series of important new commitments incurred by executive agreement or declaration.[10]

Under the executive agreement of 1953, an attack on the joint Spanish-American facilities would be regarded as a "matter of common concern."[11]

. . . under the executive agreement of 1953, the bases are maintained "jointly" by the United States and Spain. . . . It is not difficult to envision a situation in which the need to protect American servicemen would lead to large-scale military intervention in Spain and, as a result, to another military enterprise unauthorized by Congress.[12]

The distinction between the actual force of a treaty and that of an executive agreement is often indistinguishable indeed, especially when conflict is imminent. What is important to observe here is that treaty relationships may be continually changing according to both foreign and domestic developments. The definition of U.S. interests in foreign countries continually changes as well, as the president enters into executive agreements with foreign heads of state. As we shall see in the following section, some of the executive agreements augment or further delineate a treaty, or they may even be stand-alone quasitreaties carrying the full obligation of the United States for activities and actions normally covered by a treaty.

EXECUTIVE AGREEMENTS AS QUASITREATIES

Executive agreements have been used to extend the penumbra of a treaty. President Lyndon Johnson sent a message to Congress on August 5, 1964, requesting a congressional resolution "to give convincing evidence to the aggressive Communist nations, and to the world as a whole, that our policy in Southeast Asia will be carried forward—and that the peace and security of the area will be preserved."[13]

In that message to Congress, President Johnson made claims regarding the commitments of the United States to support the nations covered by the SEATO Treaty. Recall that hostilities involving U.S. aircraft, naval vessels, and ground troops had been well established already. His request for a resolution of support cited similar resolutions including those involving the threat to Formosa in 1955, the threat to the Middle East in 1957, and the threat in Cuba in 1962. The thrust of his request is indicated in the following passage:[14]

Our commitments in the area are well known to the Congress. They were first made in 1954 by President Eisenhower. They were further defined in the Southeast Asia Collective Defense Treaty approved by the Senate in February 1955. This treaty with its accompanying protocol obligates the United States and other members to act in accordance with their constitutional processes to meet Communist aggression against any of the parties or protocol states. I recommend a resolution expressing the support of the Congress for all necessary action to protect our Armed Forces and to assist nations covered by the SEATO Treaty.

After having heard President Johnson's message read by the presiding officer, Senator Fulbright requested that S.J. Res. 198, referred to as the Gulf of Tonkin Resolution and presented below as Exhibit 4.3, be read into the record and referred to the Committee on Foreign Relations and to the Committee on Armed Services, sitting jointly. After the resolution was read into the record, heated debate ensued throughout August 5 and August 6. The first and most eloquent dissenter was Senator Morse, who objected to the resolution on the basis of his belief that the resolution was indirectly a declaration of war and that it violated Article I, Section 8, of the U.S. Constitution.

Exhibit 4.3
Gulf of Tonkin Resolution—S.J. Res. 189

Whereas naval units of the Communist regime in Vietnam, in violation of the principles of the Charter of the United Nations and of international law, have deliberately and repeatedly attacked United States naval vessels lawfully present in international waters, and have thereby created a serious threat to international peace:

Whereas these attacks are part of a deliberate and systematic campaign of aggression that the Communist regime in North Vietnam has been waging against its neighbors and the nations joined with them in the collective defense of their freedom:

Whereas the United States is assisting the peoples of southeast Asia to protect their freedom and has no territorial, military or political ambitions in that area, but desires only that these peoples should be left in peace to work out their own destinies in their own way: Now, therefore, be it

Resolved by the Senate and House of Representatives of the United States of America in Congress assembled, That the Congress approves and supports the determination of the President, as Commander in Chief, to take all necessary measures to repel any armed attack against the forces of the United States and to prevent further aggression.

SEC. 2. The United States regards as vital to its national interest and to world peace the maintenance of international peace and security in southeast Asia. Consonant with the Constitution and the Charter of the United Nations and in accordance with its obligations under the Southeast Asia Collective Defense Treaty, the United States is, therefore, prepared, as the President determines, to take all necessary steps, including the use of armed force, to assist any member or protocol state of the Southeast Asia Collective Defense Treaty requesting assistance in defense of its freedom.

SEC. 3. This resolution shall expire when the President shall determine that the peace and security of the area is reasonably assured by international conditions created by action of the United Nations or otherwise, except that it may be terminated earlier by concurrent resolution of the Congress.

Source: Congressional Record—Senate (August 6, 1964): 18133.

On August 6, Senator Javits went right to the core of the war powers issue and into the basis for the authority to include Cambodia, Laos, and Vietnam in any armed intervention by the United States in the following questions to Senator Fulbright, the floor manager for the requested resolution from President Johnson. Even though Javits supported the resolution, his questions provide evidence of President Johnson's extension of treaty obligations by executive agreement not subject to approval by the Senate. Senator Javits queried Senator Fulbright as follows:[15]

My question is this: To the extent that the Senator may know—and be permitted to disclose—are we not implementing the Southeast Asia Collective Defense Treaty? This treaty has eight countries who are parties to it including the United States— three in the area, the rest in Europe, Australia, and New Zealand, and ourselves. The inclusion of Cambodia, Laos, and Vietnam is by protocol. That is, the protection of the treaty is extended to them, though they are not parties to it.

Is it that the President may take all necessary steps, including the use of Armed Forces, to assist any member or protocol state, which would include Laos, Cambodia, and Vietnam, in the Southeast Asia Collective Defense Treaty, that may request assistance in defense of its freedom?

We may note that Senator Javits indicated that Cambodia, Laos, and Vietnam were not included as signatories in the SEATO Treaty, but were being made a part of the U.S. obligation under the treaty by "protocol" or through executive agreements. Senator Fulbright's forthright answer to Senator Javits's question contradicts President Johnson's statements regarding Laos, South Vietnam, and, by inference, Cambodia in the following response:[16]

First, this particular action was not taken in consultation with the other signatories of the Southeast Asia Treaty. It was an act for which we took the responsibility. It had nothing to do with the treaty. The fact that we are present in the area grows, at least in part, out of our obligations under the treaty. That is one of the reasons why we are in the area, and have been for a number of years. But we would have the right to be there without the treaty. As to the contribution of the protocol states— there are three, as the Senator from New York has said. Under the Laotian Agreement of 1962, Laos is out of the treaty. Cambodia has renounced any desire to be protected by the United States. So actually this is a technical way of saying that we are assisting South Vietnam, because that country is all that is left. That phrase means South Vietnam.

Senator Fulbright could not have made a better argument for an executive taking independent action—"this particular action was not taken in consultation with the other signatories of the Southeast Asia Treaty"—and without either the advice or the consent of the Senate—"It had nothing to do with the treaty." Laos was not a party to the SEATO Treaty, by its own action in 1962, yet the resolution would cover U.S. assistance and armed forces to counter Communist aggression in Laos. Whether the resolution in fact amounted to a declaration of war against North Vietnam will be discussed in Chapter 10. It is sufficient here to indicate, however, the force of the executive agreements in committing armed forces at the discretion of the executive.

The executive agreements which extended the use of armed forces to nations other than the signatories to the Southeast Asia Collective Defense (SEATO) Treaty ultimately would cost the United States tens of billions of dollars, thousands of lives, and countless political and diplomatic casualties.

Time has a way of dimming one's view of the details of such a long, drawn-out experience such as the nation's nightmare Vietnam involvement. A more recent example of the force of mutual defense executive agreements, still quite vivid in the minds of Americans of this generation, is that of the Iraqi invasion of Kuwait of August 2, 1990. It contains all of the elements of the continuing constitutional conflict between the executive and the Congress. The world watched the drama being played out on television in "real time"; even the congressional debates were seen on the C-SPAN and CNN television networks while they were happening. The players, the issues, and the action on the battlefield could be monitored hour by hour on television throughout the world. Remarkably, with the hour-by-hour television coverage of the debates in the House of Representatives, with members of the president's cabinet on "talk shows" in and around the Washington area, and with military strategists appearing in almost every imaginable television and radio venue, people worldwide were aware of the constitutional issues and the mood of Congress at the instant they were being acted out in Washington.

Even though the constitutional issues associated with Desert Shield/Desert Storm will be discussed at length in Chapters 8 and 9, the context and extent of the executive agreements that President Bush established with Saudi Arabia and Kuwait illustrate the prominence of the executive agreement as an instrument of the president's war power. This Middle Eastern conflict additionally presents a clear picture—perhaps a prophetic one—of the manner in which the U.S. armed forces are first introduced on a small scale and then incremented in a gradual, but certain, buildup to a major involvement that often assumes the proportions of a full-scale war.

President George Bush, as contrasted with President Lyndon Johnson and President Richard Nixon, was open and "up front" regarding his agreements with the coalition forces and the governments of Saudi Arabia and Kuwait.[17] His straightforward personal manner was also a trademark of his presidential administration. He has been characterized as not wanting power, but rather sincerely wanting to serve. Perhaps this is one of the main reasons that Saddam Hussein's August 2, 1990, invasion of Kuwait and Hussein's flaunting his power over a defenseless Kuwait were so repugnant to President Bush, who responded immediately with personal and national indignation.

Bush argued that (1) the Iraqi invasion of Kuwait was a "defining moment" in post–Cold War international relations—a test of the post–Cold War world order; (2) the Iraqi invasion was a threat to the international community in view of Kuwait's oil supply to the world and Iraq's monopoly position on the world oil supply; (3) Kuwait was a peaceful nation and the aggression had to be stopped, with the Kuwaiti government wholly restored; and (4) a show of force by the world community against Saddam Hussein should send the message of international solidarity against such aggression.

The Security Council of the United Nations took immediate (on the day of the August 2 invasion) action by demanding Iraq's cessation of aggression and unconditional withdrawal from Kuwait and by imposing mandatory economic sanctions on Iraq. On August 7, President Bush dispatched troops to Saudi Arabia through executive agreements with Saudi Arabia and Kuwait. As the hostilities intensified and as U.S. troops deployed to Saudi Arabia steadily increased, the president signed an executive agreement with Saudi Arabia for the Saudi purchase of $2.2 billion in advanced weapons.

While Desert Shield and Desert Storm will be discussed at length in Chapters 8 and 9 from the point of view of the president's authority as commander in chief, events already depicted here and in the previous sections of this chapter support the argument that U.S. obligations through executive agreements can equal or even exceed those in a formal treaty.

Finally, Senator Gale McGee, in his testimony before the Foreign Relations Committee of the U.S. Senate, reiterates the increasing importance of the executive agreement as a direct relationship with the rising power of America as a world leader:[18]

without exception the trend toward a stronger and stronger executive role in foreign policy has coincided with the rising preeminence of the United States in world politics during the 20th century. Presidents Theodore Roosevelt, Taft, and Wilson expanded that role materially. But the most significant changes have occurred since the beginning of World War II. Under President Franklin Roosevelt the use of the executive agreements experienced a sharp increase. In particular his commitments to the transfer of destroyers for bases, the extension of the Monroe Doctrine principle to Iceland and Greenland, and the "shoot on sight" edict to American naval forces in the Atlantic are often cited.

The president, as the voice of the people, can obtain support for his actions during an attack on what are thought to be American interests. The notion of giving assistance to a small nation in distress is part of the fabric of the American culture and sense of fair play. The conflict in responding to these situations, however, is that they raise questions such as these: How much and what type of assistance should the president provide on his own authority before he consults with and actively seeks the advice and consent of Congress? Can Congress expect that the executive will be able to predict when a provision of assistance or humanitarian aid to a requesting nation can lead to acts of war involving the United States?

NOTES

1. Constitution of the United States of America, Articles I, II, and VI; Francis Wilcox, and Richard Frank, eds., *The Constitution and the Conduct of Foreign Policy: An Inquiry by a Panel of the American Society of International Law* (New York: Praeger, 1976); Francis Wilcox, *Congress, the Executive and Foreign Policy* (New York: Harper & Row, 1971); "Congress, the President, and the Power to Commit Forces to Combat," note, *Harvard Law Review* 81 (June 1968): 1771–1805; Barry Goldwater, "President's Ability to Protect America's Freedoms—the Warmaking Power," *Law and Social Order* 2 (1971): 423–449; Norman Graebner, "The President as Commander in Chief: A Study in Power," *Journal of Military History* 57:1 (January 1993): 111–132; Ludwell John III, "Abraham Lincoln and the Development of Presidential War-Making Powers: Prize Cases," *Civil War History* (September 1989): 208–224.

2. Max Farrand, *The Records of the Federal Convention of 1787*, Vol. 2, rev. ed., passim (New Haven, Conn.: Yale University Press, 1937); Edward Corwin, *The President: Office and Powers 1787–1957* (New York: New York University

Press, 1957); Carl March, "A Note on Treaty Ratification," *American Political Science Review* 47 (1953): 1130; Alexander Hamilton, John Jay, and James Madison, *The Federalist: A Commentary on THE CONSTITUTION OF THE UNITED STATES Being a Collection of Essays Written in Support of the Constitution Agreed Upon September 17, 1787, by the Federal Convention* (Washington, D.C.: Robert B. Luce, Inc., 1976); James Madison, *Notes of Debates in the Federal Convention of 1787 Reported by James Madison* (Athens: Ohio University Press, 1966); reprint of House Document No. 398, *Documents Illustrative of the Formation of the Union of the American States* (Washington, D.C.: Government Printing Office, 1927).

    3. *Foster v. Neilson*, 2 Pet. (27 U.S.) 253 (1829); 112 U.S. 580 (1884); *Annals of Congress* 31 (1818): 106; *Fourteen Diamond Rings v. United States*, 183 U.S. 176 (1901); Taylor Reveley III, "Prepared Statement," in *The War Power after 200 Years: Congress and the President at a Constitutional Impasse*, Hearings before the Special Subcommittee on War Powers of the Senate Committee on Foreign Relations, 100th Cong., 2nd Sess. (Washington, D.C.: U.S. Government Printing Office, 1989).

    4. Louis Fisher, *The President and Congress: Power and Policy* (New York: The Free Press, 1972): 42–43. See also Edward Corwin, *The President: Office and Powers 1787–1957* (New York: New York University Press, 1957), and Washington's own account of the incident in John Fitzpatrick, ed., *The Diaries of George Washington*, 4 vols. (Boston: Houghton Mifflin, 1925), and John Fitzpatrick, ed., *The Writings of George Washington*, 39 vols. (Washington, D.C.: U.S. Government Printing Office, 1931–1944).

    5. William Maclay, "Account by William Maclay of President George Washington's First Attempt to Obtain the Advice and Consent of the Senate to a Treaty," in William Goldsmith, ed., *The Growth of Presidential Power: A Documented History*, 3 vols. (New York: Chelsea House Publishers, 1974): 392–395.

    6. Louis Fisher, *President and Congress: Power and Policy* (New York: Free Press, 1972), Table 1, p. 45; Louis Fisher, "Congressional Participation in the Treaty Process," *University of Pennsylvania Law Review* 137 (1989): 1511; John Murphy, "Treaties and International Agreements Other Than Treaties: Constitutional Allocation of Power and Responsibility among the President, the House of Representatives, and the Senate," 23 *University of Kansas Law Review* 221 (1975); Joseph Tomain, "Executive Agreements and the Bypassing of Congress," 8 *Journal of International Law and Economics* 129 (1973); Solomon Slonin, "Congressional-Executive Agreements," 14 *Columbia Journal of Transnational Law* 434 (1975).

    7. Lester Jayson, et al., eds., *The Constitution of the United States of America: Analysis and Interpretation*, U.S. Senate Doc. No. 92–82 (Washington, D.C.: U.S. Government Printing Office, 1973): 511; U.S. Senate Committee on Foreign Relations, "Treaties and Other International Agreements: The Role of the United States Senate," 98th Cong., 2nd Sess., Committee Print (Washington, D.C.: U.S. Government Printing Office, June 1984); Craig Mathews, "The Constitutional

Power of the President to Conclude International Agreements," *Yale Law Journal* 64 (1955): 345; Arthur Bestor, "Separation of Powers in the Domain of Foreign Affairs: The Original Intent of the Constitution Historically Examined," 5 *Seton Hall Law Review* 529 (1974); Richard Cohen, "Self-Executing Executive Agreements: A Separation of Powers Problem," 24 *Buffalo Law Review* 137 (1974).

8. U.S. Senate Committee on Foreign Relations, *Documents Relating to the War Power of Congress, the President's Authority as Commander-in-Chief and the War in Indochina*, 91st Cong., 2nd Sess. (Washington, D.C.: U.S. Government Printing Office, 1970): 26 (hereafter in this chapter, this document will be referred to as *Documents Relating to the War Power*); Anthony Austin, *The President's War: The Story of the Tonkin Gulf Resolution and How the Nation Was Trapped in Vietnam* (Philadelphia: J. B. Lippincott, 1971); Alexander Bickel, et al., "Indochina: The Constitutional Crisis," *Congressional Record* (daily ed.) 116 (May 13, 1970): S7117–S7123, Part II, *Congressional Record* (daily ed.) 116 (May 20, 1970): S7538–S7541; Eugene Dverin, ed., *The Senate's War Powers: Debate on Cambodia from the Congressional Record* (Chicago: Markham Publishing Company, 1971).

9. U.S. Senate Committee on Foreign Relations, *Documents Relating to the War Power*, p. 27; Samuel Rosenman, ed., *The Public Papers and Addresses of Franklin D. Roosevelt* (New York: Harper & Brothers, 1950).

10. U.S. Senate Committee on Foreign Relations, *Documents Relating to the War Power*, p. 27; Warren Kimball, "Franklin Roosevelt: 'Dr. Win-the-War,'" in Joseph Dawson, *Commanders in Chief: Presidential Leadership in Modern Wars* (Lawrence: University Press of Kansas, 1993): 87–105; Solomon Slonin, "Congressional-Executive Agreements," 14 *Columbia Journal of Transnational Law* 434 (1975); John Murphy, "Treaties and International Agreements Other Than Treaties: Constitutional Allocation of Power and Responsibility among the President, the House of Representatives, and the Senate," 23 *University of Kansas Law Review* 221 (1975).

11. U.S. Senate Committee on Foreign Relations, *Documents Relating to the War Power*, p. 28; U.S. Department of State Historical Studies Division, *Armed Actions Taken by the United States without a Declaration of War, 1789–1967*, Res. Proj. No. 806A (Washington, D.C.: U.S. Government Printing Office, 1967).

12. U.S. Senate Committee on Foreign Relations, *Documents Relating to the War Power*, p. 29; Harry S. Truman, *Memoirs*, Vol. 2 (Garden City, N.Y.: Doubleday, 1956); Robert Donovan, *Tumultuous Years: The Presidency of Harry S. Truman, 1949–1953* (New York: W. W. Norton, 1982); Merlo Pusey, *Eisenhower the President* (New York: Macmillan, 1956); James Sundquist, *Politics and Policy: The Eisenhower, Kennedy, and Johnson Years* (Washington: The Brookings Institution, 1968).

13. Lyndon Johnson, Message from the President of the United States to the Congress, *Congressional Record*—Senate (August 5, 1964): 18132; Larry Berman, *Lyndon Johnson's War: The Road to Stalemate in Vietnam* (New York: Norton, 1989); Richard Evans and Robert Novak, *Lyndon B. Johnson: The Exercise of Power* (New York: The New American Liberty, 1966); Lyndon Johnson,

The Vantage Point: Perspectives on the Presidency, 1963–1969 (New York: Holt, Rinehart & Winston, 1971).

14. Lyndon Johnson, Message from the President of the United States to the Congress in *Congressional Record*—Senate (August 5, 1964): 18132. He actually got all he asked for in the Gulf of Tonkin Resolution—S. J. Res. 198 found in *Congressional Record*—Senate (August 6, 1964): 18133; see also Anthony Austin, *The President's War: The Story of the Tonkin Gulf Resolution and How the Nation Was Trapped in Vietnam* (Philadelphia: J. B. Lippincott, 1971); U.S. Senate Foreign Relations Committee, "Hearings on the Southeast Asia Collective Defense Treaty," 83rd Cong., 2nd Sess., November 11, 1954 (Washington, D.C.: U.S. Government Printing Office, 1954); U.S. Senate Foreign Relations Committee, "Hearings on U.S. Commitments to Foreign Powers," 90th Cong., 1st Sess., August 16–September 19, 1967 (Washington, D.C.: U.S. Government Printing Office, 1967); U.S. Senate Foreign Relations Committee, "National Commitments," Senate Report No. 797, 90th Cong., 1st Sess., November 20, 1967 (Washington, D.C.: U.S. Government Printing Office, 1967).

15. *Congressional Record*—Senate (August 6, 1964): 18404, and Anthony Austin, *The President's War: The Story of the Tonkin Gulf Resolution and How the Nation Was Trapped in Vietnam* (Philadelphia: J. B. Lippincott, 1971); Larry Berman, *Lyndon Johnson's War: The Road to Stalemate in Vietnam* (New York: Norton, 1989).

16. *Congressional Record*—Senate (August 6, 1964): 18404; Thomas Eagleton, "Congress and War Powers," *Missouri Law Review* 37 (Winter 1972): 1–32; Thomas Eagleton, "The August 15 Compromise and the War Powers of Congress," *St. Louis University Law Journal* 18 (Fall 1973): 1–11; Thomas Eagleton, *War and Presidential Power: A Chronicle of Congressional Surrender* (New York: Liveright, 1974); John Ely, *On Taking Up Arms and Taking Responsibility: Constitutional Lessons of Vietnam and Its Aftermath* (Princeton, N.J.: Princeton University Press, 1993); Larry Cable, *Conflict of Myths: The Development of American Counterinsurgency Doctrine and the Vietnam War* (New York: New York University Press, 1986); Alexander Bickel, "The Constitution and the War," *Commentary* 54 (July 1972): 49–55; Alexander Bickel, et al., "Indochina: The Constitutional Crisis," *Congressional Record* (daily ed.) 116 (May 13, 1970): S7117–S7123, Part II, *Congressional Record* (daily ed.) 116 (May 20, 1970): S7538–S7541.

17. George Bush, "Letter to Congressional Leaders Reporting on the National Emergency with Respect to Iraq," *Public Papers of the Presidents of the United States: George Bush* (Washington, D.C.: U.S. Government Printing Office, 1992): 131–133; George Bush, "Statement on Allied Military Action in the Persian Gulf, January 16, 1991," *Public Papers of the Presidents of the United States: George Bush* (Washington, D.C.: U.S. Government Printing Office, 1992): 42; Michael Glennon, "The Gulf War and the Constitution," *Foreign Affairs* 70:2 (Spring 1991): 84–101; Joan Biskupic, "Constitution's Conflicting Clauses Underscored by Iraq Crisis: Provisions on Waging War Leave a Basic Question

Unanswered, Does Congress or the President Call the Shot?" *Congressional Quarterly Weekly Report* (January 5, 1991): 33–36; Gregory Bowens, "House Backs Measure Allowing U.S. Role in U.N. Operation," *Congressional Quarterly Weekly Report* (May 29, 1993): 1373; Dick Cheney, "Legislative-Executive Relations in National Security: Work Together to Govern," *Vital Speeches* 56:11 (March 15, 1990): 334–336; George Church, "Trip Wires to War: What Would It Take for the U.S. to Attack Iraq, and How Would Bush Square the Decision with the U.N. and Congress?" *Time* (October 29, 1990): 48–51; Gregory Bowens, and Carroll Doherty, "Bombing, Widely Backed on Hill, Reopens War Powers Debate," *Congressional Quarterly Weekly Report* 51:27 (July 3, 1993): 1750–1751. Compare the works just cited with John Ely, "The (Troubled) Constitutionality of the War They Told Us About," *Stanford Law Review* 42:4 (April 1990): 876–926; John Ely, "The Unconstitutionality of the War They Didn't Tell Us About," *Stanford Law Review* 42:5 (May 1990): 1111–1148; James Nathan, "Salvaging the War Powers Resolution," *Presidential Studies Quarterly* 23:2 (Spring 1993): 235–268.

18. Gale McGee, "Minority Views of Senator Gale McGee on the National Commitments Resolution," in U.S. Senate Committee on Foreign Relations, *Documents Relating to the War Power,* p. 35; Myres McDougal, and Asher Lans, "Treaties and Congressional-Executive or Presidential Agreements: Interchangeable Instruments of National Policy," *Yale Law Journal* 54 (1945): 181, 534; U.S. Senate Committee on Foreign Relations, "Treaties and Other International Agreements: The Role of the United States Senate," 98th Cong., 2nd Sess., Committee Print (Washington, D.C.: U.S. Government Printing Office, June 1984); U.S. Senate Foreign Relations Committee, "Hearings on U.S. Commitments to Foreign Powers," 90th Cong., 1st Sess., August 16–September 19, 1967 (Washington, D.C.: U.S. Government Printing Office, 1967); Richard Cohen, "Self-Executing Executive Agreements: A Separation of Powers Problem," *Buffalo Law Review* 24 (1979): 137.

Chapter 5

United Nations Obligations

DUMBARTON OAKS PROPOSALS

The Dumbarton Oaks Proposals were the precursor to the United Nations Charter and provide most of the language that is found in the final form of the Charter.[1] The beginning sentence of the Dumbarton Oaks Proposals is as follows: "There should be established an international organization under the title of The United Nations, the Charter of which should contain provisions necessary to give effect to the proposals which follow."[2]

This was the beginning of the United Nations Organization. The actual Charter would be signed at the United Nations Conference on International Organizations in San Francisco, California, on June 26, 1945. The uniqueness of this organization is found in the list of member nations. Unlike all other peacekeeping organizations, this one includes most of the nations of the world as its members. Its Charter and resolutions passed by the Security Council have been used as a basis for the United States to employ armed forces throughout the world, usually to "protect U.S. interests."

The United Nations, especially during the Cold War, had as many detractors as supporters in America and throughout the world. This was primarily due to the ineffectiveness and slowness with which the United Nations handled matters of conflict. Among the five permanent members of the United Nations Security Council—the United States of America, China (The Republic of China—Taiwan—until 1971, the People's Republic of China since 1971), France, the Union of Soviet Socialist Republics, and the United Kingdom of Great Britain and Northern Ireland—it was almost certain that the Soviet Union or the People's Republic of China would veto any use of force against a Communist country no matter whether there was "just cause" or not. For this reason, the United Nations was a source of contention in Congress and among the American people for most of its existence between 1945 and 1988.

With United Nations intervention in the Iraqi-Kuwaiti crisis in 1990, the American attitude toward the United Nations has changed favorably. There are still those who believe that the United States should not bear the major share of the support for the day-to-day operations of the United Nations. They cite Article 2, Sections 1 and 2:[3]

1. The Organization is based on the principle of the sovereign equality of all its Members.
2. All Members, in order to ensure to all of them the rights and benefits resulting from membership, shall fulfil in good faith the obligations assumed by them in accordance with the present Charter.

Additionally, there have been serious controversies regarding the effectiveness of recent secretaries-general of the United Nations. Despite these reservations, there is general agreement that the benefits of such an organization still outweigh its costs, especially recently.

UNITED NATIONS TREATY OBLIGATIONS ON MEMBER NATIONS

Much of the form and language in the current United Nations Charter was taken, as stated earlier, from the Dumbarton Oaks Proposals, and also from the League of Nations framework—the former having the greater influence. After almost a half century of operation, one would have to concede that the United Nations Organization has weathered some severe storms and managed to survive. The Cold War and the almost certain vetoes by the Soviet Union or the People's Republic of China of any major peacekeeping initiatives by the United States, especially in areas with a dominant Communist influence, had created suspicion in the minds of many nations that the United Nations was a venue more for propaganda than for peaceful resolution of disputes and issues.[4]

Despite the shortcomings of the United Nations, membership in that organization has provided much of the justification for the president to exercise his war powers in international conflicts. An example are the identical letters President George Bush sent to the Speaker of the U.S. House of Representatives, Thomas S. Foley, to the president pro tempore of the U.S. Senate, Robert C. Byrd, to the Senate majority leader, George J. Mitchell, to the Senate Republican leader, Robert Dole, and to the House

Republican leader, Robert H. Michel, outlining his authority and activity in the Desert Shield/Desert Storm use of force upon the invasion of Kuwait by Iraq. The text of that letter is presented below:[5]

January 16, 1991

Dear Mr. Speaker: (Dear Mr. President:)

Pursuant to section 2(b) of the Authorization for Use of Military Force Against Iraq Resolution (H.J. Res. 77, Public Law 120–1), I have concluded that:

1. the United States has used all appropriate diplomatic and other peaceful means to obtain compliance by Iraq with U.N. Security Council Resolutions 660, 661, 662, 664, 665, 666, 667, 669, 670, 674, 677, and 678; and

2. that those efforts have not been and would not be successful in obtaining such compliance. Enclosed is a report that supports my decision.

Sincerely,

GEORGE BUSH

The reader is asked to observe the references to the twelve resolutions of the United Nations. While these will be examined in depth in Chapter 8, it is important to note that the meeting of November 29, 1990, on Resolution 678 was "the first time in history that a US Secretary of State has presided over a council session."[6] Additionally, it was only the fourth time in the United Nations' history that all five of the permanent members of the Security Council had met together. Such resolutions are perceived by member nations as treaty obligations under the articles of the Charter ratified by them.

As a member of the United Nations and as one of the five permanent members (United States, U.K., France, China, USSR) of the United Nations Security Council, the United States is bound by the articles of that organization's Charter. When Congress approved membership in the United Nations, it was fully cognizant of the obligations and responsibilities associated with being a signatory to the Charter.[7] The Charter explicitly obligates member nations to a commitment of resources when called upon after the Security Council has made a determination that a Chapter VII action is appropriate and involves (1) a threat to the peace, (2) a breach of the peace, or (3) an act of aggression.

When it has been established that there has been a violation of the United Nations Charter provisions involving any of the three items just listed by one member against another, the United Nations Security Council steps in to help facilitate a solution. It does not, for all practical purposes, have troops of its own to use in conflict resolution.

UNITED NATIONS CHAPTER VII ACTION

Since the focus of this book is war powers, we will not discuss at length the specific settlement of disputes covered in Chapter VI of the United Nations Charter. This does not in the least diminish the importance of that chapter, since any dispute between or among nations, in the language of Article 33, "shall, first of all, seek a solution by negotiation, enquiry, mediation, conciliation, arbitration, judicial settlement, resort to regional agencies or arrangements, or other peaceful means of their own choice." So the parties need not resort to the use of force if a dispute can be settled satisfactorily under the provisions of Chapter VI. The next tier of remedies under the United Nations Charter appears in Articles 39 through 51 of Chapter VII.

Chapter VII of the United Nations Charter is comprised of Articles 39 through 51. Article 39 is a "triggering" article which "shall determine the existence of any threat to the peace, breach of the peace, or act of aggression and shall make recommendations, or decide what measures shall be taken" when a dispute arises between or among organization members.[8] Notice in particular that the language above specifically provides the Security Council the following responsibilities under Article 39:

1. To determine the existence of:
    a. a threat to the peace
    b. a breach of the peace
    c. an act of aggression
2. To make recommendations or decide what measures shall be taken to maintain or restore international peace and security.

It should be noted that these two responsibilities are the major responsibilities of the Security Council, since they provide the Security Council with the authority to call upon members to take any appropriate action to maintain or restore international peace and security. There has been discussion regarding whether the Security Council has not only the responsibility but the duty, under Article 39, to determine which of the measures contained in the remaining articles of Chapter VII must be taken by the members. Saying it another way, the Security Council should not make a determination under Article 39 unless it can be assured that the members are actually willing and able to carry out the additional measures contained in the remaining articles of Chapter VII.[9]

Although the Security Council is the organ with the responsibility for the determination whether a conflict is a threat to the peace, a breach of the peace, or an act of aggression, the General Assembly of the United Nations has called to the attention of the Security Council situations for which the General Assembly has desired sanctions. The Security Council has not always responded favorably to such actions.[10]

One might say that Article 40 is analogous to a cease-fire, enabling the Security Council to take appropriate action to defuse a volatile situation. The Security Council calls upon the parties to comply with provisional measures "without prejudice" to the rights, claims, or positions of the parties involved.

By the time Article 41 is determined to be appropriate, the situation has called for serious action, but not involving the use of armed forces to give effect to the Security Council's decision. The actions here are typically characterized as economic and/or political sanctions. Of the twelve Security Council resolutions mentioned in the letter from President George Bush presented above, the following dealt specifically with Article 41–type sanctions:[11]

1. S.C. Res. 661, August 6, 1990, imposed economic sanctions and authorized nonmilitary measures to enforce them.
2. S.C. Res. 674, October 29, 1990, held Iraq responsible for all financial losses resulting from invasion and sought evidence of human rights abuses by Iraqi troops in Kuwait.

Article 42 provides for added stronger measures in the event that the measures under Article 41 proved to be ineffective. Article 42 begins as follows: "Should the Security Council consider that measures provided for in Article 41 would be inadequate or have proved to be inadequate, . . . " These are essentially the type of actions referred to in President Bush's letter above. Notice that S.C. Res. 665 and S.C. Res. 670 augment those under Article 41: (1) S.C. Res. 665, August 25, 1990, outlawed all trade with Iraq by land, sea, and air and barred financial dealings with all United Nations members; (2) S.C. Res. 670, September 25, 1990, tightened the embargo on air traffic and authorized detention of Iraq's merchant fleet.

Article 42 measures are thought to require "special agreements" under Article 43 to specify military enforcement measures. Notice the language of Article 43: "All Members . . . undertake to make available to the Security Council . . . in accordance with a special agreement or agreements, armed forces . . ." This notion is particularly compelling when one examines the language in the beginning of Article 106: "Pending the coming into force of such special agreements referred to in Article 43 as in the opinion of the Security Council enable it to begin the exercise of its responsibilities under Article 42, . . ." The language is not clear, however, regarding whether a member is under a legal obligation to provide the Security Council with armed forces involuntarily.

Articles 48 and 49 call upon the members to carry out the decisions of the Security Council individually, cooperatively through mutual assistance, or through appropriate international agencies of which they are members. The common thread through these articles and, indeed, throughout all the articles in Chapter VII is that of member implementation of Security Council decisions and/or determinations.

AUTHORITY TO CALL ARMED FORCES

To what extent should a member nation of the United Nations feel compelled to provide armed forces should the Security Council make a determination that such is needed to respond to a threat to peace, a breach of peace, or an act of aggression? The issue of whether the Security Council's request for armed forces and assistance is legally binding cannot be resolved easily. Perhaps this is the crux of the dispute between Congress and the president when the president uses U.S. armed forces to respond to a United Nations Security Council resolution. In a subsequent chapter, we look at this issue from the congressional point of view that this is a form of "delegated authority" and is not expressly permitted by the Constitution of the United States. Here, however, we examine the obligation and responsibility from the point of view of member nations.

By December 17, 1990, Iraq had occupied Kuwait for over four months, despite the Security Council's twelve resolutions condemning the invasion and calling for Iraq's immediate and unconditional withdrawal from Kuwait. The twelve resolutions (660, 661, 662, 664, 665, 666, 667, 669, 670, 674, 677, 678) included S.C. Res. 678 authorizing "member states cooperating with the government of Kuwait to use 'all necessary means' to uphold the above resolutions."[12] On that date, December 17, 1990, and during its ministerial meeting, the North Atlantic Council issued a statement affirming its members' support for the action taken under United Nations Resolution 678.[13]

The wording of the North Atlantic Council statement is particularly interesting and important, since it underlines the force of treaty and executive agreements for the use of armed forces to counter aggression and secure or maintain the peace. Attention is drawn specifically to the phrases "commitment," "complying fully with the mandatory United Nations decisions," "called on all governments to provide appropriate support in implementing the resolutions," and "an armed attack against one of our states shall be considered an attack against them all."[14] Portions of the North Atlantic

Council statement made in Brussels, Belgium, on December 17, 1990, follow:[15]

1. Iraq's invasion and brutal occupation of Kuwait represent a flagrant violation of international law and the Charter of the United Nations. . . . We condemn Iraq's persistent contempt for the Resolutions of the United Nations Security Council, which reflect the overwhelming solidarity and commitment of the international community.

2. The responsibility now lies with the government of Iraq to ensure peace by complying fully with the mandatory United Nations decisions.

3. We firmly support Resolution 678 and all other relevant Resolutions adopted by the Security Council. . . .

4. Security Council Resolution 678 has authorized the use of all necessary means if Iraq does not comply before that date, and has expressly called on all governments to provide appropriate support in implementing the resolutions adopted by the Security Council. Our countries will continue to respond positively to this United Nations request. Furthermore, each of us will continue to maintain and enforce the economic sanctions. . . .

5. We note that the crisis in the Gulf poses a potential threat to one of our allies . . . an armed attack against one of our states shall be considered an attack against them all.

The words used in the North Atlantic Council statement indicate that the obligation of a member to respond to a call for assistance in accordance with resolutions of a treaty organization is a binding obligation. They also indicate that the Council believes that use of armed force to respond to a treaty organization obligation is appropriate. The issue raised by the obligation to assist, based on the treaty organization's resolution(s), is whether, in the case of the United States, deploying U.S. forces is an action reflecting a "delegation" of emergency powers and responsibilities to the commander in chief. Much of the testimony during the hearings by the U.S. Senate Committee on Foreign Relations on the president's authority as commander in chief and the war in Indochina centered around the question of whether a treaty in effect acts as a delegation of congressional responsibility. The Honorable Justice William H. Rehnquist, Chief Justice of the U. S. Supreme Court, who was, at the time of the Indochina hearings, assistant attorney general, Office of Legal Counsel, testified regarding the delegation issue as follows:[16]

Congress may of course authorize Presidential action by declaration of war. But it is abundantly clear that its authorization of Presidential action may take other forms. From the example of the Fifth Congress' delegation to President Adams of the power to stop French vessels on the high seas, through the legislative acts authorizing President Eisenhower to use troops in Lebanon and in Formosa, and authorizing President Kennedy to use armed forces in connection with the Cuban missile crisis, to the Gulf of Tonkin Resolution in 1964, both Congress and the President have made it clear that it is the substance of Congressional authorization, and not the form which that authorization takes, which determines the extent to which Congress has exercised its portion of the war power.

The notion that an advance authorization by Congress of military operations is some sort of an invalid delegation of congressional war power is untenable in the light of decided cases.

Justice Rehnquist cited *United States v. Curtiss-Wright Corporation*, 299 U.S. 304 (1936)(specifically at 315 and 318) to support his argument.[17] He argued that even though the *Schechter Poultry Corporation v. United States*, 295 U.S. 495 (1935) "held that Congress in *delegating powers dealing with domestic affairs* must establish standards for administrative guidance, this principle does not obtain in the field of external affairs [emphasis added]."[18] He went on to argue that the authorization passes from Congress to Congress according to the immediacy of the situation. His conclusion was that President Nixon's authority regarding the Cambodian incursion was based on activities "jointly authorized by the two branches of government between which the powers of the Constitution divided the 'war power.'"[19] Rehnquist's arguments are given more weight in the light of comparison of the more recent *INS v. Chadha* and the earlier, classic *United States v. Anderson*, *Stewart v. Kahn*, and *Lichter v. United States*. These latter cases argue that emergency powers remain with the president and that the courts are reluctant to get into the conflict between Congress and the president regarding when a state of war is over.[20]

We examine the matter of the obligation to provide armed forces when called on by the United Nations Security Council and other treaty organizations in Chapter 8. It presents an analysis of the interrelationship of resolutions of treaty organizations and executive agreements committing U.S. troops in the recent invasion of Kuwait by Iraq. The invasion of Kuwait by Iraq was certainly an act of aggression and was considered a war between Kuwait and Iraq, but should the intervention of the United States on behalf of Kuwait and Saudi Arabia have been considered war with Iraq? If it was war, then Congress should have declared it war. If it was not war, was it necessary for President Bush to obtain approval of Congress in order to proceed to help Kuwait and Saudi Arabia repel the aggression?

President George Bush, in his letter of February 11, 1991, to congressional leaders, Thomas Foley, Speaker of the House of Representatives, and

Dan Quayle, president of the Senate, regarding his report to Congress on the national emergency caused by the invasion of Kuwait by Iraq, wrote as follows:[21]

8. The invasion of Kuwait and the continuing illegal occupation of that country by Saddam Hussein continue to pose an unusual and extraordinary threat to the national security and foreign policy of the United States. The United States remains committed to a multilateral resolution of this crisis through its actions implementing the binding decisions of the United Nations Security Council with respect to Iraq and Kuwait. I shall continue to exercise the powers at my disposal to apply economic sanctions against Iraq and occupied Kuwait as long as these measures are appropriate, . . .

Twelve days after the above letter was transmitted to the congressional leaders, President Bush addressed the nation at 10 p.m. in the Briefing Room of the White House over both radio and television with the following message (excerpts):[22]

Regrettably, the noon deadline passed without the agreement of the Government of Iraq to meet demands of United Nations Security Council Resolution 660, as set forth in the specific terms spelled out by the coalition to withdraw unconditionally from Kuwait. . . . I have therefore directed General Norman Schwarzkopf, in conjunction with coalition forces, to use all forces available including ground forces to eject the Iraqi army from Kuwait."

In view of the almost certain offensive measures anticipated to be taken by U.S. armed forces and given the events since August 2, 1990, should the War Powers Resolution have been triggered at any time before or after the letter to Congress?

NOTES

1. U.S. Department of State, *Bulletin XI*, Washington, October 7, 1944.

2. U.S. Department of State, *Charter of the United Nations* (Washington, D.C.: U.S. Government Printing Office, 1945) (hereafter in this chapter, this document will be referred to as *United Nations Charter*).

3. Ibid., Chapter I, Article 2, Sections 1, 2; George Church, "Trip Wires to War: What Would It Take for the U.S. to Attack Iraq, and How Would Bush Square the Decision with the U.N. and Congress?" *Time* (October 29, 1990): 48–51; Lori Damrosch, "Constitutional Control of Military Actions: A Comparative Dimension," *American Journal of International Law* 85:1 (January 1991): 74–88; Thomas Franck, and Faiza Patel, "UN Police Action in Lieu of War: 'The Old Order Changeth,'" *American Journal of International Law* 81:1 (January

1991): 63–74; Michael Glennon, "The Constitution and Chapter VII of the United Nations Charter," *American Journal of International Law* 85:1 (January 1991): 74–88; Bert Rockman, "Mobilizing Political Support for U.S. National Security," *Armed Forces and Society* 14 (Fall 1987): 17–41.

4. Compare Michael Glennon, "The Constitution and Chapter VII of the United Nations Charter," *American Journal of International Law* 85:1 (January 1991): 74–88; Oscar Schachter, "United Nations Law in the Gulf Conflict," *American Journal of International Law* 85:3 (July 1991): 452–473; Zbigniew Brzezinski, *Power and Principle: Memoirs of the National Security Advisor* (New York: Farrar, Strauss & Giroux, 1983); U.S. House of Representatives, House Committee on International Relations, "Hearings: Seizure of the *Mayaguez*," 94th Cong., 2nd Sess. (Washington, D.C.: U.S. Government Printing Office, 1974).

5. George Bush, "Statement on Allied Military Action in the Persian Gulf, January 16, 1991," in *Public Papers of the Presidents of the United States: George Bush* (Washington, D.C.: U.S. Government Printing Office, 1992): 42; George Bush, "Letter to Congressional Leaders Reporting on the National Emergency with Respect to Iraq," in *Public Papers of the Presidents of the United States: George Bush* (Washington, D.C.: U.S. Government Printing Office, 1992): 131–133; Gregory Bowens, "House Backs Measure Allowing U.S. Role in U.N. Operation," *Congressional Quarterly Weekly Report* (May 29, 1993): 1373; Burns Weston, "Security Council Resolution 678 and Persian Gulf Decision Making: Precarious Legitimacy," *American Journal of International Law* 85:3 (July 1991): 516–535; U.S. Department of State, "The Gulf Crisis: UN Security Council Actions," *U.S. Department of State Dispatch* 1:14 (December 3, 1990): 296.

6. *United Nations Charter*, Chapter V, Article 23, Section 1, lists permanent members. See also excerpted articles below in this chapter. See also "Secretary Baker's Meetings with Security Council Members," *U.S. Department of State Dispatch* 1:14 (December 3, 1990): 301.

7. Signed by the United States at the United Nations Conference on International Organization in San Francisco, June 26, 1945. Part of the preamble to the Charter states as follows: "Accordingly, our respective Governments, through representatives assembled in the city of San Francisco, who have exhibited their full powers found to be in good and due form, have agreed to the present Charter of the United Nations and do hereby establish an international Organization to be known as the United Nations."

8. *United Nations Charter*, Chapter VII, Section 39; see also United Nations, *Provisional Records of the Security Council*, U.N. Doc. S/PV.3046 (New York: United Nations, January 31, 1992).

9. In order of meetings of the Security Council—SCOR, 3rd Yr., 296th Mtg., May 19, 1948; SCOR, 3rd. Yr., 298th Mtg., May 20, 1948; and SCOR, 3rd. Yr., 309th Mtg., May 20, 1948, for the cases for the United States, France, Belgium, and the U.K., respectively.

10. Compare G.A. (General Assembly) Res. 1899(XVIII), November 13, 1963, and G.A. Res. 2074(XX), December 17, 1965, with G.A. Res. 377(V), November 3, 1950, and G.A. Res. 498(V), February 1, 1951.

11. "The Gulf Crisis: UN Security Council Actions," *U.S. Department of State Dispatch* 1:14 (December 3, 1990): 296. By the time of these sanctions, the U.S. public was ready to recommend the maximum use of force. See George Church, "Trip Wires to War: What Would It Take for the U.S. to Attack Iraq, and How Would Bush Square the Decision with the U.N. and Congress?" *Time* (October 29, 1990): 48–51; Dick Cheney, "Legislative-Executive Relations in National Security: Work Together to Govern," *Vital Speeches* 56:11 (March 15, 1990): 334–336.

12. "The Gulf Crisis: UN Security Council Actions," *U.S. Department of State Dispatch* 1:14 (December 3, 1990): 296. Compare Carroll Doherty, "Uncertain Congress Confronts President's Gulf Strategy," *Congressional Quarterly Weekly Report* 48:46 (November 17, 1990): 3879–3882; Carroll Doherty, "Congress Faces Grave Choices as Clock Ticks toward War: Institutional Pride and Constitutional Authority at Stake as Capitol Hill Searches for Role in Gulf Crisis," *Congressional Quarterly Weekly Report* (January 5, 1991): 7–9; "Congress Approves Resolution Authorizing Use of Force," *Congressional Quarterly Weekly Report* 49:2 (January 12, 1991): 131.

13. U.S. Department of State, "North Atlantic Council Statement on the Gulf," *U.S. Department of State Dispatch* 1:17 (December 24, 1990): 354. With the support of NATO and of the Security Council of the United Nations, president Bush needed only a mandate from the Congress of the United States to have near unanimous national and international support for an "all-out" major offensive against the Iraqi forces. President Bush had put together a twenty-eight–member coalition of nations. They were poised for the January 15 deadline for Saddam Huessin to get out of Kuwait.

14. Ibid. The language is the same as that used by President Lyndon Johnson in his August 5, 1964, letter to the U.S. Congress indicating the obligation of the United States under the provisions of the SEATO Treaty. His second proposition in that letter stated, "A threat to any nation in that region is a threat to all, and a threat to us."

15. Ibid. Proposition 5 of the NATO statement refers to the same phrase used in the United Nations Charter and in the SEATO Treaty, and was repeated by President Johnson in the citation above.

16. U.S. Senate, "Statement by William H. Rehnquist, Assistant Attorney General Office of Legal Counsel, on the President's Constitutional Authority to Order the Attack on the Cambodian Sanctuaries," in U.S. Senate Committee on Foreign Relations, *Documents Relating to the War Power of Congress, the President's Authority as Commander-in-Chief and the War in Indochina*, 91st Cong., 2nd Sess. (Washington, D.C.: U.S. Government Printing Office, 1970): 180–181. (Hereafter in this chapter, the work *Document . . .* will be referred to as *Documents Relating to the War Power*.) See Rehnquist's earlier statements in William

Rehnquist, "The Constitutional Issues—Administration Position," *New York University Law Review* 45 (June 1970): 628–639.

17. U.S. Senate, "Statement by William H. Rehnquist, Assistant Attorney General Office of Legal Counsel, on the President's Constitutional Authority to Order the Attack on the Cambodian Sanctuaries," in U.S. Senate Committee on Foreign Relations, *Documents Relating to the War Power,* p. 181.

18. Ibid., and Louis Fisher, *The Politics of Shared Power: Congress and the Executive* (Washington: Congressional Quarterly Press, 1981); Louis Fisher, "Delegating Power to the President," *Journal of Public Law* 19 (1970): 251; Douglas Weeks, "Legislative Power versus Delegated Legislative Power," *Georgetown Law Journal* 25 (1937): 314; Maurice Merrill, "Standards—A Safeguard for the Exercise of Delegated Power," *Nebraska Law Review* 47 (1968): 469; Douglas Rosenberg, "Delegation and Regulatory Reform: Letting the President Change the Rules," *Yale Law Journal* 89 (1980): 561.

19. U.S. Senate, "Statement by William H. Rehnquist, Assistant Attorney General Office of Legal Counsel, on the President's Constitutional Authority to Order the Attack on the Cambodian Sanctuaries," in U.S. Senate Committee on Foreign Relations, *Documents Relating to the War Power,* pp. 181–182; Francis Wormuth, *The Vietnam War: The President versus the Constitution* (Santa Barbara, Calif.: Center for the Study of Democratic Institutions, 1968); Stanley Faulkner, "War in Vietnam: Is It Constitutional?" *Georgetown Law Journal* 56 (June 1968): 1132–1143; John Ely, *On Taking Up Arms and Taking Responsibility: Constitutional Lessons of Vietnam and Its Aftermath* (Princeton, N.J.: Princeton University Press, 1993); Alexander Bickel, et al., "Indochina: The Constitutional Crisis," *Congressional Record* (daily ed.) 116 (May 20, 1970): S7117–S7123, Part II, *Congressional Record* (daily ed.) 116 (May 20, 1970): S7538–S7541.

20. *INS v. Chadha*, 462 U.S. 919 (1983); *United States v. Anderson*, 9 Wall. 56 (1870); *Stewart v. Kahn*, 11 Wall. 493 (1870); *Lichter v. United States*, 344 U.S. 742 (1947); Louis Fisher, *Constitutional Conflicts between Congress and the President*, 3rd ed. (Lawrence: University Press of Kansas, 1991); Thomas Franck, "Courts and Foreign Policy," *Foreign Policy* (Summer 1991): 66–86; Ludwell John III, "Abraham Lindoln and the Development of Presidential War-Making Powers: Prize Cases," *Civil War History* (September 1989): 208–224.

21. George Bush, "Letter to Congressional Leaders Reporting on the National Emergency with Respect to Iraq," in *Public Papers of the Presidents of the United States: George Bush* (Washington, D.C.: U.S. Government Printing Office, 1992): 133; Richard Lacayo, "A Reluctant Go-Ahead: As Hopes for Peace Fade, a Divided Congress Authorizes the President to Lead the United States into Battle," *Time* (January 21, 1991): 32–33; Richard Lacayo, "On the Fence: The President Says He Can Take America to War without Asking Congress. The Lawmakers Disagree—But Most Would Rather Not Take a Public Stand At All," *Time* (January 14, 1991): 12–14; Joan Biskupic, "Constitution's Conflicting Clauses Underscored by Iraq Crisis: Provisions on Waging War Leave a Basic Question

Unanswered, Does Congress or the President Call the Shot?" *Congressional Quarterly Weekly Report* (January 5, 1991): 33–36.

22. George Bush, "Address to the Nation Announcing Allied Military Ground Action in the Persian Gulf—February 23, 1991," in *Public Papers of the Presidents of the United States: George Bush* (Washington, D.C.: U.S. Government Printing Office, 1992): 171.

PART III

Congress and War Powers

Chapter 6

The War Powers Resolution

In previous chapters we observed that constitutional powers of the Congress and of the executive are both joint and separate. What further complicates the exercise of each entity's powers is the fact that through the constitutional treaty process, the responsibility and powers of Congress, the president, and third parties are even more intertwined. Some constitutional scholars argue that a treaty, after the advice and consent of the Senate is attached thereto, carries with it collateral responsibilities of enforcement—armed, if necessary. One of the main arguments in the Vietnam conflict for continuing to expand the use of armed force was that Congress had authorized such actions through the Southeast Asia Collective Defense Treaty (SEATO) of 1954 and subsequently through the Tonkin Gulf Resolution (passed by the House of Representatives on August 6, 1964, and by the Senate on August 7, 1964). Additionally, there were a number of congressional appropriations for the military in Vietnam which tended to lend some credibility to the claim that Congress approved of the actions taken or planned by the executive.

It is virtually impossible to objectively analyze the appropriateness of the actions taken by the executive during the Vietnam conflict without examining the explicit language of the SEATO treaty and the Gulf of Tonkin Resolution. The language, the implied intent, and the scope of covered activities are cast in the light of the United States going to the assistance of a nation for which a treaty relationship/obligation existed. Understanding the war powers of the Congress or of the president in his roles of chief executive and commander in chief requires acknowledging and understanding the context surrounding the request for U.S. assistance by South Vietnam. It may be added also that this SEATO Treaty relationship between the United States and the cosignatories, especially South Vietnam, was not just a recent relationship. It had existed since its signing in Manila on September 8, 1954 (it was approved by the Senate on February 19, 1955).

SEATO AND THE GULF OF TONKIN

Unlike Operation Desert Shield and Operation Desert Storm, discussed in Chapters 8 and 9, the use of armed forces in Southeast Asia was pursuant to obligations under the Southeast Asia Collective Defense Treaty of 1955 rather than pursuant to obligations under the United Nations Charter.[1] As the record will show, the use of the United Nations as a means of implementing peacekeeping efforts was viewed with skepticism, to say the least.[2]

With hostilities increasing by assaults from North Vietnam on both Laos and South Vietnam, casualties were mounting for the U.S. troops, vessels, and aircraft. The American public had not quite understood the magnitude of the operations in a land so far away—in Southeast Asia. It is hard to imagine today, but people did not even know how to pronounce the names of the major areas of hostilities in Southeast Asia in which our troops were serving. It was in this setting that President Lyndon Johnson sent a special message to Congress requesting support for the U.S. operations in Southeast Asia. Due to the letter's length, only excerpts are included here, but enough is presented to indicate the rationale and constitutional authority for making the request.[3]

Exhibit 6.1
Letter from President Lyndon Johnson to Congress—August 5, 1964

To the Congress of the United States:

These latest actions of the North Vietnamese regime have given a new and grave turn to the already serious situation in southeast Asia. Our commitments in that area are well known to the Congress. They were first made in 1954 by President Eisenhower. They were further defined in the Southeast Asia Collective Defense Treaty approved by the Senate in 1955.

This treaty with its accompanying protocol obligates the United States and other members to act in accordance with their constitutional processes *to meet Communist aggression against any of the parties or protocol states* [emphasis added].

Our policy in southeast Asia has been consistent and unchanged since 1954. I summarized it on June 2 in four simple propositions:

1. America keeps her word. Here as elsewhere, we must and shall honor our commitments.

2. The issue is the future of southeast Asia as a whole. *A threat to any nation in that region is a threat to all, and a threat to us* [emphasis added].

3. Our purpose is peace. We have no military, political, or territorial ambitions in the area.

4. This is not just a jungle war, but a struggle for freedom on every front of human activity. Our military and economic assistance to South Vietnam and Laos in particular has the purpose of helping these countries *to repel aggression* and strengthen their independence [emphasis added].

I recommend a resolution expressing the support of the Congress for *all necessary action to protect our Armed Forces* and to assist nations covered by the SEATO Treaty [emphasis added]. . . .

The resolution could well be based upon similar resolutions enacted by the Congress in the past—to meet the threat to Formosa in 1955, to meet the threat to the Middle East in 1957, and to meet the threat in Cuba in 1962. It could state in the simplest terms the resolve and support of the Congress for action to deal appropriately with attacks against our Armed Forces and to defend freedom and preserve peace in southeast Asia in accordance with the obligations of the United States under the Southeast Asia Treaty. . . .

LYNDON B. JOHNSON

THE WHITE HOUSE
August 5, 1964

The language and rationale of the request by President Johnson is similar to that of President Bush in requesting a resolution from Congress for Desert Storm in that (1) both are responding to aggression or to the threat of aggression against a member of a treaty or protocol nation, (2) both respond to obligations under treaties calling for mutual assistance, (3) both state equivalently that "a threat to any nation in that region is a threat to all, and a threat to us," and (4) both request congressional support for "all necessary action to protect our Armed Forces and to assist nations." Those who argue that the executive has continually and increasingly encroached on congressional prerogatives would argue also that both presidents, without the advice and consent of Congress, used armed forces on foreign soil and, after having placed our troops in harm's way, came to Congress for support to "protect American lives and interests."

The debate that followed the reading of President Johnson's letter to Congress was one of the most unusual in recent memory for a number of reasons. All participants were thoroughly knowledgeable regarding the constitutional issues involved, the precedents in Congress leading to this and other requests by President Eisenhower and President Kennedy, the treaty implications of our presence in Southeast Asia (particularly in Vietnam), and the scenario of hostilities leading up to the confrontations in the Gulf of Tonkin. The major players in that debate were Senators Fulbright, Stennis, Morse, Javits, Miller, and Nelson. By far the most eloquent of the arguments were those of Senator Morse, who heatedly argued that the proposed resolution was a "blank check" for the president to take any action he wanted to in Southeast Asia without oversight by the Congress.[4]

Before going too far in discussing some of the more important provisions of the Gulf of Tonkin Resolution, we must first check the actual language of the resolution. It is presented below.[5]

Exhibit 6.2
Gulf of Tonkin Resolution—S.J. Res. 189

P.L. 88–408 (78 Stat. 384)

A Joint Resolution to Promote the Maintenance of International Peace and Security in Southeast Asia.

Whereas naval units of the Communist regime in Vietnam, in violation of the principles of the Charter of the United Nations and of international law, have deliberately and repeatedly attacked United States naval vessels lawfully present in international waters, and have thereby created a serious threat to international peace;

Whereas these attacks are part of a deliberate and systematic campaign of aggression that the Communist regime in North Vietnam has been waging against its neighbors and the nations joined with them in the collective defense of their freedom;

Whereas the United States is assisting the peoples of southeast Asia to protect their freedom and has no territorial, military or political ambitions in that area, but desires only that these peoples should be left in peace to work out their own destinies in their own way; Now, therefore, be it

Resolved by the Senate and House of Representatives of the United States of America in Congress assembled, That the Congress approves and supports the determination of the President, as Commander in Chief, to take all necessary measures to repel any armed attack against the forces of the United States and to prevent further aggression.

SEC. 2. The United States regards as vital to its national interest and to world peace the maintenance of international peace and security in southeast Asia. Consonant with the Constitution and the Charter of the United Nations and in accordance with its obligations under the Southeast Asia Collective Defense Treaty, the United States is, therefore, prepared, as the President determines, to take all necessary steps, including the use of armed force, to assist any member or protocol state of the Southeast Asia Collective Defense Treaty requesting assistance in defense of its freedom.

SEC. 3. This resolution shall expire when the President shall determine that the peace and security of the area is reasonably assured by international conditions created by action of the United Nations or otherwise, except that it may be terminated earlier by concurrent resolution of the Congress."

Source: Congressional Record 110 (1964): 18133; P.L. 88–408 (78 Stat. 384), August 7, 1964.

The preamble to S.J. Res. 189 (1964) just cited makes only a passing reference to the United Nations Charter and international law. By contrast, the preamble to the authorization given to President Bush in Desert Storm, H.J. Res. 77 (1991), specifically cites Article 51 of the United Nations Charter, and United Nations Security Council Resolution 678.[6] The actual authorization given President Johnson was more sweeping than that given President Bush. President Johnson was authorized "to take all necessary measures to repel any armed attack against the forces of the United States and to prevent further aggression."[7] In the Desert Storm authorization, the president was authorized "to use United States Armed Forces pursuant to United Nations Security Council Resolution 678 (1990)."[8] Noteworthy also is the fact that the Gulf of Tonkin Resolution would expire only after a determination by the president that it should be terminated.

Some of the arguments against the Gulf of Tonkin Resolution were: (1) a fear that the resolution called for a predated declaration of war, (2) that it was a delegation of congressional duties to determine issues of war or peace, (3) that it authorized the president to make war without a declaration of war, and (4) that it was a unilateral action unsanctioned by the United Nations and unaccompanied by allies of the United States.[9]

Even though Senator Miller indicated to Senator Fulbright that he would vote for the resolution, he raised questions regarding the open-ended phrase "to take all necessary measures to repel any armed attack."[10] He argued that the phrase (1) does not mention against whom an armed attack will be conducted, (2) does not indicate whether further aggression will be required, and (3) does not indicate when the authorization will expire. Senator Fulbright attempted to allay Senate reservations with the following explanation:[11]

Mr. FULBRIGHT. Section 1 deals, in general, with attacks on U.S. forces and the aggression against us. Section 2 deals with the attacks on SEATO, of which we are a part. We have a dual role. We are a sovereign power. Our forces are in the Gulf of Tonkin, and the aggression there is one thing. We are also part of SEATO. This is not spelled out, but that is the general idea, I believe, that is expressed in the two sections.

Mr. MILLER. But there is no intention expressed other than to prevent further aggression and stop the present aggression in southeast Asia.

Mr. FULBRIGHT. That is correct.

The irony of the above exchange is that President Richard Nixon used the Gulf of Tonkin Resolution to carry armed aggression into Cambodia. It seems that Senator Miller's skepticism was quite properly warranted and Senator Fulbright's explanation was grossly incorrect. The authority under the Gulf of Tonkin Resolution continued until Congress repealed it on January 12, 1971. Interesting (and entertaining) debate regarding efforts to repeal the resolution can be found in the transcript of remarks by Senator Stennis and Senator Ervin, along with a humorous description of the debate on a radio program, in the *Congressional Record* for June 22, 1970.[12]

The sequel to the congressional approval of the Gulf of Tonkin Resolution involves the remarks of President Lyndon Johnson in the East Room of the White House on August 10, 1964, upon the signing of S.J. Res. 189. When he addressed the American people he indicated that the resolution stood "squarely on the corners of the Constitution," and "confirms and reinforces powers of the Presidency."[13] The language and the nuance of the Gulf of Tonkin Resolution and its delegation of authority reflected the feeling in Congress that the president was in a better position to assess the potential for aggression and peaceful solutions than the collective Congress. A careful reading of Section IV, "The Theoretical Bases for Unilateral Presidential Action," in *Documents Relating to the War Power of Congress, the President's Authority as Commander-in-Chief and the War in Indochina* indicates that although the Congress thought that the president actually did "have primary responsibility in the modern world for the handling of foreign policy, he should not have the discretion to initiate war as an instrument of foreign policy."[14]

Is it any wonder that President Johnson and subsequently President Nixon might have received mixed messages regarding the sense of Congress involving actions taken or planned in the Vietnam conflict? The Gulf of Tonkin Resolution essentially amounted to a "blank check" to the executive to conduct military operations until the president "shall determine that the peace and security of the area is reasonably assured." The resolution gave the president the prerogative to determine the following:[15]

1. The appropriate war policy to be determined
2. The question of determination of war and peace
3. The scope of limited war
4. The decision regarding whether there would be limited war or general war
5. The choice of adversary

To top the list off, Congress even gave the president $700 million to implement the provisions of the Gulf of Tonkin Resolution. Two years after Senator Fulbright maneuvered the Gulf of Tonkin Resolution through Congress, he was quoted as saying, "Each time Senators have raised questions about successive escalations of the war, we have had the blank check of August 7, 1964, waved in our faces as supposed evidence of the overwhelming support of the Congress for a policy in Southeast Asia."[16]

As the date of the document just cited will indicate, by 1970 the number of human casualties and the amount of national resources pumped into the "undeclared war" in Vietnam had split the nation apart politically. Congress and the president were being held accountable for what America by now had characterized as "the senseless war in Vietnam." It was in this context, coupled with the Watergate scandal of President Richard Nixon, that the War Powers Resolution, presented below in Exhibit 6.3, was passed over the presidential veto.

Exhibit 6.3
The War Powers Resolution—P.L. 93–148

JOINT RESOLUTION

Concerning the war powers of Congress and the President.

Resolved by the Senate and House of Representatives of the United States of America in Congress assembled,

SHORT TITLE

Section 1. This joint resolution may be cited as the "War Powers Resolution."

PURPOSE AND POLICY

Sec. 2.(a) It is the purpose of this joint resolution to fulfill the intent of the framers of the Constitution of the United States and insure that the collective judgement of both the Congress and the President will apply to the introduction of United States Armed Forces into hostilities, or into situations where imminent involvement in hostilities is clearly indicated by the circumstances, and to the continued use of such forces in hostilities or in such situations.

(b) Under article I, section 8, of the Constitution, it is specifically provided that the Congress shall have the power to make all laws necessary and proper for carrying into execution, not only its own powers but also all other powers vested by the Constitution in the government of the United States, or in any department or officer thereof.

(c) The constitutional powers of the President as Commander-in-Chief to introduce United States Armed Forces into hostilities, or into situations where imminent involvement in hostilities is clearly indicated by the circumstances, are exercised only pursuant to (1) a declaration of war, (2) specific statutory authorization, or (3) a national emergency created by attack upon the United States, its territories or possessions, or its armed forces.

CONSULTATION

Sec. 3. The President in every possible instance shall consult with Congress before introducing United States Armed Forces into hostilities or into situations where imminent involvement in hostilities is clearly indicated by the circumstances, and after every such introduction shall consult regularly with the Congress until United States Armed Forces are no longer engaged in hostilities or have been removed from such situations.

REPORTING

Sec. 4.(a) In the absence of a declaration of war, in any case in which the United States Armed Forces are introduced—

(1) into hostilities or into situations where imminent involvement in hostilities is clearly indicated by the circumstances;

(2) into the territory, airspace or waters of a foreign nation, while equipped for combat, except for deployments which relate solely to supply, replacement, repair, or training such forces; or

(3) in numbers which substantially enlarge United States Armed Forces equipped for combat already located in a foreign nation;

The President shall submit within 48 hours to the Speaker of the House of Representatives and to the President pro tempore of the Senate a report, in writing, setting forth—

(A) the circumstances necessitating the introduction of United States Armed Forces;

(B) the constitutional and legislative authority under which such introduction took place; and

(C) the estimated scope and duration of the hostilities or involvement.

(b) The President shall provide such other information as Congress may request in the fulfillment of its constitutional responsibilities with respect to committing the Nation to War and to the use of United States Armed Forces abroad.

(c) Whenever United States Armed Forces are introduced into hostilities or into any situation described in subsection (a) of this section, the President shall so long as such armed forces continue to be engaged in such hostilities or situation, report to Congress periodically on the status of such hostilities or situation as well as on the scope and duration of such hostilities or situation, but in no event shall he report to Congress less often than once every six months.

Sec. 5.(a) Each report submitted pursuant to section 4(a)(1) shall be transmitted to the Speaker of the House of Representatives and to the President pro tempore of the Senate on the same calendar day. Each report so transmitted shall be referred to the Committee on Foreign Affairs of the House of Representatives and to the Committee on Foreign Relations of the Senate for appropriate action. If, when the report is transmitted, the Congress had adjourned sine die or has adjourned for any period in excess of three calendar days, the Speaker of the House of Representatives and the President pro tempore of the Senate, if they deem it advisable (or if petitioned by at least 30 percent of the membership of their respective Houses) shall jointly request the President to convene Congress in order that it may consider the report and take appropriate action pursuant to this section.

(b) Within sixty calendar days after a report is submitted or is required to be submitted pursuant to section 4(a)(1), whichever is earlier, the President shall terminate any use of United States Armed Forces with respect to which such report was submitted (or required to be submitted), unless the Congress (1) has declared war or has enacted a specific authorization for such use of United States Armed Forces, (2) has extended by law such sixty-day period, or (3) is physically unable to meet as a result of an armed attack upon the United States. Such sixty-day period shall be extended for not more than an additional thirty days if the President determines and certifies to the Congress in writing that unavoidable military necessity respecting the safety of the United States Armed Forces requires the continued use of such armed forces in the course of bringing about a prompt removal of such forces.

(c) Notwithstanding subsection (b), at any time that United States Armed Forces are engaged in hostilities outside the territory of the United States, its possessions and territories without a declaration of war or specific statutory authorization, such forces shall be removed by the President if the Congress so directs by concurrent resolution.

CONGRESSIONAL PRIORITY PROCEDURES FOR JOINT RESOLUTION OR BILL

Sec. 6. [This section establishes the technical procedures for introducing an expedited bill or joint resolution in Congress under Section 5(b) of the War Powers Resolution.]

CONGRESSIONAL PRIORITY PROCEDURES FOR CONCURRENT RESOLUTION

Sec. 7. [This section establishes the technical procedures for introducing an expedited concurrent resolution in Congress under Section 5(b) of the War Powers Resolution.]

INTERPRETATION OF JOINT RESOLUTION

Sec. 8.(a) Authority to introduce United States Armed Forces into hostilities or into situations wherein involvement in hostilities is clearly indicated by the circumstances shall not be inferred—

(1) from any provision of law (whether or not in effect before the date of the enactment of this joint resolution) including any provision contained in any appropriation act, unless such provision specifically authorizes the introduction of United States Armed Forces into hostilities or into such situations and states that it is intended to constitute specific statutory authorization within the meaning of this joint resolution; or

(2) from any treaty heretofore or hereafter ratified unless such treaty is implemented by legislation specifically authorizing the introduction of United States Armed Forces into hostilities or into such situations and stating that it is intended to constitute specific statutory authorization within the meaning of this joint resolution.

(b) Nothing in this joint resolution shall be construed to require any further specific statutory authorization to permit members of United States Armed Forces to participate jointly with members of the armed forces of one or more foreign countries in the headquarters operations of high-level military commands which were established prior to the date of enactment of this joint resolution and pursuant to the United Nations Charter or any treaty ratified by the United States prior to such date.

(c) For purposes of this joint resolution, the term "introduction of United States Armed Forces" includes the assignment of members of such armed forces to command, coordinate, participate in the movement of, or accompany the regular or irregular military forces of any foreign country or government when such military forces are engaged, or there exists an imminent threat that such forces will become engaged, in hostilities.

(d) Nothing in this joint resolution—

(1) is intended to alter the constitutional authority of the Congress or of the President, or the provisions of existing treaties; or

(2) shall be construed as granting any authority to the President with respect to the introduction of United States Armed Forces into hostilities or into situations wherein involvement in hostilities is clearly indicated by the circumstances which authority he would not have had in the absence of this joint resolution.

SEPARABILITY CLAUSE

Sec. 9. If any provision of this joint resolution or the application thereof to any person or circumstance is held invalid, the remainder of the joint resolution and the application of such provision to any other person or circumstance shall not be affected thereby.

EFFECTIVE DATE

Sec. 10. This joint resolution shall take effect on the date of its enactment.

Enacted November 7, 1973 over the veto of President Richard M. Nixon. H.J. Res. 542, 87 Stat. 555 (1973)

Section 5(a) simply outlines the procedures for submission of the Section 4(a)(1) report to Congress. It additionally outlines the procedure for Congress to be convened when it is necessary for it to consider such a report and to take appropriate action. It has not created serious controversy either inside or outside the White House.

CONSTITUTIONAL IMPEDIMENTS OF SECTION 5(B)

In sharp contrast to Section 5(a), Sections 5(b) and 5(c) are the most controversial sections of the War Powers Resolution. Attention is drawn to the phrase "the President shall terminate any use of United States Armed Forces," that is, Congress is *requiring* the president to terminate the use of U.S. armed forces (1) within sixty days after submitting a Section 4(a)(1) report, or (2) within sixty days of when a report was "required to be submitted" *in the opinion of Congress*. This is viewed as usurping the presidential prerogative of determining when U.S. armed forces have been deployed "into hostilities or into situations where imminent involvement in hostilities is clearly indicated by the circumstances."[17] The president, some members of Congress, and some constitutional scholars argue that this provision—calling for Congress to make this determination—violates the "commander in chief" clause of the Constitution.[18]

What are the congressional alternatives during the sixty-day with-drawal period called for in Section 5(b)? Four alternatives are outlined in the resolution itself: (1) Congress can declare war. Since, under the Constitution, Congress has the power to declare war, it can do so without a presidential signature. (2) Congress can specifically authorize the use of armed forces. There are numerous examples, presented in the previous and following chapters, of these authorizations. Joint resolutions are appropriate for this purpose, but the form of the authorizations is not spelled out in Section 5(b). (3) Congress can extend by law the sixty-day period. This alternative can also be implemented with a joint resolution or bill. (4) If Congress "is physically unable to meet as a result of an armed attack upon the United States" the sixty-day period may be extended.

It should be noted from the language of Section 5(b) that the president himself may, unilaterally, extend the sixty-day period by thirty days by providing Congress, in writing, with an appropriate determination or certification that such is warranted. A problem with the interpretation of the phrase "shall terminate any use of United States Armed Forces" is that it is not clear that a full or partial withdrawal is included in the concept of "termination of use."[19] Additionally, there is some question regarding whether the "termination of use" is associated with a very specific, narrowly defined situation for which the Section 4(a)(1) report was submitted or was required to have been submitted, or whether it is associated with the broader context of ongoing hostilities or imminent hostilities.

CONCURRENT RESOLUTION IN SECTION 5(C)

Section 5(c) is even more suspect to the executive, some members of Congress, and constitutional scholars because it contains the provision "such forces shall be removed by the President if the Congress so directs by concurrent resolution."[20] It is argued that the concurrent resolution was used to avoid having to "present" such a resolution to the president for his signature (as in the case of a joint resolution or bill) and to avoid having to muster a two-thirds vote in each house to override a presidential veto. In several cases, including especially *INS v. Chadha* (1983) and *U.S. Senate v. Federal Trade Commission* (1983), such uses of the concurrent resolution were held to violate the "presentment clause."[21]

Those who favor replacing the concurrent resolution with a joint resolution, which must be presented to the president, argue that the president could veto such a joint resolution and thereby require a two-thirds majority in both houses of Congress to override the veto. The argument continues that the president, therefore, could continue with the action in question, despite congressional opposition, by mustering enough votes to have *one-third plus one vote in either of the houses of Congress*. They point to the case where President Nixon chose to continue combat activities in Cambodia and Laos despite a congressional bill to cut off appropriations for such activities. In that case, President Nixon vetoed the bill providing for a cutoff of appropriations for any activities in Cambodia and Laos, and Congress had to revise the bill so that funds were available for another forty-five days.[22]

Even though the concurrent resolution provision in Section 5(c) may not be constitutionally binding, it still may be an effective way for the Congress to express the "sense of the Congress" regarding the presidential use of force in a given situation. Laying aside the "one-third plus one vote" argument cited above, it would seem reasonable to believe that a president would weigh carefully the commitment of armed forces for very long if that is all the support that he could find in Congress. Very often the force of political power is greater than the force of constitutional power—535 members of Congress could take their cases to the people and have the people give the president a political mandate to withdraw or face political "suicide" in the next election not only for himself, but also for candidates of his political party.

The following chapters present documents and arguments which indicate the positions of Congress and the president regarding the necessity for the president to respond to the provisions of the War Powers Resolution in operations in Somalia and Iraq. In each of these situations, U.S. armed forces were involved in hostilities, but Section 4(a)(1) of the War Powers Resolution was not voluntarily triggered by the president.

NOTES

1. Refer to the third paragraph in President Lyndon B. Johnson's letter to Congress of August 5, 1964, in "Special Message to the Congress on U.S. Policy in Southeast Asia—August 5, 1964," in *Public Papers of the Presidents of the United States: Lyndon B. Johnson* (August 5, 1964), Vol. II (Washington, D.C.: U.S. Government Printing Office, 1963–1964): 930–932, and "To Promote the Maintenance of International Peace and Security in Southeast Asia—Message from the President" (H. Doc. No. 333) (August 5, 1964) *Congressional Record—Senate* 110 (Washington, D.C.: U.S. Government Printing Office, 1964): 18132. See also notes *passim* throughout Chapters 5 and 6 of this book and Southeast Asia Collective Defense Treaty (SEATO), 6 U.S.T. 81, T.I.A.S. No. 3170, 209 U.N.T.S. 28 (effective February 19, 1955); U.S. Senate Foreign Relations Committee, "Hearings on the Southeast Asia Collective Defense Treaty," 83rd Cong., 2nd Sess., November 11, 1954 (Washington, D.C.: U.S. Government Printing Office, 1954).

2. See the testimony surrounding the Gulf of Tonkin Resolution in "To Promote the Maintenance of International Peace and Security in Southeast Asia—Message from the President" (H. Doc. No. 333) (August 5, 6, 1964) *Congressional Record—Senate*, (Washington, D.C.: U.S. Government Printing Office, 1964): 18132–18416; Lori Damrosch, "Constitutional Control of Military Actions: A Comparative Dimension," *American Journal of International Law* 85:1 (January 1991): 74–88; Carroll Doherty, "Congress Faces Grave Choices As Clock Ticks toward War: Institutional Pride and Constitutional Authority at Stake As Capitol Hill Searches for Role in Gulf Crisis," *Congressional Quarterly Weekly Report* (January 5, 1991): 7–9; Carroll Doherty, "Uncertain Congress Confronts President's Gulf Strategy," *Congressional Quarterly Weekly Report* 48:46 (November 17, 1990): 3879–3882.

3. "To Promote the Maintenance of International Peace and Security in Southeast Asia—Message from the President (H. Doc. No. 333) (August 5, 6, 1964) *Congressional Record—Senate* 110 (Washington, D.C.: U.S. Government Printing Office, 1964): 18132; James Burns, *Presidential Government: The Crucible of Leadership* (Boston: Houghton Mifflin, 1966); Thomas Eagleton, "The August 15 Compromise and the War Powers of Congress," *St. Louis University Law Journal* 18 (Fall 1973): 1–11; Richard Evans, and Robert Novak, *Lyndon B. Johnson: The Exercise of Power* (New York: The New American Liberty, 1966).

4. "To Promote the Maintenance of International Peace and Security in Southeast Asia—Message from the President" (H. Doc. No. 333) (August 5, 6, 1964) *Congressional Record—Senate* 110 (Washington, D.C.: U.S. Government Printing Office, 1964): 18133–18139; *Public Papers of the Presidents of the*

United States: Lyndon B. Johnson, 1963–1964, 2 vols. (Washington, D.C.: U.S. Government Printing Office, 1965); Louis Fisher, "Delegating Power to the President," *Journal of Public Law* 19 (1970): 251; William Rehnquist, "Statement by William H. Rehnquist, Assistant Attorney General Office of Legal Counsel, on the President's Constitutional Authority to Order the Attack on the Cambodian Sanctuaries," in U.S. Senate, *Documents Relating to the War Power of Congress, the President's Authority as Commander-in-Chief and the War in Indochina*, 91st Cong., 2nd Sess. (Washington, D.C.: U.S. Government Printing Office, 1970): 182–185; Harry Summers, Jr., *On Strategy: A Critical Analysis of the Vietnam War* (Novato, Calif.: Presidio Press, 1982).

5. *Congressional Record* 110 (1964): 18133; P.L. 33–408 (78 Stat. 384), August 7, 1964. Vote was 414 for, 0 opposed in the House of Representatives and 88 for, 2 opposed in the Senate. Anthony Austin, *The President's War: The Story of the Tonkin Gulf Resolution and How the Nation Was Trapped in Vietnam* (Philadelphia: J. B. Lippincott, 1971); U.S. Senate Foreign Relations Committee, "Hearings on the Gulf of Tonkin, the 1964 Incidents," 90th Cong., 2nd Sess., February 20, 1968 (Washington, D.C.: U.S. Government Printing Office, 1968).

6. U.S. House of Representatives, "Authorization for Use of Military Force against Iraq Resolution," P.L. 102–1 (H.J. Res. 77), January 14, 1991; Burns Weston, "Security Council Resolution 678 and Persian Gulf Decision Making: Precarious Legitimacy," *American Journal of International Law* 85:3 (July 1991): 516–535; Oscar Schachter, "United Nations Law in the Gulf Conflict," *American Journal of International Law* 85:3 (July 1991): 452–473; Patrick James, and John Oneal, "The Influence of Domestic and International Politics on the President's Use of Force," *Journal of Conflict Resolution* 35:2 (June 1991): 307–332.

7. U.S. Senate, *Congressional Record* 110 (1964): 18133; P.L. 33–408 (78 Stat. 384), August 7, 1964, Section 1. One of the single best sources for the text of the Gulf of Tonkin Resolution and the SEATO Treaty are presented in U.S. House of Representatives, *The War Powers Resolution: A Special Study of the Committee on Foreign Affairs* (Committee Print), Committee on Foreign Affairs (Washington, D.C.: U.S. Government Printing Office, 1982), Chapters 1–3. For the U.S. Senate hearings associated with this matter, review U.S. Senate, *Documents Relating to the War Power of Congress, the President's Authority as Commander-in-Chief and the War in Indochina*, Committee on Foreign Relations, 91st Cong., 2nd Sess. (Washington, D.C.: U.S. Government Printing Office, 1970). An interesting historical setting is provided in Anthony Austin, *The President's War: The Story of the Tonkin Gulf Resolution and How the Nation Was Trapped in Vietnam* (Philadelphia: J. B. Lippincott, 1971).

8. U.S. House of Representatives. "Authorization for Use of Military Force against Iraq Resolution," P.L. 102–1 (H J. Res. 77), January 14, 1991, Sec. 2(a); U.S. Department of State, "The Gulf Crisis: UN Security Council Actions," *U.S. Department of State Dispatch* 1:14 (December 3, 1990): 296;

George Bush, "Statement on Allied Military Action in the Persian Gulf, January 16, 1991," in *Public Papers of the Presidents of the United States: George Bush* (Washington, D.C.: U.S. Government Printing Office, 1992): 42; "Congress Approves Resolution Authorizing Use of Force," *Congressional Quarterly Weekly Report* 49:2 (January 12, 1991): 131; Oscar Schachter, "United Nations Law in the Gulf Conflict," *American Journal of International Law* 85:3 (July 1991): 452–473; "The Waiting Game," *Commonweal* (November 23, 1990): 675–676; Paul Savoy, "Peacekeepers for the Gulf," *The Nation* (November 26, 1990): 642–644; "The War Powers Act," *Congressional Digest* 66:12 (December 1987): 290–291.

9. "To Promote the Maintenance of International Peace and Security in Southeast Asia—Message from the President" (H. Doc. No. 333) (August 5, 6, 1964) *Congressional Record—Senate* 110 (Washington, D.C.: U.S. Government Printing Office, 1964): 18132–18416; Anthony Austin, *The President's War: The Story of the Tonkin Gulf Resolution and How the Nation Was Trapped in Vietnam* (Philadelphia: J. R. Lippincott, 1971); Alexander Bickel, et al., "Indochina: The Constitutional Crisis," *Congressional Record* (daily ed.) 116 (May 13, 1970): S7117–S7123, Part II, *Congressional Record* (daily ed.) 116 (May 20, 1970): S7538–S7541; and the interesting perspectives given by Senator Thomas Eagleton in Thomas Eagleton, "Congress and War Powers," *Missouri Law Review* 37 (Winter 1972): 1–32, Thomas Eagleton, "The August 15 Compromise and the War Powers of Congress," *St. Louis University Law Journal* 18 (Fall 1973): 1–11; Thomas Eagleton, *War and Presidential Power: A Chronicle of Congressional Surrender* (New York: Liveright, 1974); Thomas Eagleton, "Whose Power Is War Power?" *Foreign Policy* 8 (Fall 1972): 23–32.

10. "To Promote the Maintenance of International Peace and Security in Southeast Asia—Message from the President" (H. Doc. No. 333) (August 5, 6, 1964) *Congressional Reccord—Senate* (Washington, D.C.: U.S. Government Printing Office, 1964): 18405. Miller was not alone in his opposition to the "blank check" language. Representative Clement Zablocki, Senator Ernest Gruening, Senator Sam Ervin, Senator Daniel Brewster, Senator Wayne Morse, and Senator Gaylord Nelson strongly opposed the language. See U.S. House of Representatives, *The War Powers Resolution: A Special Study of the Committee on Foreign Affairs* (Committee Print), Committee on Foreign Affairs, especially pp. 1–6. Senator Wayne Morse even went as far as stating: "I believe that history will record that we have made a great mistake by subverting and circumventing the Constitution of the United States *** by means of this resolution. As I argued earlier today at great length, we are in effect giving the President *** warmaking powers in the absence of a declaration of war." Cited in U.S. House of Representatives, *The War Powers Resolution: A Special Study of the Committee on Foreign Affairs* (Committee Print), Committee on Foreign Affairs, p. 5, and in *Congressional Record*, August 7, 1963, pp. 18403–18404.

11. "To Promote the Maintenance of International Peace and Security in Southeast Asia—Message from the President" (H. Doc. No. 333) (August 5, 6,

1964) *Congressional Record—Senate* (Washington, D.C.: U.S. Government Printing Office, 1964): 18406; U.S. House of Representatives, *The War Powers Resolution: A Special Study of the Committee on Foreign Affairs* (Committee Print), Committee on Foreign Affairs, pp. 1–16. Tragically, Senator William Fulbright, who devotedly led the floor fights to push the Gulf of Tonkin Resolution through opposition, became disenchanted with President Johnson's Vietnam policy and was quoted in the just cited work, page 10, as saying, "I believe the Presidency has become a dangerously powerful office, more urgently in need of reform than any other institution of American Government." This statement and his subsequent actions caused a never-to-be-healed split in the longtime relationship between himself and Lyndon Johnson.

12. *Congressional Record* 116 (1970): 20750, 22567.

13. "Remarks upon Signing Joint Resolution of the Maintenance of Peace and Security in Southeast Asia—August 10, 1964," in *Public Papers of the Presidents of the United States: Lyndon B. Johnson, 1963–1964*, 2 vols. (Washington, D.C.: U.S. Government Printing Office, 1965): 946–947. Interesting insights regarding the events just before, during, and just after the signing of the Gulf of Tonkin Resolution are given in: Thomas Eagleton, *War and Presidential Power: A Chronicle of Congressional Surrender* (New York: Liveright, 1974); Eugene Rostow, *Peace in the Balance: The Future of American Foreign Policy* (New York: Simon & Schuster, 1972); Donald Morgan, *Congress and the Constitution: A Study of Responsibility* (Cambridge, Mass.: Harvard University Press, 1966).

14. U.S. Senate, *Documents Relating to the War Power of Congress, the President's Authority as Commander-in-Chief and the War in Indochina*, Committee on Foreign Relations, 91st Cong., 2nd Sess. (Washington, D.C.: U.S. Government Printing Office, 1970): 78–82. Secretaty of State Dean Rusk and Senator William Fulbright were two of the most respected personages on Capitol Hill at the time and the public believed that they were both sincere and right in their assertion that the language was appropriate for a commander in chief in a time of national and international crisis. Additionally, Secretary of Defense Robert McNamara had credibility in his assessments of the military issues in Vietnam in particular and in Southeast Asia in general. Leonard Meeker of the Department of state sent a memorandum to the Senate Foreign Relations Committee on March 8, 1966, outlining his views of the constitutionality of U.S. involvement. He stated (in part): "The President of the United States has full authority to commit U.S. forces in the collective defense of South Vietnam. This authority stems from the constitutional powers of the President. . . . These duties carry very broad powers, including the power to deploy American forces abroad and commit them to military operations when the President deems such action necessary to maintain security and defense of the United States." See U.S. House of Representatives, *The War Powers Resolution: A Special Study of the Committee on Foreign Affairs* (Committee Print), Committee on Foreign Affairs, p. 13.

15. U.S. Senate, *Documents Relating to the War Power of Congress, the President's Authority as Commander-in-Chief and the War in Indochina*,

96   *War Powers*

Committee on Foreign Relations, 247, 160–164. Schlesinger was critical of this "blank check" given by congress in Arthur Schlesinger, Jr., *The Imperial Presidency* (Boston: Houghton Mifflin, 1973), *passim*, especially p. 184. See also John Ely, *On Taking Up Arms and Taking Responsibility: Constitutional Lessons of Vietnam and Its Aftermath* (Princeton, N.J.: Princeton University Press, 1993), Chapters 2 and 4; U.S. Senate Foreign Relations Committee, "Hearings on U.S. Commitments to Foreign Powers," 90th Cong., 1st Sess., August 16–September 19, 1967 (Washington, D.C.: U.S. Government Printing Office, 1967); U.S. Senate Foreign Relations Committee, "National Commitments," Senate Report No. 797, 90th Cong., 1st Sess., November 20, 1967 (Washington, D.C.: U.S. Government Printing Office, 1967).

16. U.S. Senate, *Documents Relating to the War Power of Congress, the President's Authority as Commander-in-Chief and the War in Indochina*, Committee on Foreign Relations (Washington, D.C.: U.S. Government Printing Office, 1970): 161. Much to the chagrin of Senator Fulbright, Senators Daniel Brewster, Jacob Javitz, Wayne Morse, and others were right in their misgivings about the Gulf of Tonkin Resolution. Less than a year from its passage, on March 3 through March 6, 1965, the Pentagon announced that "more than 100 U.S. jets had bombed North Vietnamese munitions depots." U.S. House of Representatives, *The War Powers Resolution: A Special Study of the Committee on Foreign Affairs* (Committee Print), Committee on Foreign Affairs, p. 7. This was an *offensive* action. Thousands of American troops were on Vietnamese soil. The "blank check" that Congress had given to President Johnson had turned into an "all-out war." See John Stennis, and William Fulbright, *The Role of Congress in Foreign Policy* (Washington, D.C.: American Enterprise Institute, 1971); Anthony Austin, *The President's War: The Story of the Tonkin Gulf Resolution and How the Nation Was Trapped in Vietnam* (Philadelphia: J. B. Lippincott, 1971); U.S. Senate Foreign Relations Committee, "Hearings on the Gulf of Tonkin, the 1964 Incidents," 90th Cong., 2nd Sess., February 20, 1968 (Washington, D.C.: U.S. Government Printing Office, 1968).

17. War Powers Resolution, Section 4(a)(1). See arguments of Leonard Meeker, legal advisor for the Department of State in U.S. Department of State, "The Legality of United States Participation in the Defense of Viet-Nam," *Department of State Bulletin* (March 28, 1966): 474–489; U.S. House of Representatives, *Congress, the President, and the War Powers*, Hearings before the House Subcommittee on National Security Policy and Scientific Developments of the Committee on Foreign Affairs, 91st Cong., 2nd sess. (Washington, D.C.: U.S. Government Printing Office, 1970); U.S. Senate Foreign Relations Committee, "Hearings on U.S. Commitments to Foreign Powers," 90th Cong., 1st Sess., August 16–September 19, pp. 128–131. One will gain a special insight into President Johnson's view of the his authority with or without the Gulf of Tonkin Resolution in remarks made at a weekly press conference on August 18, 1967, and in the hearings just cited.

18. See especially the arguments in U.S. House of Representatives, *War Powers: Origins, Purposes, and Applications: Hearings before the Subcommittee on Arms Control, International Security and Science of the Committee on Foreign Affairs*, 100th Cong., 2nd Sess., August 4, 1988, and September 27, 1988 (Washington, D.C.: U.S. Government Printing Office, 1989); U.S. House of Representatives, *The War Powers Resolution: A Special Study of the Committee on Foreign Affairs* (Committee Print), Committee on Foreign Affairs; U.S. Senate Foreign Relations Committee, "Hearings on U.S Commitments to Foreign Powers," 90th Cong., 1st Sess., August 16–September 19, 1967 (Washington, D.C.: U.S. Government Printing Office, 1967); U.S. Senate, *Documents Relating to the War Power of Congress, the President's Authority as Commander-in-Chief and the War in Indochina*, Committee on Foreign Relations, 91st Cong., 2nd Sess. (Washington, D.C.: U.S. Government Printing Office, 1970); U.S. Senate, *War Powers*, S. Rept. 93–220, 93rd Cong., 1st Sess. (Washington, D.C.: U.S. Government Printing Office, 1973); U.S. Senate, *War Powers Legislation*, Hearings before the Senate Foreign Relations Committee, 92nd Cong., 1st Sess. (Washington, D.C.: U.S. Government Printing Office, 1971); Arthur Bestor, "Separation of Powers in the Domain of Foreign Affairs: The Original Intent of the Constitution Historically Examined," *Seton Hall Law Review* 5 (1974): 529; "Congress, the President, and the Power to Commit Forces to Combat," Note. *Harvard Law Review* 81 (June 1968): 1771–1805; Louis Fisher, *President and Congress* (New York: Free Press, 1972).

19. See the arguments in Appendix 3 of U.S. House of Representatives, *War Powers: Origins, Purposes, and Applications: Hearings before the Subcommittee on Arms Control, International Security and Science of the Committee on Foreign Affairs*, 100th Cong., 2nd Sess., August 4, 1988, and September 27, 1988 (Washington, D.C.: U.S. Government Printing Office, 1989): 230–239; William D. Rogers, "The Constitutionality of the Cambodian Incursion," *American Journal of International Law* 65 (January 1971): 26–37; Richard M. Nixon, "U.S. Foreign Policy for the 1970's: A New Strategy for Peace," *Message from the President of the United States Transmitting a Report on Foreign Relations*, House Document No. 91–258 (Feburary 18, 1970); Thomas Eagleton, *War and Presidential Power: A Chronicle of Congressional Surrender* (New York: Liveright, 1974); William P. Rogers, "Congress, the President, and the War Powers," *California Law Review* 59 (September 1971): 1194–1214; Stuart Keown, "The President, the Congress, and the Power to Declare War," *University of Kansas Law Review* 16 (November 1967): 82–97.

20. Robert Turner, *The War Powers Resolution: Its Implementation in Theory and Practice* (Philadelphia: Philadelphia Foreign Policy Research Institute, 1983); Robert Turner, "The War Powers Resolution: Unconstitutional, Unnecessary and Unhelpful," *Loyola of Los Angeles Law Review* 17 (1984): 683; Elliot Richardson, "Testimony of Elliot L. Richardson on the War Powers Resolution: Conflicting Constitutional Powers, the War Powers and U.S. Foreign Policy," in U.S. House of Representatives, *War Powers: Origins, Purposes, and applications: Hearings*

before the Subcommittee on Arms Control, International Security and Science of the Committee on Foreign Affairs, 100th Cong., 2nd Sess., August 4, 1988, and September 27, 1988 (Washington, D.C.: U.S. Government Printing Office, 1987): 138–206; John Ely, On Taking Up Arms and Taking Responsibility: Constitutional Lessons of Vietnam and Its Aftermath (Princeton, N.J.: Princeton University Press, 1993), Chapter 4; U.S. Senate, War Powers, S. Rept. 93–220, 93rd Cong., 1st Sess. (Washington, D.C.: U.S. Government Printing Office, 1973); U.S. Senate, War Powers Legislation, Hearings before the Senate Foreign Relations Committee, 92nd Cong., 1st Sess. (Washington, D.C.: U.S. Government Printing Office, 1971).

21. See also the wide range of argument associated with the "legislative veto" in Louis Fisher, Constitutional Conflicts between Congress and the President, 3rd ed. (Lawrence: University Press of Kansas, 1991); U.S. Senate, Documents Relating to the War Power of Congress, the President's Authority as Commander-in-Chief and the War in Indochina, Committee on Foreign Relations, 91st Cong., 2nd Sess. (Washington, D.C.: U.S. Government Printing Office, 1970), passim; 99 Stat. 448, sec. 801 (1985); 131 Congressional Record 131 (1985): 14947–14948; and compare U.S. House of Representatives, "War Powers: A Text of Compliance: Hearings before the House Committee on International Relations," 94th Cong., 1st Sess. (1975): 91 and U.S. Senate, The War Power after 200 Years: Congress and the President at a Constitutional Impasse, Hearings before the Special Subcommittee on War Powers of the Senate Committee on Foreign Relations, 100th Cong., 2nd Sess. (Washington, D.C.: U.S. Government Printing Office, 1989); Joseph Cooper, and Ann Cooper, "The Legislative Veto and the Constitution," George Washington Law Review 30 (1962): 467; Frederick Kaiser, "Congressional Control of Executive Actions in the Aftermath of the Chadha Decision," Administive Law Review 36 (1984): 239; Donald Elliot, "INS v. Chadha: The Administrative Constitution, the Constitution, and the Legislative Veto," Supreme Court Review (1983): 125; Cornelius Cotter and Malcolm Smith, "Administrative Accountability to Congress: The Concurrent Resolution," Western Political Quarterly 9 (1956): 955.

22. It is interesting to see the development of judicial thought in Holtzman v. Schlesinger, 361 F. Supp. 553 (E.D.N.Y. 1973) through Holtzman v. Schlesinger, 484 F. 2d 1307 (2d Cir. 1973), cert. denied, 416 U.S. 936 (1974); Rankin Gibson, "Congressional Concurrent Resolution: An Aid to Statutory Interpretation?" American Bar Association Journal 37(1951): 421; Frederick Kaiser, "Congressional Control of Executive Actions in the Aftermath of the Chadha Decision," Administrative Law Review 36 (1984): 239; U.S. House of Representatives, House Committee on Rules, Studies on the Legislative Veto, Committee Print (February 1980); Richard M. Nixon, Six Crises (New York: Pyramid Books, 1968); Richard Evans, and Robert Novak, Nixon in the White House: The Frustration of Power (New York: Random House, 1971); John Lehman, The Executive, Congress, and Foreign Policy: Studies of the Nixon Administration (New York: Praeger, 1976); William D. Rogers, "The Consti-

tutionality of the Cambodian Incursion," *American Journal of International Law* 65(January 1971): 26–37; Arthur Schlesinger, Jr., *The Imperial Presidency* (Boston: Houghton Mifflin, 1973).

Prior Consultation and Reporting

The series of congressional hearings on the War Powers Resolution after a major "use of armed forces" engagement reflected the impatience of Congress with the president's responses to congressional requests for compliance with the provisions of the resolution. Conflicts involving hostilities between or among sovereign states typically start out with ruptures in diplomacy and increase in intensity and scope by uneven increments.[1] The United States has typically intervened in the early stages of such conflicts during periods in which hostilities (translated "war") have not been imminent.[2] Quick reaction and strategic implementation requirements have typically required the president to take immediate and decisive action based on intelligence from many sources including intelligence agencies, the Joint Chiefs of Staff, foreign ministers, the United Nations Security Council, appropriate mutual defense treaty organizations, and the president's own national security advisors.[3] Congress has been continually concerned that the collective congressional body is not included in this "information loop" and is not collectively consulted (advice and consent?) prior to proposed armed force deployment.[4] Important, germane questions to be answered involve issues such as the following: How much information needs to be exchanged in prior consultation? Must all parties to the consultation be active participants in the information exchange? Must the president himself be a participant in the consultation? Is the time interval between consultation and action an important element in consultation? Is consultation perceived as permission to act?

Issues raised by these questions will be studied in this chapter through testimony before congressional committees and from correspondence between Congress and the executive and its representatives. Perhaps the greatest insights into the whole notion of consultation and reporting under the War Powers Resolution are obtained from documented correspondence between Dante Fascell, chairman of the Committee on Foreign Affairs, and George P. Schultz, secretary of state, and the ensuing exchange of questions and answers triggered by that letter. We will review that correspondence in a subsequent section.

CONSULTATION WITH CONGRESS

Senator Byrd made a statement in a press release that fairly accurately reflects the sense of Congress on presidential consultation before making a commitment of armed forces: "The fact is that no President has effectively consulted on a regular basis with the Congress, and by consultation, I mean the exploration of a consensus prior to a decision to commit U.S. forces in a situation. Instead, the Congress has almost always been treated to after-the-fact consultation, which is not consultation at all."[5]

We will start our analyses with an examination of U.S. Senate and U.S. House of Representatives testimony and other relevant documents and sources relating to the president's uses of armed force. In these documents, we should be able to determine whether there has been enough consultation between the president and Congress to both satisfy the provisions of the War Powers Resolution and to provide the president with the advice and consent of Congress as might be appropriate to the given conflict.

Cyrus Vance, secretary of state between 1977 and 1980 under President Jimmy Carter, pointed out that between 1973, the year of the passing of the War Powers Resolution, and the end of 1987 (fourteen years), Presidents Ford, Carter, and Reagan reported ten military actions to Congress. These actions included operations in Da Nang, Phnom Penh, and Saigon, the *Mayaguez* recapture, the Iran mission that was aborted, multilateral peacekeeping operations in the Sinai and Lebanon, AWACS planes in Chad, and the invasion of Grenada.[6] Vance, in the *War Powers: Origins, Purposes, and Applications* just cited in note 6, indicated that in none of these cases did the president adequately consult with Congress *prior* to the introduction of armed forces into hostilities.

Robert F. Turner, in a very long prepared statement before the Subcommittee on Arms Control, International Security and Science of the Committee on Foreign Affairs of the House of Representatives, took a different stand on the question of whether the president should be required to consult with Congress subject to the timetable of Congress. He argued as follows:[7]

But it is both illegal and in my view unseemly for Congress to by law attempt to compel the President of the United States to "consult" on a timetable established by Congress. The President is head of a great co-equal branch of the American Government, and he (or she) deserves to be treated with the dignity appropriate to that office. Congress and the President should seek to cooperate in a spirit of comity out of mutual realization that the safety and security of the nation requires a joint effort. But for either side to "demand" that the other "appear on call" is to belittle the constitutional authority of a co-equal and incompatible without doctrine of separation of powers.

Elliot Richardson listed three broad scenarios for which the president might consult with Congress.[8] Under the first scenario, the president is faced with a "quick reaction" use of force that is usually a single stroke, such as the air strikes against Libya. In such a case, secrecy and speed are paramount and the president cannot be expected to conduct extensive prior consultation with Congress. The second scenario is one in which the time between the decision to deploy armed forces and the time of actual deployment is only hours, or two or three days at most. In this case, the presidential consultation need not be extensive prior to the action. The third scenario is one for which the president may have a longer period during which he is concerned with the decision to deploy or not and any logistic considerations associated with such action. This is a situation for which the president should carry on rather extensive consultation with the Congress on a step-by-step basis. How this consultation is to be actually implemented and by whom in the executive and Congress is not fully outlined by Richardson.

As an example of the nature of consultation and some of the parties involved we might observe the manner in which President Gerald Ford communicated with Congress. On April 30, 1975, President Gerald R. Ford wrote to the Speaker of the House of Representatives, Carl Albert, outlining the activities surrounding the withdrawal and evacuation of some 1,400 U.S. citizens and approximately 5,500 third country nationals and South Vietnamese from the U.S. Embassy in Saigon on April 29, 1975. Subsequent to the evacuation of April 29, the SS *Mayaguez* was fired upon by a Cambodian motor torpedo boat from the new Khmer Communist government. This incident of May 12, 1975, occurred just two weeks after the evacuation. President Ford was notified regarding the action at 7:40 a.m. He called a meeting of the National Security Council shortly after noon.[9] By 10:30 the next morning, President Ford had met again with the National Security Council and ordered "U.S. forces to interdict any boat coming or going to Koh Tang Island."[10] The National Security Council met again at 10:40 p.m. and learned that an "Air Force helicopter enroute to Utapao had crashed killing all 23 Americans on board."[11] By 5:15 p.m. on May 14, assault forces had landed on Koh Tang, and by 9 p.m. other marines had boarded the *Mayaguez*. By 11:30 p.m. the entire crew of the *Mayaguez* was safe aboard the *Wilson*. At 12:27 a.m. on May 15, President Ford made a broadcast from the White House indicating that the ship and crew had been safely recovered but were still under hostile fire.[12]

On May 15, President Ford sent a letter to the Speaker of the House of Representatives, Carl Albert, outlining the action that he had taken. The third paragraph of that letter began as follows: "In accordance with my desire that the Congress be informed on this matter and taking note of Section 4(a)(1) of the War Powers Resolution, I wish to report to you . . ."[13] He ended his letter with the statement, "This operation was ordered and conducted pursuant to the President's constitutional Executive power and his authority as Commander-in-Chief of the United States Armed Forces."[14]

President Ford was subsequently severely criticized for taking the action without consultation with the Congress and obtaining their advice and consent to take offensive action in this situation. In his fascinating and intriguing book, *A Time to Heal*, Ford reflects on the *Mayaguez* incident and offers several reasons why, in the heat of a conflict, a president cannot immediately respond to Congress in the form and according to the timetable desired by as follows Congress.[15] The reasons he gives are as follows:[16]

1. Legislators have so many other concerns that it is impractical to expect them to be as well versed in fast-breaking developments as those in the executive branch who deal with foreign policy and national security situations every day.

2. It is impossible to wait for a congressional consensus when its leadership so often is scattered around the world.

3. There is a risk of disclosure of sensitive information through insecure means of communication. "Members of Congress *** [sic] might also confuse what they hear on the radio *** [sic] with what they are told on a highly classified basis by the White House."

4. By delaying action to consult with Congress, the consequences for the Nation in an emergency might be much worse.

5. There is a question of how consultations with a handful of congressional leaders can bind the entire Congress to support a course of action—especially given the independence of younger Members.

6. Congress has little to gain and much to lose politically by involving itself deeply in crisis management.

7. Neither foreign policy nor military operations can be commanded by 535 Members of Congress on Capitol Hill "even if they all happen to be on Capitol Hill when they are needed."

Perhaps if we took a chronological look at the consultation process involving a "quick reaction" situation faced by the president, it may clarify some of the reasons why the executive is concerned with going before Congress to obtain its "advice and consent." There never has been, however, a clear definition of who Congress is with regard to consultation. Could it mean the Congress as a whole? Could it mean leaders of both houses of Congress? Could it mean leaders of both political parties? Could it mean the Senate? Some combination of all the above?

CONSULTATION ON THE *MAYAGUEZ* INCIDENT

Day 2: May 13

Reading the documents associated with the *Mayaguez* incident reveals that many members of Congress were contacted by the White House staff and Secretary of State Kissinger.[17] On Day 2 (May 13) of the incident, Kissinger held a news conference and discussed the developments up to that point. Later in the day, he referred to the incident in an address before the Kansas City International Relations Council.[18] Starting at 5:30 the same day, President Ford directed White House aides to contact congressional leaders; ten in the House and eleven in the Senate were contacted and informed regarding developments surrounding the *Mayaguez* incident.[19]

Day 3: May 14

Beginning at about 11:15 a.m., the White House congressional liaison staff contacted twenty-one congressional leaders and informed them of developments concerning the *Mayaguez*, its crew, and action taken. Specific comments from those contacted were recorded by the White House staff and brought to the attention of the president.[20] Between 2 p.m. and 5 p.m., Deputy Assistant Secretary of Defense Morton Abramowitz and Deputy Assistant Secretary of State Robert Miller went before the House Foreign Affairs Committee and the House Armed Services Committee. About that same time, Colonel Zane Finkelstein, legal and legislative assistant to the Joint Chiefs of Staff, and Acting Assistant Secretary of State J. Owen Zurhellen went before the Foreign Relations Committee. Between 6:30 p.m. and 7:00 p.m., President Ford met with congressional leaders in the Cabinet Room of the White House and gave them a two–hour briefing regarding developments surrounding the *Mayaguez* incident.[21]

Day 4: May 15

At 2 a.m. President Ford signed and dispatched a letter personally addressed to Speaker of the House Albert and President Pro Tempore of the Senate Eastland. This letter was the letter mentioned earlier outlining the events leading up to and including the rescue of the crew of the *Mayaguez*.[22]

The sequel to the story of the executive contacts is that some members of Congress believed that the contacts made by the White House had encompassed consultation within the meaning of the War Powers Resolution. Those who did not think so criticized the White House contacts on several grounds: (1) The contacts were low level in nature, that is, they were made by liaison aides mainly. Ctitics thought that the president should have made the contacts himself. (2) The contacts were largely made after the fact, that is, the contacts were made after decisions had already been made by the president. (3) Members of Congress felt that there was not enough of the spirit of executive-legislative rapport shared during this episode.[23]

Was this quality consultation? Members of Congress felt that the president should have conducted face-to-face meetings with them prior to any major commitment. From that perspective, the consultation was not quality consultation. Did the consultation that actually took place fulfill the requirements of the War Powers Resolution? After the dust settled on this issue, most in Congress believed that the consultation that did take place did, in fact, constitute "consultation" according to the strict language of the War Powers Resolution, but it could have been more participative with Congress. Could the president have taken this action without regard to the War Powers Resolution as an exercise of "repelling hostile enemy actions against American citizens"?

Since the action was taken to free captured Americans, most in Congress believed that the president did have inherent powers permitting him to do so. "Reflecting the view of most Congressmen, Speaker Carl Albert told newsmen that the *Mayaguez* operation was legal under the Commander in Chief clause of the Constitution. Representative Zablocki commended the President for 'the reasoned use of force.'"[24] "Senator Frank Church supported the administration's contention that the strikes against Cambodian gunboats on day 3 of the crisis did not violate the Cooper-Church restrictions."

CONGRESS REQUESTS STATE DEPARTMENT ANSWERS

Perhaps the greatest insights into the complex notion of consultation and reporting under the War Powers Resolution are obtained from the exchanges between the Committee on Foreign Affairs of the House of Representatives and the Department of State concerning the deaths of thirty-seven U.S. servicemen on the USS *Stark* in the Persian Gulf. On May 20, 1987, Secretary of State George Shultz sent a letter to then Speaker of the House of Representatives Jim Wright describing the Iraqi aircraft missile attack on the USS *Stark* while it was on a legitimate patrol in the Persian Gulf.[25]

On September 21, 1987, four months after Secretary Schultz's letter was received by Speaker Wright, Dante B. Fascell, chairman of the House of Representatives Committee on Foreign Affairs, wrote a letter to Secretary Schultz which included an attachment requesting answers to seven questions regarding the War Powers Resolution consultation and reporting associated with the *Stark* incident. The State Department response, dated March 30, 1988, some six months later, was not signed by Secretary of State George Shultz; it was signed by J. Edward Fox, assistant secretary, legislative affairs.[26]

The questions posed by Fascell, and the response by Fox are very germane to an understanding of their respective views regarding the War Powers Resolution's consultation and reporting obligation. Fox's Department of State reply gave both a constitutional and a legal reason why the president was not bound by the War Powers Resolution in the action he took. The final sentence in Fox's reply to Fascell gives the essence of the president's view of his reporting obligation under the War Powers Resolution. It states, "A report on this action 'consistent with the War Powers Resolution' was provided to Congress."[27] We notice that the phrase "consistent with . . ." rather than "in accordance with . . ." has been the pattern of responses by all presidents from President Nixon to the present president. They actually comply with the reporting provision of the War Powers Resolution without acknowledging its authority over their actions.

It is also remarkable to note that there was a six-month period between the request for information by Fascell and a written reply by the State Department. Even though the situations described by Fox actually did involve "hostilities" within the meaning of the War Powers Resolution, Section 4(a)(1) was never formally triggered. The State Department's position was that a report submitted "consistent with the War Powers Resolution" was sufficient to satisfy any reporting (and perhaps consultation) requirement of the War Powers Resolution.

An array of distinguished witnesses testified before the Subcommittee on Arms Control, International Security and Science of the Committee on Foreign Affairs of the House of Representatives regarding "War Powers: Origins, Purposes, and Applications" on August 4 and September 27, 1988. In an exchange between former Secretary of State Cyrus Vance and Representative Stephen Solarz during those hearings, Representative Solarz seemed to capture the essence of presidential reporting under the War Powers Resolution by observing, "So far as I can recall, no president in the last fifteen years has ever submitted a notification clearly and unequivocally triggering that requirement [Section 4(a)(1) of the War Powers Resolution]. In the absence of presidential compliance with that provision of the law, we end up in a sort of legal and constitutional 'no man's land,' and nobody seems to think the clock is running. If you try to go to court, as Mr. Weiss and other Members have, you run into problems of standing and political questions."[28] Representative Solarz could make the same statement today. Presidents Jimmy Carter, Ronald Reagan, George Bush, and Bill Clinton have used the same phrase, "consistent with the War Powers Resolution," instead of specifically triggering the resolution.

The following two chapters of this book are a departure from the first seven chapters. Since none of the literature has placed the consultation between Congress and the executive in a time line for a given operation, it is hard to judge whether the timing and content of consultation has satisfied the spirit of the War Powers Resolution and the spirit of good faith. Operations Desert Shield and Desert Storm have all of the elements of a full-scale "defensive turned offensive" operation requiring U.S. armed forces. We will use that conflict to observe and evaluate whether consultation was timely, informative, and offered in the spirit of complying with the moral obligations of the War Powers Resolution.

NOTES

1. U.S. House of Representatives, "The Crisis in Somalia: Markup on S.J. Res. 45—Authorizing the Use of U.S. Armed Forces in Somalia," Hearing before the Committee on Foreign Affairs, 103rd Cong., 1st Sess., May 5, 1993 (Washington, D.C.: U.S. Government Printing Office, 1993). See especially the opening statements of Hon. Toby Roth and Hon. Donald M. Payne. (Hereafter in this chapter, this document will be referred to as "The Crisis in Somalia.") Allison Graham, *Essence of Decision: Explaining the Cuban Missile Crisis* (Boston: Little, Brown, 1971); Dan Caldwell, "A Research Note on the Quarantine of Cuba, October 1962," *International Studies Quarterly* XXII (December 1978): 625–633; Jimmy Carter, *Keeping Faith: Memoirs of a President* (New York: Bantam Books, 1982); Ronald Elving, "America's Most Frequent Fight Has Been the Undeclared War," *Congressional Quarterly Weekly Report* 49:1 (January 5, 1991): 37–39; George Church, "Trip Wires to War: What Would It Take for the U.S. to Attack Iraq, and How Would Bush Square the Decision with the U.N. and Congress?" *Time* (October 29, 1990): 48–51; David Detzer, *The Brink: Cuban Missile Crisis, 1962* (New York: Thomas Y. Crowell, 1979).

2. U.S. House of Representatives, "The Crisis in Somalia," "Prepared Statement of Hon. Herman J. Cohen" and "Prepared Statement of Lois Richards," pp. 50–54. See also U.S. Senate, "Joint Chiefs of Staff Briefing on Current Military Operations in Somalia, Iraq, and Yugoslavia," Hearing before the Committee on Armed Services, 103rd Cong., 1st Sess., January 29, 1993 (Washington, D.C.: U.S. Government Printing Office, 1993); Ronald Elving, "America's Most Frequent Fight Has Been the Undeclared War," *Congressional Quarterly Weekly Report* 49:1 (January 5, 1991): 37–39; Thomas Franck, and Faiza Patel, "UN Police Action in Lieu of War: 'The Old Order Changeth,'" *American Journal of International Law* 81:1 (January 1991): 63–74; Harry S. Truman, *Memoirs*, Vol. 2 (Garden City, N.Y.: Doubleday, 1956); U.S. House of Representatives, House Select Committee to Investigate Covert Arms Transactions with Iran and Senate Select Committee on Secret Military Assistance to Iran and the Nicaraguan Opposition, *Report of the Congressional Committees Investigating the Iran-Contra Affair with Supplemental, Minority, and Additional Views*, 100th Cong., 1st Sess., H. Rept. 100–433, S. Rept. 100–216 (Washington, D.C.: U.S. Government Printing Office, 1987).

3. U.S. House of Representatives, "The Crisis in Somalia; U.S. House of Representatives, *Intelligence Oversight Act of 1988*, H. Rept. 100–705, 100th Cong., 2nd Sess. (Washington, D.C.: U.S. Government Printing Office, 1988); U.S. House of Representatives, *U.S. Intelligence Performance on Central America: Achievements and Selected Instances of Concern*, Committee Print, Subcommittee on Oversight and Evaluation of the House Permanent Select Committee on Intelligence, 97th Cong., 2nd Sess. (Washington, D.C.: U.S. Government Printing Office, 1982); U.S. Senate, *Meeting the Espionage Challenge: A Review of United States Counterintelligence and Security Programs*, S. Rept. 99–522, Senate Select Committee on Intelligence, 99th Cong., 2nd Sess. (Washington, D.C.: U.S. Government Printing Office, 1986); U.S. Senate, *Report of the Select Committee on Intelligence, U.S. Senate, Jan. 1, 1983 to Dec. 31, 1984*, S. Rept. 98–665, 98th Cong., 2nd Sess. (Washington, D.C.: U.S. Government Printing Office, 1984); U.S. House of Representatives, *War Powers, Libya, and State-Sponsored Terrorism*, Hearings before the Subcommittee on Arms Control, International Security and Science of the House Committee on Foreign Affairs, 99th Cong., 2nd Sess. (Washington, D.C.: U.S. Government Printing Office, 1986); U.S. Senate, *Supplementary Detailed Staff Reports on Foreign and Military Intelligence—bk. 4—Final Report*, S. Rept. 94–755, Senate Select Committee to Study Governmental Operations with Respect to Intelligence Activities, 94th Cong., 2nd Sess. (Washington, D.C.: U.S. Government Printing Office, 1976).

4. See Sections IV and V of Cyrus Vance, "Striking the Balance: Congress and the President under the War Powers Resolution," in Appendix 5 of U.S. House of Representatives, *War Powers: Origins, Purposes, and Applications: Hearings before the Subcommittee on Arms Control, International Security and Science of the Committee on Foreign Affairs,* 100th Cong., 2nd Sess., August 4, 1988, and September 27, 1988 (Washington, D.C.: U.S. Government Printing Office, 1989):

288–304 (hereafter in this chapter, this document will be referred to as *War Powers*); John Murphy, "Knowledge Is Power: Foreign Policy and Information Interchange among Congress, the Executive Branch, and the Public," *Tulane Law Review* 49 (1975): 505; Irving Younger, "Congressional Investigations and Executive Secrecy: A Study in the Separation of Powers," *University of Pittsburg Law Review* 20 (1959): 755. Most of the arguments in U.S. House of Representatives, *The War Powers Resolution: A Special Study of the Committee on Foreign Affairs* (Committee Print), Committee on Foreign Affairs (Washington, D.C.: U.S. Government Printing Office, 1982), deals with incidents for which the Congress feels that the president did not consult with Congress in good faith, that is, Congress was only informed *ex post facto* regarding military action already taken. (Hereafter in this chapter, this document will be referred to as *The War Powers Resolution: A Special Study*.)

5. Leon Leighton, "The Enduring Vitality of the War Powers Resolution: The Inadequacy of H.J. Res. 601 and S.J. Res. 323," in U.S. House of Representatives, *War Powers:* 305–358; U.S. House of Representatives, *The War Powers Resolution*. A major part of U.S. House of Representatives, *The War Powers Resolution: Relevant Documents, Correspondence, Reports* (Committee Print), Subcommittee on International Security and Scientific Affairs of the House Committee on Foreign Affairs, 98th Cong., 1st Sess. (Washington, D.C.: U.S. Government Printing Office, 1983), is devoted to correspondence among senators, representatives, presidents, and cabinet members regarding consultation associated with the War Powers Resolution. It is one of the richest sources of "firsthand" correspondence between Congress and the executive, especially the correspondence by Presidents Gerald Ford, Jimmy Carter, and Ronald Reagan. (Hereafter in this chapter, this document will be referred to as *The War Powers Resolution: Relevant Documents.*)

6. Cyrus Vance, "Striking the Balance: Congress and the President under the War Powers Resolution," in Appendix 5 of U.S. House of Representatives, *War Powers:* 296–297; U.S. Department of State Historical Studies Division, *Armed Actions Taken by the United States without a Declaration of War, 1789–1967*, Res. Proj. No. 806A (Washington, D.C.: U.S. Government Printing Office, 1967); Cyrus Vance, *Hard Choices: Critical Years in American Foreign Policy* (New York: Simon & Schuster, 1983); Gregory Treverton, *Covert Action: The Limits of Intervention in the Postwar World* (New York: Basic Books, 1987); Gerald Ford, *A Time to Heal* (New York: Harper & Row, 1979); Jimmy Carter, *Keeping Faith: Memoirs of a President* (New York: Bantam Books, 1982); and for correspondence from President Jimmy Carter, President Gerald Ford, and President Ronald Reagan, see U.S. House of Representatives, *The War Powers Resolution: Relevant Documents:* 40–108.

7. Robert Turner, "The War Powers Resolution: Its Origin and Purpose," in U.S. House of Representatives, *War Powers:* 113. His full statement is contained in pp. 55–113 of this source. Particularly insightful is Robert Turner, "The War Powers Resolution: Unconstitutional, Unnecessary and Unhelpful," *Loyola of Los*

Angeles Law Review 17 (1984): 683. After President Reagan introduced U.S. troops into El Salvador, some members of Congress thought the president had triggered the sixty-to-ninety-day time limit and should have filed a report under Section 4(a)(1) of the War Powers Resolution. Representative Mike Lowry and 110 other members of Congress took the matter to court (*Lowry v. Reagan* C.A. No. 87–219 [12/18/89], slip opinion at 13). The court dismissed the suit on the grounds that it was a nonjusticiable political question.

8. Elliot Richardson, "The War Powers Resolution: Conflicting Constitutional Powers, the War Powers and U.S. Foreign Policy," testimony in U.S. House of Representatives, *War Powers:* 138–206; U.S. House of Representatives, *War Powers, Libya, and State-Sponsored Terrorism*, Hearings before the Subcommittee on Arms Control, International Security and Science of the House Committee on Foreign Affairs, 99th Cong., 2nd Sess. (Washington, D.C.: U.S. Government Printing Office, 1986); U.S. House of Representatives, *Report of the Congressional Committees Investigating the Iran-Contra Affair with Supplemental, Minority, and Additional Views*, H. Rept. 100–433, S. Rept. 100–216, 100th Cong., 1st Sess. (Washington, D.C.: U.S. Government Printing Office, 1987); Michael Rubner, "The Reagan Administration, the 1973 War Powers Resolution, and the Invasion of Grenada," *Political Science Quarterly* 100 (Winter 1985–1986): 627–47; William D. Rogers, "The Constitutionality of the Cambodian Incursion," *American Journal of International Law* 65 (January 1971): 26–37; Lowell Weicker, John Warner, Frank Murkowski, and John McCain, "Should Congress Move to Invoke the War Powers Resolution?" *Congressional Digest* 66:12 (December 1987): 296–303.

9. U.S. House of Representatives, "Chapter 8. The *Mayaguez* Incident and the War Powers Resolution," in *The War Powers Resolution: A Special Study:* 205–214. In this special study by the Foreign Affairs Committee, the *Mayaguez* incident is broken down into four subheadings: I. *Mayaguez*: Four Days of Capture and Rescue. II. *Mayaguez* and Congressional Consultation. III. Presidential Authority to Rescue Americans Abroad. IV. *Mayaguez* as a Test of the War Powers Resolution. It is the single best source for this incident. See also Gerald Ford, *A Time to Heal* (New York: Harper & Row, 1979); U.S. House of Representatives, House Committee on International Relations, "Hearings: Seizure of the *Mayaguez*," 94th Cong., 2nd Sess. (Washington, D.C.: U.S. Government Printing office, 1974). Robert Turner quotes Senate Republican leader Hugh Scott regarding the *Mayaguez* incident: "We were informed. We were alerted. We were advised. We were notified. We were telephoned. It was discussed with us. I don't know whether that's consultation or not. We were advised that certain actions would be taken using the minimum force necessary." Turner then commented that that was not what he thought consultation ought to be. From U.S. House of Representatives, *War Powers:* 43.

10. U.S. House of Representatives. Committee on Foreign Affairs, "Chapter 8. The *Mayaguez* Incident and the War Powers Resolution," in *The War Powers Resolution: A Special Study:* 206. A copy of President Gerald Ford's letter to

Speaker Carl Albert is given in "Report Dated May 15, 1975, from former President Gerald R. Ford to Hon. Carl Albert, former Speaker of the House of Representatives, in Compliance with Section 4(a)(1) of the War Powers Resolution, Relative to the *Mayaguez* Incident," in U.S. House of Representatives, *The War Powers Resolution: Relevant Documents:* 45–46.

11. U.S. House of Representatives Committee on Foreign Affairs, "Chapter 8. The *Mayaguez* Incident and the War Powers Resolution," in *The War Powers Resolution: A Special Study:* 206.

12. Ibid., pp. 206–207.

13. "Report Dated May 15, 1975, from Former President Gerald R. Ford to Hon. Carl Albert, former Speaker of the House of Representatives, in Compliance with Section 4(a)(1) of the War Powers Resolution, Relative to the *Mayaguez* Incident," in U.S. House of Representatives, *The War Powers Resolution: Relevant Documents:* 45–46. Compare this wording with that in President Ronald Reagan's letter to Speaker "Tip" O'Neill in "Report Dated August 24, 1982, from President Ronald Reagan to Hon. Thomas P. O'Neill, Speaker of the House of Representatives, Consistent with the War Powers Resolution, Relative to Use of United States Armed Forces in Lebanon," in ibid., pp. 60–61. A portion of President Reagan's letter stated, "In accordance with my desire that the Congress be fully informed on this matter, and consistent with the War Powers Resolution, I am hereby providing a report on the deployment and mission of these members of the United States Armed Forces." A study of the papers of President Jimmy Carter, President George Bush, and President Bill Clinton will reveal the same kind of language in their reports to Congress after the deployment of armed forces on foreign soil.

14. U.S. House of Representatives, "Chapter 8. The *Mayaguez* Incident and the War Powers Resolution," in *The War Powers Resolution: A Special Study:* 46.

15. Gerald Ford, *A Time to Heal* (New York: Harper & Row, 1979). See also Robert Hartmann, *Palace Politics: An Inside Account of the Ford Years* (New York: McGraw-Hill, 1980); Kenneth Holland, "The War Powers Resolution: An Infringement on the President's Constitutional and Prerogative Powers," in Gordon Hoxie, ed., *The Presidency and National Security Policy* (New York: Center for the Study of the Presidency, 1984): 378–400; Pat Holt, *The War Powers Resolution: The Role of Congress in U.S. Armed Intervention* (Washington, D.C.: American Enterprise Institute, 1978).

16. "*Mayaguez* Consultation: The Executive View," in U.S. House of Representatives, *The War Powers Resolution: A Special Study:* 213–214; Arthur Bestor, "'Advice' from the Very Beginning, 'Consent' When the End Is Achieved," *American Journal of International Law* 83:4 (October 1989): 750–757; Arthur Bestor, "Separation of Powers in the Domain of Foreign Affairs: The Original Intent of the Constitution Historically Examined," *Seton Hall Law Review* 5 (1974): 529.

17. "*Mayaguez* and Congressional Consultation," in U.S. House of Representatives, *The War Powers Resolution: A Special Study:* 208. Robert Turner, in

his paper "The War Powers Resolution: Its Origins and Purpose," in U.S. House of Representatives, *War Powers:* 133, states: "There are many uses of armed force which lead to involvement in 'hostilities' which are clearly within the independent authority of the Commander in Chief and are not subject to congressional regulation. (The *Mayaguez* rescue is but one example.) . . . But it is both illegal and in my view unseemly for Congress to by law attempt to compel the President of the United States to 'consult' on a timetable established by Congress. The President is the head of a great co-equal branch of the American Government, and he (or she) deserves to be treated with the dignity appropriate to that office."

18. U.S. House of Representatives, "Chapter 8. The *Mayaguez* Incident and the War Powers Resolution," in *The War Powers Resolution: A Special Study:* 208. Secretary of State Henry Kissinger had been carrying on a running dialogue with Hon. Thomas E. Morgan, former chairman of the Committee on Foreign Affairs, U.S. House of Representatives, and Hon. J. W. Fulbright, former chair of the Senate Committee on Foreign Relations, in a series of memoranda cited below, all from U.S. House of Representatives, *The War Powers Resolution: Relevant Documents.* Those communications are (1) "Letter of July 16, 1974, to Former Secretary of State Henry A. Kissinger, from Hon. Thomas E. Morgan, Former Chairman, Committee on Foreign Affairs, and Hon. J. W. Fulbright, Former Chairman, Committee on Foreign Relations," p. 37; (2) "Letter of September 7, 1974, to Hon. Thomas E. Morgan, Former Chairman, Committee on Foreign Affairs, from Secretary of State Henry A. Kissinger," p. 38; (3) "Letter of October 7, 1974, to Hon. Thomas E. Morgan, Former Chairman, Committee on Foreign Affairs, from Former Secretary of State Henry A. Kissinger," p. 39.

19. "*Mayaguez* and Congressional Consultation," in U.S. House of Representatives, *The War Powers Resolution: A Special Study*: 208.

20. Ibid., p. 209.

21. U.S. House of Representatives, "Chapter 8. The *Mayaguez* Incident and the War Powers Resolution," in *The War Powers Resolution: A Special Study:* 210. Members of Congress have argued that they were not consulted regarding action to be taken or actions taken by the president, but this two-hour session did involve a discussion of the *Mayaguez* incident and possible alternatives that could be implemented.

22. U.S. House of Representatives, "Chapter 8. The *Mayaguez* Incident and the War Powers Resolution," in *The War Powers Resolution: A Special Study:* 210; and "Report Dated May 15, 1975, from Former President Gerald R. Ford to Hon. Carl Albert, Former Speaker of the House of Representatives, in Compliance with Section 4(a)(1) of the War Powers Resolution, Relative to the *Mayaguez* Incident," in U.S. House of Representatives, *The War Powers Resolution: Relevant Documents:* 45–46.

23. "*Mayaguez* and Congressional Consultation," in U.S. House of Representatives, *The War Powers Resolution: A Special Study:* 211–212; Arthur Bestor, "'Advice' from the Very Beginning, 'Consent' When the End Is Achieved," *American Journal of International Law* 83:4 (October 1989): 750–757; Gerald

Ford, *A Time to Heal* (New York: Harper & Row, 1979); Louis Fisher, *The Constitution between Friends: Congress, the President, and the Law* (New York: St. Martin's Press, 1978); U.S. House of Representatives, House Committee on International Relations, "Hearings: Seizure of the *Mayaguez*," 94th Cong., 2nd Sess. (Washington, D.C.: U.S. Government Printing office, 1974).

24. "Presidential Authority to Rescue Americans Abroad," in U.S. House of Representatives, *The War Powers Resolution: A Special Study:* 216. Although it is true that most of the senators and representatives did agree with President Ford's handling of the affair, there was some opposition: "Ranged on the other side of the issue were legislators who contended that President Ford had acted illegally. Representative Elizabeth Holtzman testified that the use of force to recover the *Mayaguez* violated the Cooper-Church restriction on funds for the Indochina conflict. Representative John Seiberling, Democrat of Ohio, said the President had ignored the funding statutes in the *Mayaguez* rescue as well as in the evacuation from Saigon." Ibid.

25. "Report Dated May 20, 1987 from Secretary of State George P. Shultz to Hon. Jim Wright, Speaker of the House of Representatives, Relative to the Iraq Aircraft Missile Attack on the U.S.S. *Stark* in the Persian Gulf on May 17, 1987," in U.S. House of Representatives, *The War Powers Resolution: Relevant Documents:* pp. 91–92.

26. U.S. House of Representatives, *The War Powers Resolution: Relevant Documents:* 93–99. The letters cited are (1) "Letter of September 21, 1987 to Secretary of State George P. Shultz from Hon. Dante B. Fascell, Chairman, Committee on Foreign Affairs Regarding Legal Advice in Connection with the U.S. Military Presence in the Persian Gulf and the War Powers Resolution," (2) "Letter to Chairman Fascell from Assistant Secretary of State J. Edward Fox Dated March 30, 1987 Responding to Chairman Fascell's September 21, 1987 Letter." This second letter by Fox (pp. 96–99) is most insightful since it repeats Fascell's questions and gives the State Department's military, legal, and constitutional answers to the questions.

27. Ibid. The answer to Question 6 contained the following statements: "Congressional leaders were consulted before the U.S. operation commenced and the President reported to Congress 'consistent with the War Powers Resolution' on October 20. In so doing, the President reserved his constitutional rights and responsibilities as Commander-in-Chief of U.S. armed forces and with respect to the conduct of foreign relations."

28. U.S. House of Representatives, *War Powers:* 219; "Broken Clock," *The New Republic* (September 10, 1990): 12–13; Zbigniew Brzezinski, *Power and Principle: Memoirs of the National Security Advisor* (New York: Farrar, Strauss & Giroux, 1983); George Church, "Trip Wires to War: What Would It Take for the U.S. to Attack Iraq, and How Would Bush Square the Decision with the U.N. and Congress?" *Time* (October 29, 1990): 48–51; Donald Elliot, "*INS v. Chadha*: The Administrative Constitution, the Constitution, and the Legislative Veto," *Supreme Court Review* 125 (1983): 125–176; Louis Fisher, *Constitutional Conflicts be-*

tween Congress and the President, 3rd ed. (Lawrence: University Press of Kansas, 1991); Thomas Franck, "Courts and Foreign Policy," *Foreign Policy* (Summer 1991): 66–86; Michael Glennon, "The Use of Custom in Resolving Separation of Powers Disputes," *Boston University Law Review* 64 (1984): 109; Frederick Kaiser, "Congressional Control of Executive Actions in the Aftermath of the *Chadha* Decision," *Administration Law Review* 36 (1984): 239; Nicholas Katzenbach, "Comparative Roles of the President and the Congress in Foreign Affairs," *Department of State Bulletin* 47 (September 11, 1967): 333–336; Harold Koh, "Why the President (Almost) Always Wins in Foreign Affairs: Lessons of the Iran-Contra Affair," *Yale Law Journal* 97 (June 1988): 1292–1297.

PART IV

Executive War Powers

Chapter 8

Desert Shield, the President, the United Nations

In the previous seven chapters of this book, we have considered the issues surrounding the war powers controversy from the point of view of the Constitution, treaties, executive orders, and testimony and documents from the various arms of the U.S. Congress. By now, the reader may have begun to realize that Congress has, to a large degree, by its actions (or inactions) during actual U.S. intervention into foreign conflict, let the president take the initiative in foreign conflicts in his role as commander in chief. While many in Congress would like the president to come to Congress to ask for approval before any armed forces are used in a potentially hostile foreign environment, few believe that the president may be forced to do so under the provisions of the U.S. Constitution or through provisions of the War Powers Resolution. Indeed, most believe that the president needs to seek congressional approval only under the most narrow range of circumstances. It seems that in the years since the passage of the War Powers Resolution, notwithstanding a bit of saber rattling, Congress and the president have almost grasped the concept that "compliance with reservations is compliance nevertheless, and have agreed to live with it."

For those who still believe that there should be more consultation between the executive and Congress during intervention into foreign conflict, this chapter and the next one leave the formal legal and constitutional issues and present a microscopic view of consultation between the Congress and the executive during the Desert Shield and Desert Storm response to the United Nations' and Kuwait's request for assistance against the invasion by Iraq. The main question to be kept in mind while reading these chapters is, "Was there good faith consultation by both the president and the Congress before and during intervention with United States armed forces into the Iraqi-Kuwaiti conflict?"

Operations Desert Shield and Desert Storm are two distinct military as well as political operations. Desert Shield was defensive and was conducted under the authority of the president as chief executive and commander in chief of the U.S. armed forces and under the authority and responsibilities of the United Nations Charter. Desert Storm was offensive and was conducted under the authority just mentioned and also with a joint resolution of support from Congress. We examine Desert Shield in this chapter and Desert Storm in the following chapter.

DESERT SHIELD

The two-part U.S. operation to liberate Kuwait and protect Saudi Arabia after the Iraqi invasion in August 1990, Desert Shield and Desert Storm, is and will be held as the greatest military victory for America in roughly the last half century. This operation also provided constitutional scholars, military strategists, and the world community with a perfect example of the execution of the powers and responsibilities of the president as commander in chief of America's armed forces. Every element of the constitutional controversy over war powers is present, is recent, and is well documented in all media—print news, television, radio, congressional committee reports, and so on. Desert Shield and Desert Storm also provide well-documented insight into the mixture of diplomatic, political, military, and moral issues involved in the events leading up to the war, the conduct of the war itself, and the diplomatic, political, military, and moral residue of the war.

The assistance given Kuwait is a compelling example of the progression of involvement into hostilities by U.S. armed forces and the nebulous concept of war. There is no controversy regarding a stronger nation's obligation to help a weaker nation when the weaker nation calls for help. In addition, almost everyone would argue that nations have a moral obligation to provide humanitarian assistance for the wounded, displaced, hungry, and those impoverished by the ravages of war. Experience has shown, however, that action taken in the spirit of goodwill often leads to a progression of involvement that changes the nature of the participation of a nation from humanitarian assistance to defensive combat assistance, then to offensive combat assistance. This is exactly the pattern of involvement by the United States in response to the Iraqi invasion of Kuwait and the request for American assistance by the government of Kuwait.

In the past, Congress has witnessed the involvement of the United States and is well aware of the military action taken without its consent (or even against its will). The 210 instances of U.S. military involvement without congressional consent presented in Appendix C are persuasive evidence that these military actions can gain momentum quickly and can involve major outlays of national funds and significant amounts of our national military and civilian resources. Such was the case with the Iraqi invasion of Kuwait. The United States had some intelligence that Saddam Hussein had been conducting maneuvers near the Kuwaiti border for some time. The pace and scope of the buildup did not seem to indicate that an invasion was impending. As the following detailed, chronological account will show, Iraqi forces increased sharply and the ensuing invasion was both swift and unexpected.

The chronology of events that followed the invasion will provide concrete evidence of the nature and timing of consultation between the president and Congress during this conflict. Was there timely and meaningful consultation between the president and Congress? Was the intent, if not the letter, of the War Powers Resolution taken into account by both the president and Congress? What obligation do both the president and Congress have to observe the articles of the treaty with the United Nations?

RESPONSE TO THE INVASION OF KUWAIT

The interactions between the president of the United States, George Bush, and the Security Council of the United Nations after the invasion of Kuwait by Iraq illustrate almost every facet of the war powers struggle between the president and Congress. President Bush was forthright and open about his view of his authority as chief executive and commander in chief when he took each action. His presidential papers[1] establish this characteristic throughout his tenure in office but even more so during his command of Desert Shield and Desert Storm.[2]

PRESIDENT BUSH DECLARES NATIONAL EMERGENCY

August 2, 1990

Saddam Hussein led Iraqi troops into Kuwaiti territory. The emir of Kuwait fled to refuge in Saudi Arabia. President Bush issued Executive Order No. 12722 (55 FR 31803) declaring a national emergency to deal with the invasion of Kuwait by Iraq, on the basis of "the threat to national security and foreign policy of the United States."[3] President Bush also issued Executive Order No. 12723 (55 FR 31805) "blocking all property of the Government of Kuwait then or thereafter in the United States or in the possession or control of a U.S. person."[4] In his letter to Thomas Foley, Speaker of the House of Representatives, and to Dan Quayle, president of the Senate, President Bush stated, "The declaration of the national emergency on August 2, 1990, was made pursuant to the authority vested in me as President by the Constitution and laws of the United States, including the International Emergency Economic Powers Act (50 U.S.C. 1701 et seq.), the National Emergencies Act (50 U.S.C. 1601 et seq.), and section 301 of title 3 of the United States Code."[5]

The United Nations Security Council issued S.C. Resolution 660 condemning the Iraqi invasion of Kuwait and demanding an immediate and unconditional withdrawal. The verbatim text of that resolution is presented in Exhibit 8.1.[6] (See Appendix B for the texts of all Security Council resolutions relevant to Desert Storm and Desert Shield.)

Exhibit 8.1
United Nations Security Council Resolution 660

(August 2, 1990)

The Security Council,

Alarmed by the invasion of Kuwait on 2 August 1990 by the military forces of Iraq,

Determining that there exists a breach of international peace and security as regards the Iraqi invasion of Kuwait,

Acting under Articles 39 and 40 of the Charter of the United Nations,

1. *Condemns* the Iraqi invasion of Kuwait;

2. *Demands* that Iraq withdraw immediately and unconditionally all its forces to the positions in which they were located on 1 August 1990;

3. *Calls upon* Iraq and Kuwait to begin immediately intensive negotiations for the resolution of their differences and supports all efforts in this regard, and especially those of the League of Arab States;

4. *Decides* to meet again as necessary to consider further steps to ensure compliance with the present resolution.

VOTE: 14 for, 0 against, 1 abstention (Yemen)

Source: U.S. Department of State, U.S. Department of State Dispatch 1:2 (September 10, 1990): 75.

August 3, 1990

Secretary of State James Baker and USSR Foreign Minister Eduard Shevardnadze met in Moscow to discuss the Iraqi invasion and issue a joint statement to call a halt to the shipment of arms to Iraq by nations sympathetic to Iraq.[7] President Bush also reported the declaration of national emergency of August 2, 1990, and the imposition of sanctions against Iraq in a letter to Congress outlining both his authority and rationale for doing so. Excerpts from President Bush's letter to the Congress are given in Exhibit 8.2.[8]

Exhibit 8.2
President Bush Declares National Emergency

To the Congress of the United States

Pursuant to section 204(b) of the International Emergency Economic Powers Act, 50 U.S.C. section 1703(b), and section 201 of the National Emergencies Act, 50 U.S.C. section 1621, I hereby report that I have exercised my statutory authority to declare a national emergency and to issue two Executive orders that:

—prohibit exports and imports of goods and services between the United States and Iraq and the purchase of Iraqi goods by U.S. persons for sale in third countries;

—prohibit transactions related to travel to or from Iraq, except for transactions necessary for journalistic travel or prompt departure from Iraq;

—prohibit transactions related to transportation to or from Iraq, or the use of vessels or aircraft registered in Iraq by U.S. persons;

—prohibit the performance of any contract in support of Government of Iraq projects;

—ban all extensions of credit and loans by U.S. persons to the Government of Iraq;

—block all property of the Government of Iraq now or hereafter located in the United States or in the possession or control of U.S. persons, including their foreign branches; and

—prohibit all transfers or other transactions involving assets belonging to the Government of Kuwait now or hereafter located in the United States or in the possession or control of U.S. persons, including their foreign branches. . . .

The measures we are taking to block Iraqi assets will have the effect of expressing our outrage at Iraq's actions, and will prevent that government from drawing on monies and properties within U.S. control to support its campaign of military aggression against a neighboring state. . . .

At the same time, in order to protect the property of the legitimate Government of Kuwait from possible seizure, diversion, or misuse by Iraq, and with the approval of the Kuwaiti government, we are blocking Kuwaiti assets within the jurisdiction of the United States or in the possession or control of U.S. persons. . . .

George Bush

The White House
August 3, 1990

Source: George Bush, "Message to the Congress on the Declaration of a National Emergency with Respect to Iraq," in *Public Papers of the Presidents of the United States: George Bush* (Washington, D.C.: U.S. Government Printing Office, 1991): 1094–1095.

August 6, 1990

The United Nations Security Council issued S.C. Resolution 661 imposing economic sanctions on both Kuwait and Iraq—members of the United Nations should neither export nor import products from Kuwait or Iraq. The Security Council Resolution additionally authorized nonmilitary measures to enforce the trade sanctions. The vote was thirteen for and none against the resolution. Yemen and Cuba abstained. Portions of that resolution are presented below:[9]

The Security Council,

Reaffirming its resolution 660 (1990) of 2 August 1990, . . .

Affirming the inherent right of individual or collective self-defence, in response to the armed attack by Iraq against Kuwait, in accordance with Article 51 of the Charter,

Acting under Chapter VII of the Charter of the United Nations,

Determines that Iraq so far has failed to comply with paragraph 2 of Resolution 660 (1990) and has usurped the authority of the legitimate Government of Kuwait;

2. *Decides*, as a consequence, to take the following measures to secure compliance of Iraq with paragraph 2 of Resolution 660 (1990) and restore the authority of the legitimate Government of Kuwait;

3. *Decides* that all States shall prevent: . . . [The sanctions are listed here.]

9. *Decides* that, notwithstanding paragraphs 4 through 8 above, nothing in the present Resolution shall prohibit assistance to the legitimate Government of Kuwait, and calls upon all states:

(a) To take appropriate measures to protect assets of the legitimate Government of Kuwait and its agencies;

(b) Not to recognize any regime set up by the occupying Power.

What is significant about this Security Council resolution is the phrase "Acting under Chapter VII of the Charter of the United Nations." This phrase, triggered by Articles 39 and 40 of Security Council Resolution 660, provides that a member nation is authorized to use "all necessary means" to restore peace. Technically, it also provides that a member nation may take offensive action, not just defensive action, against an aggressor nation to protect the peace of another member nation. This United Nations Chapter VII authorization is what the United States needed to intensify its activities to assist Saudi Arabia and Kuwait against the Iraqi invasion.

TROOPS DEPLOYED TO SAUDI ARABIA

August 7, 1990

President Bush deployed U.S. armed forces to Saudi Arabia to protect Saudi Arabia from invasion by Iraq and to have a staging area for troops for repelling Iraq's occupation of Kuwait. President Bush's letter outlining the deployment of troops was not sent to Congress until August 9, 1990. [Excerpts from that letter are reproduced below under the heading "August 9, 1990."] The Gulf Cooperation Council issued a statement calling for the withdrawal of Iraq from Kuwait.

August 8, 1990

Iraq declared that Kuwait has been annexed to Iraq through a "comprehensive and eternal merger." This phrase was used in United Nations S.C. Resolution 662 below.

Upon learning of the annexation of Kuwait to Iraq, President Bush addressed the nation from the Oval Office of the White House. Key portions of that address illustrate the U.S. commitment made by President Bush and the authority upon which he deployed the armed forces to Saudi Arabia. They also indicate that he had already consulted with Congress regarding his actions in the matter. Excerpts from the address follow:[10]

And this past Monday, the United Nations Security Council approved for the first time in 23 years mandatory sanctions under Chapter VII of the United Nations Charter. These Sanctions, now enshrined in international law have the potential to deny Iraq the fruits of aggression while sharply limiting its ability to either import or export anything of value, especially oil.

I pledge here today that the United States will do its part to see that these sanctions are effective and to induce Iraq to withdraw without delay from Kuwait. Let me make it clear: The sovereign independence of Saudi Arabia is of vital interest to the

United States. This decision, which I shared with the congressional leadership grows out of the longstanding friendship and security relationship between the United States and Saudi Arabia. . . . Through their presence, as well as through training and exercises, these multinational forces will enhance the overall capability of Saudi Armed Forces to defend the Kingdom.

We know that when President Bush said, "This decision, which I shared with the congressional leadership . . . ," there was some consultation with the Congress in the form of contact with the leadership. While it may be argued that there might not have been enough discussion, we do know that Congress was consulted. The address additionally served to prepare the American public for military actions which might be needed to provide for the peace and security of Saudi Arabia as well as for Kuwait. This action would be taken to maintain the "friendship and security relationship" of Saudi Arabia.

August 9, 1990

United Nations Security Council issued S.C. Resolution 662 declaring Iraq's annexation of Kuwait null and void. The vote was unanimous, that is fifteen for and none against. Portions of the text of that resolution are presented here:[11]

Exhibit 8.3
United Nations Security Council Resolution 662 (Excerpts)

The Security Council,

Recalling its Resolutions 660 (1990) and 661 (1990),

Gravely alarmed by the declaration by Iraq of a "comprehensive and eternal merger" with Kuwait,

Demanding, once again, that Iraq withdraw immediately and unconditionally all its forces to the positions in which they were located on 1 August 1990,

Determined to bring the occupation of Kuwait by Iraq to an end and to restore the sovereignty, independence and territorial integrity of Kuwait,

Determined also to restore the authority of the legitimate Government of Kuwait,

1. *Decides* that annexation of Kuwait by Iraq under any form and whatever pretext has no legal validity, and is considered null and void;

2. *Calls upon* all States, international organizations and specialized agencies not to recognize that annexation and to refrain from any action or dealing that might be interpreted as an indirect recognition of the annexation;

3. *Further demands* that Iraq rescind its actions purporting to annex Kuwait; . . .

President Bush notified Congress that the number of armed forces deployed to Saudi Arabia would increase, but that war did not seem imminent. The president imposed further sanctions on Iraq in the Mediterranean Sea. The list of added sanctions was quite substantial in the light of sanctions already in effect. A portion of the letter sent from President Bush to the Speaker of the House of Representatives and to the president of the Senate is presented here and indicates the authority used by the president to take his added sanctions action:[12]

Today, I have taken additional steps to respond to these developments and to ensure that the economic measures we are taking with respect to Iraq and Kuwait conform to United Nations Security Council Resolution 661 of August 6, 1990. Specifically, pursuant to section 204(b) of the International Emergency Economic Powers Act, 50 U.S.C. section 1703(b), section 201 of the National Emergencies Act, 50 U.S.C. section 1621, and the United Nations Participation Act, 22 U.S.C. section 287(c), I have issued two Executive orders.

The letter to the the Speaker of the House of Representatives and to the president of the Senate conforms to the notice requirements of Section 4 of the War Powers Resolution regarding (1) to whom the notice is sent in the House and Senate, (2) authority for the action taken, and (3) what action was taken or is planned to be taken. While the president did not request any "permission" of Congress, this briefing does give Congress an opportunity to offer any counsel that may be appropriate to the situation. Additionally, Congress has the opportunity to call upon responsible parties in the executive and in the military to discuss the operation.

President Bush further explained his actions and intentions in his letter of February 11, 1991. We see in this letter more specific details regarding the situation in Kuwait, his authority under the U.S. Constitution to take such action, and the authority under the United Nations Charter to take such action. While only a portion of the letter is presented here, it does provide evidence that there was a continual dialogue with the leadership of Congress regarding developments in this phase of the operation:[13]

. . . on August 9, 1990, I issued Executive Orders Nos. 12724 and 12725 (55 FR 33089), to ensure that the sanctions imposed by the United States were consistent with United Nations Security Council Resolution 661 of August 6, 1990. Under these orders, additional steps were taken with regard to Iraq, and sanctions were applied to Kuwait as well to insure that no benefit to Iraq resulted from the military occupation of Kuwait. . . . The additional sanctions of August 9, 1990, were imposed pursuant to the authority vested in me by the Constitution and laws of the

United States, including the statutes cited above and the United Nations Participation Act (22 U.S.C. 287c).

It should be evident from the two communications just cited that the president was concerned about keeping Congress informed regarding every phase of activity that involved the use of armed forces. This concern underscores the executive's argument that consultation was both effective and timely. Was there time for the president to wait for a debate in the Congress before taking action with Kuwait against Iraq?

SHIPPING TO IRAQ BLOCKADED

August 12–13, 1990

President Bush ordered the U.S. Navy to halt all shipping to and from the ports providing access to Iraq. Although this action had the force of a "blockade," President Bush characterized it as a defensive measure to prohibit imports and exports to and from Iraq. As was the case in the Cuban missile crisis, there was divided opinion regarding whether the blockade action might be taken as an act of "war" and not just defensive action. Obviously, if the president had stated otherwise, there would have been the constitutional question of whether Congress had issued a declaration of war prior to an act of war being carried out by the commander in chief.

On August 12, White House Press Secretary Marlin Fitzwater released a statement regarding the "halt" of shipping, which stated in part,[14]

This morning the President received a letter from His Highness, Sheik Jabir al-Ahmad al-Jabir Al Sabah, the Amir of Kuwait, requesting on behalf of the Government of Kuwait, and in accordance with article 51 of the U.N. Charter and the right of individual and collective self-defense that the United States Government take appropriate steps as necessary to ensure that the U.N.-mandated economic sanctions against Iraq and Kuwait are immediately and effectively implemented. . . . Iraq continues to act in defiance of U.N. Resolutions 660, 661, and 662, the basis for resolving Iraq's occupation. The United States will continue to pursue the application of those resolutions in all their parts.

There was concern on the parts of Congress and the news media regarding whether "all" shipping would be halted, even if the contents of the shipping contained humanitarian aid such as food and medical supplies. If all shipping had been halted, there might have been the possibility of conflict with the provisions of United Nations Security Council Resolutions

660, 661, and 662. Learning of this concern, Fitzwater then issued the following short statement on August 13:[15]

There seems to be some confusion about what is covered in terms of our interdiction efforts. When the President said "everything," he obviously meant everything that is included in the U.N. resolution. We do not intend to go beyond the resolution. Specifically, the resolution lists those items covered and says, "but not including supplies intended strictly for medical purposes. . . ."

In his press conference in the White House Briefing Room the following day, President Bush was questioned regarding the trucks still carrying supplies through Jordan to Iraq. It had been long known and well documented that a major and strategic supply route for Iraqi forces had been established through Jordan. Even the nightly news documented convoys of trucks going to Baghdad through Jordan with impunity. Both the members of Congress and the American public were aware of the magnitude of the supply operation and that it was continuing without interruption. The president replied by asserting that UN Article 51 sanctions would continue to be carried out to the fullest extent possible.

August 18, 1990

When Iraq sealed off its borders on August 9, 1990, it was estimated that about 500 Americans were trapped in Iraq and about 3,000 Americans were trapped in Iraqi-occupied Kuwait. Many of these Americans were associated with the U.S. Embassy. Despite any other interests that the United States might have had up to August 9, the lives of American citizens now became a national interest that must be protected. Protests to Iraq were met with belligerence from Saddam Hussein. This gained the attention of the United Nations and set the stage for S.C. Resolution 664.

The Security Council issued S.C. Resolution 664 condemning Iraq for holding foreign nationals hostage and demanded their immediate release. The vote was unanimous, that is, fifteen for and none against. Excerpts from United Nations S.C. Resolution 664 (August 19, 1990) follow:[16]

Exhibit 8.4
United Nations Security Council Resolution 664 (Excerpts)

The Security Council,

Recalling the Iraqi invasion and purported annexation of Kuwait and resolutions 660, 661, and 662, . . .

Acting under Chapter VII of the United Nations Charter:

1. *Demands* that Iraq permit and facilitate the immediate departure from Kuwait and Iraq of the nationals of third countries and grant immediate and continuing access of consular officials to such nationals; . . .

3. *Reaffirms* its decision in resolution 662 (1990) that annexation of Kuwait by Iraq is null and void, . . .

During this same time, U.S. ships in the Persian Gulf and in the Gulf of Oman fired warning shots across the bows of two Iraqi tankers that appeared to be trying to violate the blockade on imports to or exports from Iraqi ports in those locations. Again, even though the United Nations had called for sanctions against Iraq, the firing of shots across the bows of Iraqi tankers could have been interpreted as an act of war committed by the United States. It could be argued that the United Nations resolutions, though intended well, did not have the force of a declaration of war by the United States. Fortunately, the tankers turned away without returning fire upon the American vessels.

CIVILIANS USED AS "HUMAN SHIELDS"

August 22, 1990

On August 19, 1990, Saddam Hussein ordered all civilian Westerners to report to strategic military sites to be used as "human shields" in the event that there was an attack from U.S. or coalition forces against Iraq. Diplomatic activity had escalated, but to no avail with regard to the occupation of Kuwait and the detention of Kuwaiti and American civilians. President Bush responded by sending the following letter to Speaker of the House of Representatives Thomas Foley and to President of the Senate Dan Quayle on August 22 outlining action he had taken and the rationale and authority for doing so:[17]

Exhibit 8.5
President Bush's Letter Mobilizing U.S. Reserves

Dear Mr. Speaker: (Dear Mr. President:)

I have today, pursuant to section 673b of title 10, United States Code, authorized the Secretary of Defense, and the Secretary of Transportation with respect to the Coast Guard when it is not operating as a service within the Department of the Navy, to order to active duty units and individual members not assigned to units of the Selected Reserve to perform such missions the Secretary of Defense may determine necessary. The deployment of United States forces to conduct operational missions in and around the Arabian Peninsula necessitates this action.

A copy of the Executive order implementing this action is attached.

Sincerely,

GEORGE BUSH

Source: George Bush, "Letter to Congressional Leaders on the Mobilization of United States Reserves—August 22, 1990," in *Public Papers of the Presidents of the United States: George Bush* (Washington, D.C.: U.S. Government Printing Office, 1991): 1156.

Placing this communication in context, we observe that this is one more instance of the constant dialogue President Bush had carried on with Congress to keep it informed regarding almost every detail of deployment of armed forces along with the rationale for doing so. The president's emergency powers as the nation's chief executive and as the commander in chief of the nation's armed forces provide authorization for the activation of the nonattached units mentioned in the letter and in the implementing executive order. The communiqués were addressed to the Speaker of the House of Representatives and to the president pro tempore of the Senate as called for under Section 5(a) of the War Powers Resolution.

August 25, 1990

In the strongest language to date, the United Nations Security Council "call[ed] upon" all members of the United Nations to stop all trade and commerce with Iraq. This was the first of the resolutions to request states to coordinate their actions "as appropriate mechanisms of the Military Staff Committee" of the United Nations. Selected portions of that resolution, United Nations S.C. Resolution 665 (August 25, 1990) are as follows:[18]

Exhibit 8.6
United Nations Security Council Resolution 665 (Excerpts)

(August 25, 1990)

The Security Council,

Recalling its resolutions 660 (1990), 661 (1990), 662 (1990) and 665 (1990) and demanding their full and immediate implementation,

Having decided in resolution 661 (1990) to impose economic sanctions under Chapter VII of the Charter of the United Nations, . . .

1. *Calling upon* those Member States cooperating with the Government of Kuwait which are deploying maritime forces to the area to use such measures commensurate to the specific circumstances as may be necessary under the authority of the Security Council to halt all inward and outward maritime shipping in order to inspect and verify their cargoes and destinations and to ensure strict implementation of the provisions related to such shipping laid down in Resolution 661 (1990); . . .

3. *Requests* all States to provide in accordance with the Charter such assistance as may be required by the States referred to in paragraph 1 of this resolution; . . .

It is interesting to note here that both S.C. Res. 662 and S.C. Res. 664 were approved unanimously, that is, fifteen for and none against, with no abstentions. Previously, Yemen had abstained in the vote on S.C. Res. 660 and Yemen and Cuba had abstained in the vote on S.C. Res. 661. Yemen and Cuba abstained also in the vote on this resolution. It is also most significant to note that President Mikhail Gorbachev gave his endorsement to the actions being taken in the Gulf crisis. A portion of the statement released by White House Press Secretary Marlin Fitzwater stated,[19] "President Gorbachev's statement yesterday supporting the United Nations sanctions was a very important development. . . . We are encouraged by the progress of events at the United Nations and by President Gorbachev's strong support."

BUSH SIGNS ACCORD WITH GORBACHEV AT HELSINKI

September 9, 1990

During a conference in Helsinki, Finland, attended by President George Bush, Secretary of State James Baker, USSR President Mikhail Gorbachev, and USSR Foreign Minister Eduard Shevardnadze, President Bush and President Gorbachev issued a joint statement denouncing the invasion of Kuwait by Iraq. A portion of that joint statement reads as follows:[20]

We are united in the belief that Iraq's aggression must not be tolerated. No peaceful international order is possible if larger states can devour their smaller neighbors. We affirm the joint statement of our Foreign Ministers of August 3, 1990, and our support for United Nations Security Council Resolutions 660, 661, 662, 664, and 665. . . . Nothing short of the complete implementation of United Nations Security Council Resolutions is acceptable.

It was universally argued in the print media in America during the time of the invasion events that the Soviet Union's posture made a significant difference in the conduct of diplomatic and military affairs. The fact that USSR President Mikhail Gorbachev and USSR Foreign Minister Eduard Shevardnadze, without reservation, stood by President George Bush's decisions and actions early on in the invasion kept the conflict from becoming a conflict between superpowers. It additionally kept Saddam Hussein from having the kind of strategic support that would have provided him with the means to take and sustain even more harsh treatment of the people and government of Kuwait. It had a major impact on the conflict and on world opinion regarding the coalition forces supporting President Bush's action.

September 11, 1990

President Bush addressed a joint session of the Congress with a moving description and analysis of events transpiring after the Iraqi invasion on August 2, 1990. In the very long and comprehensive address in the House Chamber of the Capitol, two portions stand out among the others: the first indicating President Bush's perception of the justification and authority to proceed with his plan in Kuwait and the second providing a glimpse of the personality of the man, George Bush. He remarked,

The United Nations is backing up its words with action. The Security Council has imposed mandatory economic sanctions on Iraq, designed to force Iraq to relinquish the spoils of its illegal conquest. The Security Council has also taken the decisive step of *authorizing the use of all means necessary* to ensure compliance with these sanctions [emphasis added]. . . .[21] Let me also make clear that *the United States has no quarrel with the Iraqi people*. Our quarrel is with Iraq's dictator and with his aggression. Iraq will not be permitted to annex Kuwait. That's not a threat, that's not a boast, that's just the way it's going to be [emphasis added].[22]

Anyone seeing President Bush making these statements before Congress, as the author did, would recognize the sincerity and compassion that the president had for the people of Iraq. The president made it clear by word, tone, and gesture that he wanted Saddam Hussein to withdraw from Kuwait and not have to go to the ultimate "use of force." His demeanor and language were more those of a chief executive than those of a commander in chief of the armed forces. His language also indicated that there was a genuine resignation to go to the "use of force" rather than an eager anticipation of it.

September 13, 1990

The Security Council responded to a humanitarian plea from Iraq to permit food to be supplied to the civilian population in its S.C. Resolution 666 (September 13, 1990). While the request for humanitarian aid was formally made to the United Nations, it was common knowledge that Iraq was being supplied with convoys of armed forces materiel and supplies through Jordan. Additionally, shipments of oil out of Iraq through Jordan were virtually uninterrupted, much to the consternation of the American public and members of Congress. Saddam Hussein knew the strategic importance of keeping the main thoroughfare between Jordan and Baghdad open for military and humanitarian purposes.

For the sake of brevity and since the authority to conduct armed conflict is considered only peripherally in S.C. Res. 666, only short excerpts of that resolution are presented below:[23]

Exhibit 8.7
United Nations Security Council Resolution 666 (Excerpts)

(September 13, 1990)

The Security Council,

Recalling its resolution 661 (1990), paragraph 3(c) and 4 of which apply, except in humanitarian circumstances, foodstuffs, . . .

Acting under Chapter VII of the Charter of the United Nations,

1. *Decides* that in order to make the necessary determination whether or not for the purposes of paragraph 3(c) and paragraph 4 of resolution 661 (1990) humanitarian circumstances have arisen, the Committee shall keep the situation regarding foodstuffs in Iraq and Kuwait under constant review; . . .

This resolution was in partial response to the address delivered from the Oval Office of the White House by President Bush to the people of Iraq on September 12, 1990, explaining the position of the United States. President Bush made it clear that the United States did not have a conflict with the people of Iraq, only with Saddam Hussein and their military strategists who were seeking to oppress the people of Kuwait. He emphasized again that the conflict was not just between Iraq and the United States, it was a conflict between Iraq and the rest of the world. The president remarked, "Saddam Hussein tells you that this crisis is a struggle between Iraq and America. In fact, it is Iraq against the world."[24]

September 14, 1990

Saddam Hussein's troops attacked the Canadian and European diplomatic compounds and briefly held three French diplomats hostage. This attack on the diplomatic compounds of the Canadians and Europeans was seen by the whole world as savage, wanton, and unbridled aggression without purpose. It immediately brought the invasion of Kuwait to a new level of hostility. The free world community would be outraged at the "recent violations by Iraq of diplomatic premises in Kuwait and at the abduction of personnel enjoying diplomatic immunity and foreign nationals who were present in these premises [from the language of S.C. Resolution 667, quoted in part below]."

September 16, 1990

In some of the strongest language of the United Nations Security Council to date, the Security Council issued S.C. Resolution 667 regarding the actions taken by Saddam Hussein against the diplomatic personnel. In retrospect, history records that this resolution galvanized world opinion into support for use of extreme force to counter Hussein's actions. Sections of S.C. Resolution 667 (September 16, 1990) dealing with its authority and rationale are presented in Exhibit 8.8:[25]

Exhibit 8.8
United Nations Security Council Resolution 667 (Excerpts)

(September 16, 1990)

The Security Council,

Reaffirming its resolutions 660 (1990), 661 (1990), 662 (1990), 664 (1990), 665 (1990), and 666 (1990),

Recalling the Vienna Conventions of 18 April 1961 on diplomatic relations and of 24 April 1963 on consular relations, to both of which Iraq is a party, . . .

Outraged at recent violations by Iraq of diplomatic premises in Kuwait and at the abduction of personnel enjoying diplomatic immunity and foreign nationals who were present in these premises, . . .

Determined to ensure respect for its decisions and for Article 25 of the Charter of the United Nations, . . .

Acting under Chapter VII of the Charter of the United Nations, . . .

2. *Demands* the immediate release of those foreign nationals as well as all nationals mentioned in resolution 664 (1990);

3. *Further demands* that Iraq immediately and fully comply with its international obligations under resolutions 660 (1990), 662 (1990) and 664 (1990) of the Security Council, the Vienna Conventions on diplomatic and consular relations and international law; . . .

September 24, 1990

In S.C. Resolution 669 (September 24, 1990), the United Nations Security Council relaxed the conditions of the economic sanctions called for under S.C. Resolution 661 in order to provide for humanitarian supplies and for economic assistance under Article 50 of the United Nations Charter.[26] Many in the international community believe that the timing of this resolution worked against the coalition forces, since it provided food and other relief aid to a city which was the headquarters of Saddam Hussein and a nerve center for conducting Iraqi armed forces against Kuwait. The convoys of trucks from Jordan to Baghdad contained not only humanitarian supplies but also strategic materiel for Hussein's war efforts in exchange for petroleum for Jordan. Furthermore, the government of Jordan allowed other neighboring countries to cross its borders to provide aid to the Iraqi army.

UNITED NATIONS ORDERS "ALL NECESSARY MEANS"

September 25, 1990

The United Nations Security Council tightened the embargo against commerce and assistance to Iraq by issuing S.C. Resolution 670 (September 25, 1990). The language of this resolution contained authorities not cited before in the previous eight resolutions associated with Iraq's invasion of Kuwait. Additionally the phrase "each State shall take all necessary measures" in the Security Council resolution provided member states with the authority to take offensive military action against Iraqi forces. Those portions dealing specifically with the United Nations' and its members' authority are given below:[27]

Exhibit 8.9
United Nations Security Council Resolution 670 (Excerpts)

(September 25, 1990)

The Security Council,

Reaffirming its resolutions 660 (1990), 661 (1990), 662 (1990), 664 (1990), 665 (1990), 666 (1990), and 667 (1990);

Condemning Iraq's continued occupation of Kuwait, its failure to rescind its actions and end its purported annexation and its holding of their State nationals against their will, in flagrant violation of resolutions 660 (1990), 662 (1990), 664 (1990) and 667 (1990) and of international humanitarian law; . . .

Determined to ensure respect for its decisions and the provisions of Articles 25 and 48 of the Charter of the United Nations;

Affirming that any acts of the Government of Iraq which are contrary to the above-mentioned resolutions or to Articles 25 and 48 of the Charter of the United Nations, such as Decree No. 377 of the Revolution Command Council of Iraq of 16 September 1990, are null and void; . . .

5. *Decides* that each State shall take all necessary measures to ensure that any aircraft registered in its territory or operated by an operator who has his principal place of business or permanent residence in its territory complies with the provisions of resolution 661 (1990) and the present resolution; . . .

8. *Calls upon* all States to detain any ships of Iraqi registry which enter their ports and which are being or have been used in violation of resolution 661 (1990), or to deny such ships entrance to their ports except in circumstances recognized under international law as necessary to safeguard human life; . . .

This resolution contained the strongest condemnation of Iraqi aggression against Kuwait and the diplomatic compounds of any the resolutions issued by the Security Council to date regarding this conflict. It convinced the American public that the United States could no longer play a "wait-and-see" game with Saddam Hussein. The loss of human lives, the destruction of property, the raping of young Kuwaiti women, the burning of Kuwaiti oil fields, and the flagrant disregard for diplomatic protocol and immunity cried out for world assistance. The national consensus in America was to take swift and deadly action. The U.S. Congress, for once in many decades, was solidly behind the public demand for action.

CONGRESSIONAL AND UNITED NATIONS RESOLUTIONS

Almost from the time of the invasion of Kuwait by Iraq on August 2, 1990, Congress took a wait-and-see policy with regard to actions taken by President Bush. Most of the debate centered around the president's deployment of armed forces without having obtained the advice and consent of Congress on his actions. The dynamics of the aggression by Iraq initially called for swift and decisive military action, without a doubt. Members of Congress complained, however, that the president could and should have obtained prior approval from Congress before committing armed forces in the Gulf crisis.

Each of the nine resolutions of the United Nations Security Council seemed to ratchet the public emotion and the public support for decisive armed American action higher. Saddam Hussein's actions became more belligerent with each Security Council resolution. The drama created by televised live action from the field, live action from the United Nations, countless interviews with military strategists, members of Congress, diplomats from the State Department, and representatives from the White House, including the president himself, captivated the nation's attention. People did not want another Vietnam, but, even more, they did not want to let a bully nation take widespread aggressive action against a peaceful neighbor.

Since the August 2 invasion of Kuwait, President Bush had sent several letters to Congress advising it of action that he was taking. He additionally addressed joint sessions of Congress to brief Congress and the people on developments in the Gulf crisis. Congress was well aware that Saddam Hussein knew that the United States could not conduct offensive action without some sort of support from Congress. President Bush needed and requested support for any additional actions. On October 2, 1990, after a debate that many political observers say was one of the best in recent memory, the Senate passed Senate Concurrent Resolution 147 with a vote of ninety-six to three. The preamble and text of the resolution are important in the respect that they explicitly acknowledge the obligations of the United States under the Article 51 of the United Nations Charter and the resolutions issued by the United Nations Security Council. The text of Senate Concurrent Resolution 147 is presented in Exhibit 8.10 below:[28]

Exhibit 8.10
Senate Concurrent Resolution 147—October 2, 1990

S. Con. Res. 147

Whereas on August 2, 1990, the armed forces of Iraq invaded and occupied the State of Kuwait, took large numbers of innocent hostages, and disregarded the rights of diplomats, all in clear violation of the United Nations Charter and fundamental principles of international law;

Whereas the President condemned Iraq's aggression, imposed comprehensive United States economic sanctions upon Iraq, and froze Iraqi assets in the United States;

Whereas the United Nations Security Council, in a series of five unanimously approved resolutions, condemned Iraq's actions as unlawful, imposed mandatory economic sanctions designed to compel Iraq to withdraw from Kuwait, called on all states to take appropriate measures to ensure the enforcement of sanctions, called for the immediate release of all hostages, and reaffirmed the right of individual and collective self-defense; and

Whereas, in response to requests from governments in the region exercising the right of collective self-defense as provided in Article 51 of the United Nations Charter, the President deployed United States Armed Forces in the Persian Gulf region as a part of a multilateral effort: Now, therefore, be it

Resolved by the Senate (the House of Representatives concurring), That (a) the Congress strongly approves the leadership of the President in successfully pursuing the passage of United Nations Security Council Resolutions 660, 661, 662, 664, 665, 666, 667, and 670, which call for—

(1) the immediate, complete, and unconditional withdrawal of all Iraqi forces from Kuwait;

(2) the restoration of Kuwait's sovereignty, independence, and territorial integrity;

(3) the release and safe passage of foreign nationals held hostage by Iraq;

(4) the imposition of economic sanctions, including the cessation of airline transport, against Iraq; and

(5) the maintenance of international peace and security in the Persian Gulf region.

(b) The Congress approves the actions taken by the President in support of these goals, including the involvement of the United Nations and of the friendly governments. The Congress supports continued action by the President in accordance with the decisions of the United Nations Security Council and in accordance with United States Constitutional and statutory processes, including the authorization and appropriation of funds by the Congress, to deter Iraqi aggression and to protect American lives and vital interests in the region.

(c) The Congress calls on all nations to strengthen the enforcement of the United Nations imposed sanctions against Iraq, to provide assistance for those adversely affected by enforcement of the sanctions, and to provide assistance to refugees fleeing Kuwait and Iraq.

Sec. 2. The Secretary of the Senate shall transmit a copy of this concurrent resolution to the President.

Source: U.S. Senate, *Congressional Record—Senate* 136 (October 2, 1990): S14338.

We observe that this resolution cited "Article 51 of the United Nations Charter" and "five unanimously approved resolutions" of the United Nations Security Council in the preamble. Later, in the resolution, eight Security Council resolutions dealing with the Iraqi invasion were cited. In Paragraph (b), the phrase "Congress supports continued action by the President . . . *including the authorization and appropriation of funds* [emphasis added]" seems to give the president the "consent" necessary to continue the buildup of forces and plans to repel the aggression. It was argued in the Congress in the months following the passage of this resolution that the president did not have authority to engage in hostilities and that the president's actions to engage armed forces were subject to the reporting provisions and calendar of the War Powers Resolution.

October 17, 1990

Secretary of State James Baker appeared before the Senate Foreign Relations Committee to provide that committee with an outline of the president's goals and associated strategies to achieve those goals.[29] In the exchange between the questioners and Secretary of State Baker, he was asked whether he would ask Congress to approve the use of force before offensive measures were taken against Iraq. He would not state affirmatively that the administration would seek prior congressional approval before an offensive attack on Iraq.

October 29, 1990

The United Nations Security Council issued S.C. Resolution 674 (October 29, 1990) with the following two main demands:[30]

1. Demands that the Iraqi authorities and occupying forces immediately cease and desist from taking third State nationals hostage, and mistreating and oppressing Kuwaiti and third State nationals, and from other actions such as those reported to the Council and described above, violating the decisions of this Council, the Charter of the United Nations, the Fourth Geneva Convention, the Vienna Conventions on Diplomatic and Consular Relations and international law;
2. Demands that Iraq ensure the immediate access to food, water and basic services necessary to the protection and well-being of Kuwaiti nationals and of nationals of third States in Kuwait and Iraq, including the personnel of diplomatic and consular missions in Kuwait.

On the occasion of S.C. Resolution 674, Thomas Pickering, U.S. permanent representative to the United Nations, outlined U.S. actions regarding Iraq and described atrocities being committed throughout Kuwait by Iraqi troops.[31] Reporters in Saudi Arabia gave personal interviews with Kuwaiti citizens who were able to flee Kuwait subsequent to the Iraqi invasion. They were able to provide the American television, print, and radio audience with graphic accounts of looting, raping, killing, and destruction of public and private property.

November 28, 1990

Reports from all sources in Kuwait and Saudi Arabia were verified that Saddam Hussein had been destroying all public records and that raping of Kuwaiti women by Iraqi solders was being carried out to alter the demographic composition of Kuwait. Reports carried by newspapers and television news spots included accounts of Iraqi soldiers raping Kuwaiti women and saying that they would bear Iraqi children and become part of the Iraqi nation. These actions caused the United Nations Security Council to pass S.C. Resolution 677, stating, in part, that the Security Council was: "gravely concerned at the ongoing attempt by Iraq to alter the demographic composition of the population of Kuwait and to destroy the civil records maintained by the legitimate Government of Kuwait."[32]

CONGRESSIONAL AND PRESIDENTIAL CONSULTATION

The documents and communication between the president and Congress, including the president's addresses before Congress and the testimony of the secretary of state before congressional committees, do provide compelling evidence that there was an ongoing consultative relationship between the president and Congress from the outset of the accumulation of Iraqi troops along the Kuwaiti border through all phases of the invasion. The form and substance of U.S. Senate Concurrent Resolution 147 seemed to have the weight of "advice and consent" to conduct continued action pursuant to the United Nations Security Council resolutions. Congress stated it would authorize and appropriate funds "to protect American lives and vital interests in the region."[33] Study of the debate preceding and following the passage of Senate Concurrent Resolution 471 indicates that the Congress was concerned that they were not preempting the president's responsibility to give notice of entering into hostilities in accordance with the provisions of the War Powers Resolution. Particularly insightful arguments were offered by Senators Dole, Kerry, and Biden.[34] During those debates, Senator Biden introduced a resolution entitled "Collective Security in the Persian Gulf Resolution."

Senator Biden's resolution was substantially more restrictive of presidential prerogatives than Senate Concurrent Resolution 147 in many respects, but the most significant of these was the language under Section 5(b)(1)(A–C) stating, [35]

(b) Further Authorization.—(1) Before initiating a use of force against Iraq beyond those uses authorized by subsection (a), the President shall—(A) consult and seek the advice of the Combined Congressional Leadership Group created pursuant to section 7 of this Resolution; (B) set forth to Congress and the American people his explanation of the imperatives mandating such use of force in the absence of a United Nations directive; and (C) seek a declaration of war or other statutory authorization.

This resolution clearly would have set the stage for a congressional-presidential confrontation. The Senate chose to pass Senate Concurrent Resolution 147 with the language as presented in Exhibit 8.10 above, which did not include the restrictive language that Senator Biden sought to impose on the process. We will be able to assess the implementation of that resolution coupled with the results of subsequent United Nations resolutions when we examine the decision to commit U.S. forces to action in the following chapter. Additionally, we continue to examine the consultation process between the president and Congress as the hostilities intensify between Iraq and the coalition forces. United Nations Security Council Resolution 678 and the ensuing Desert Storm operation sharply increased the urgency and volume of consultation among the president as commander in chief, the members of the armed services committees in Congress, the State Department, the Joint Chiefs of Staff, and all foreign heads of state involved in the coalition force activity.

In reviewing the events subsequent to Desert Shield in the operation called Desert Storm, it would be instructive to keep the following questions in mind with regard to the charge by members of Congress that the president did not consult with Congress during important phases of the conflict. We might ask, "Did the president satisfy all moral and legal obligations of reporting and consultation with Congress under the War Powers Resolution?" "Was there evidence that the president should have sought any further 'advice and consent' prior to any escalation of armed force activity?"

NOTES

1. George Bush, *Public Papers of the Presidents of the United States: George Bush*, 2 vols. (Washington, D.C.: U.S. Government Printing Office, 1992). There are a number of short statements about the Gulf War that add to a composite of

President Bush as commander in chief in addition to his public papers. A few of these are "War is Declared," *The Progressive* 51:11 (November 1987): 7; "War Powerless," *The Nation* (October 22, 1990): 440–441; "War Powers," *National Review* (November 19, 1990): 15; "War Powers Act and the Persian Gulf," *Congressional Digest* 66:12 (December 1987): 289; "War Powers Resolution— RIP," *National Review* (August 23, 1993): 17; "War Powers Time," *The New Republic* (May 17, 1993): 8.

2. Mike Moore, "How George Bush Won His Spurs," *Bulletin of the Atomic Scientists* 47:8 (October 1991): 26–33; Marian Leich, "War Powers," *American Journal of International Law* 85:2 (April 1991): 340–341; Joan Biskupic, "Constitution's Conflicting Clauses Underscored by Iraq Crisis: Provisions on Waging War Leave a Basic Question Unanswered, Does Congress or the President Call the Shot?" *Congressional Quarterly Weekly Report* (January 5, 1991): 33–36; "War Powers," *National Review* (November 19, 1990): 15; "War Powerless," *The Nation* (October 22, 1990): 440–441.

3. George Bush, "Letter to Congressional Leaders Reporting on the National Emergency with Respect to Iraq," in *Public Papers of the Presidents of the United States: George Bush* (Washington, D.C.: U.S. Government Printing Office, 1992): 131. (Hereafter in this chapter, this book will be referred to as *Public Papers: George Bush.*) The National Emergencies Act was passed in 1976 in order to restrict the use of presidential powers to declare national emergencies. Louis Fisher relates the following humorous incident in Congress in 1971 regarding presidential emergency powers: "It came as a surprise to many members of Congress in 1971 to learn that the United States had been in a state of declared national emergency since March 9, 1933, when President Roosevelt proclaimed an emergency at the time of the banking crisis." See Louis Fisher, *Constitutional Conflicts between Congress and the President,* 3rd ed. (Lawrence: University Press of Kansas, 1991): 259. After the passage of the National Emergencies Act, emergencies cannot extend to more than two years.

4. George Bush, "Letter to Congressional Leaders Reporting on the National Emergency with Respect to Iraq," in *Public Papers: George Bush,* 131. Since Saddam Hussein had taken control of the government of Kuwait in the invasion, this blocking of Kuwaiti assets prevented Hussein from gaining access to Kuwaiti assets outside the borders of Kuwait. This was a defensive action to prevent further damage to the government and people of Kuwait.

5. Ibid. President Bush could also have stated that this action was taken under his authority and responsibilities as commander in chief under the Constitution, and so forth. The effect would have been the same. He cited this authority to justify placing the armed forces in a state of ready alert.

6. U.S. Department of State, "UN Security Council Resolutions on Iraq's Invasion of Kuwait," *U.S. Department of State Dispatch* 1:2 (September 10, 1990): 75 (Washington, D.C.: U.S. Department of State, 1990); "The Gulf Crisis: UN Security Council Actions," *U.S. Department of State Dispatch* 1:14 (December 3, 1990): 296 (Washington, D.C.: U.S. Department of State, 1990). The key

phrase in UN Security Council Resolution 660 was "a breach of international peace and security." Additionally, the operative phrase "Acting under Articles 39 and 40 of the Charter of the United Nations" sets forth the authority for the coalition forces to take note of Iraq's invasion of Kuwait and to be ready to take defensive action to help Kuwait restore "peace and security" to its government and citizens.

7. U.S. Department of State, "US-Soviet Gulf Crisis Discussions, 1990–January 1991," *U.S. Department of State Dispatch* 2:10 (March 11, 1991): 167 (Washington, D.C.: U.S. Department of State, 1991). It was well known that Jordan was a major gateway for arms and supplies to Iraq. Soviet opposition to the blocking of arms to Iraq could have been a major, if not fatal, obstacle in trying to constrain further Iraqi action against Kuwait.

8. George Bush, "Message to the Congress on the Declaration of a National Emergency with Respect to Iraq," in *Public Papers: George Bush*: 1094–1095. See also President George Bush, "Letter to Congressional Leaders Reporting on the National Emergency with Respect to Iraq," ibid., Vol. 2, (February 11, 1991): 131.

9. U.S. Department of State, "UN Security Council Resolutions on Iraq's Invasion of Kuwait," *U.S. Department of State Dispatch* 1:2 (September 10, 1990): 75–76; "The Gulf Crisis: UN Security Council Actions," *U.S. Department of State Dispatch* 1:14 (December 3, 1990): 296. The important operative phrases here, "in accordance with Article 51 of the Charter, Acting under Chapter VII of the Charter of the United Nations," provide the United States and coalition forces additional authority to apply "sanctions" against Iraq on Kuwait's behalf and with the approval of the United Nations Security Council.

10. U.S. Department of State, "UN Security Council Resolutions on Iraq's Invasion of Kuwait," *U.S. Department of State Dispatch* 1:2 (September 10, 1990): 76. See also the discussions in the four articles cited earlier: "War Is Declared," *The Progressive* 51:11 (November 1987): 7; "War Powerless," *The Nation* (October 22, 1990): 440–441; "War Powers," *National Review* (November 19, 1990): 15; and "War Powers Act and the Persian Gulf," *Congressional Digest* 66:12 (December 1987): 289. These articles set the tone for action that everyone of any military or congressional background knew would involve "hostilities or . . . situations where imminent involvement in hostilities is clearly indicated by the circumstances"—language from P.L. 93–148, the "War Powers Resolution," Sec. 4.(a)(1), U.S. House of Representatives, *The War Powers Resolution: A Special Study of the Committee on Foreign Affairs* (Committee Print), Committee on Foreign Affairs (Washington, D.C.: U.S. Government Printing Office, 1982): 287.

11. President George Bush, "Letter to Congressional Leaders Reporting on the National Emergency with Respect to Iraq," in *Public Papers: George Bush*, Vol. 2 (February 11, 1991): 131.

12. George Bush, "Letter to Congressional Leaders on Additional Economic Measures Taken with Respect to Iraq and Kuwait," in ibid., p. 1117.

13. George Bush, "Address to the Nation Announcing the Deployment of United States Armed Forces to Saudi Arabia—August 8, 1990," in ibid., pp. 1107–1109.

14. "Statement by Press Secretary Fitzwater on the Persian Gulf Crisis—August 12, 1990," in ibid., pp. 1128–1129.

15. "Statement by Press Secretary Fitzwater on United States Interdiction of Iraqi Shipping—August 13, 1990," in ibid., p. 1129.

16. U.S. Department of State, "Resolution 664 (Aug. 18, 1990)," in "UN Security Council Resolutions on Iraq's Invasion of Kuwait," *U.S. Department of State Dispatch* 1:2 (September 10, 1990): 76.

17. George Bush, "Letter to Congressional Leaders on the Mobilization of United States Reserves—August 22, 1990," in *Public Papers: George Bush*, Vol. 1, p. 1156.

18. "Resolution 665 (Aug. 25, 1990)," in "UN Security Council Resolutions on Iraq's Invasion of Kuwait," *U.S. Department of State Dispatch* 1:2 (September 10, 1990): 76.

19. "Excerpt of a Statement by Press Secretary Fitzwater on Soviet President Mikhail Gorbachev's Endorsement of United Nations Economic Sanctions against Iraq—August 25, 1990," in *Public Papers: George Bush*, Vol. 1, p. 1165.

20. "US-USSR Statement," *U.S. Department of State Dispatch* 1:3 (September 17, 1990): 92.

21. George Bush, "Address before a Joint Session of the Congress on the Persian Gulf Crisis and the Federal Budget Deficit," in *Public Papers: George Bush*, Vol. 1, p. 1220.

22. Ibid., p. 1221.

23. U.S. Department of State, "UN Security Council Resolutions on Iraq's Invasion of Kuwait," *U.S. Department of State Dispatch* 1:4 (September 24, 1990): 112.

24. George Bush, "Taped Address to the Iraqi People," *U.S. Department of State Dispatch* 1:4 (September 24, 1990): 113.

25. U.S. Department of State, "UN Security Council Resolutions on Iraq's Invasion of Kuwait," *U.S. Department of State Dispatch* 1:4 (September 24, 1990): 112.

26. U.S. Department of State, "UN Security Council Resolutions on Iraq," *U.S. Department of State Dispatch* 1:5 (October 1, 1990):128.

27. Ibid., pp. 128–129.

28. U.S. Senate, "S. Con. Res. 147," *Congressional Record—Senate* 136 (October 2, 1990): S14338 (Washington, D.C.: U.S. Government Printing Office, 1990).

29. U.S. Department of State, "Isolation Strategy toward Iraq," *U.S. Department of State Dispatch* 1:8 (October 22, 1990): 204.

30. U.S. Department of State, "UN Security Council Condemns Actions by Iraq," *U.S. Department of State Dispatch* 1:10 (November 5, 1990): 239–240.

31. Ibid., p. 239.

32. U.S. Department of State, "UN Security Council Resolutions on Iraq," *U.S. Department of State Dispatch* 1:12 (December 3, 1990): 298.

33. U.S. Senate, "S. Con. Res. 147," *Congressional Record—Senate* 136 (October 2, 1990), in para. (b), p. S14338.

34. U.S. Senate, "Supporting the Actions Taken by the President with Respect to Iraqi Aggression against Kuwait," *Congressional Record—Senate* 136 (October 2, 1990): S14330–S14338.

35. Ibid., pp. S14334–S14335.

Chapter 9

Use of "All Necessary Means"

The threat by Saddam Hussein that chemical and nuclear weapons might be used, given any attempt by the United States and its coalition forces to attack Iraqi forces occupying Kuwait or in Iraq, was enough to give members of Congress, the United Nations Security Council, and the member nations of the United Nations and NATO serious concern. Protests for and against U.S. involvement in the conflict were at an emotional high pitch. By November 16, 1990, President Bush had determined that the developments in the Persian Gulf required additional troops and made a report to congressional leaders regarding the situation there. The portions of the letter to Speaker of the House of Representatives Thomas Foley and to President Pro Tempore of the Senate Robert Byrd that dealt with (1) the president's rationale for needing more troops, (2) his assessment of imminent hostilities, and (3) his request for congressional input follow:[1]

Exhibit 9.1
Letter from President Bush to Congress—Troop Deployment

November 16, 1990

Dear Mr. Speaker: (Dear Mr. President:)

In view of Iraq's continued occupation of Kuwait, defiance of 10 U.N. Security Council resolutions demanding unconditional withdrawal, and sustained threat to other friendly countries in the region, I determined that the U.S. deployments begun in August should continue. Accordingly, on November 8, after consultations with our Allies and coalition partners, I announced the continued deployment of U.S. Armed Forces to the Persian Gulf region.

I want to emphasize that this deployment is in line with the steady buildup of U.S. Armed Forces in the region over the last 3 months and is a continuation of the deployment described in my letter of August 9. I also want to emphasize that the mission of our Armed Forces has not changed. Our Forces are in the Gulf region in the exercise of our *inherent right of individual and collective self-defense* against Iraq's aggression and consistent with U.N. Security Council resolutions related to Iraq's on-going occupation of Kuwait [emphasis added].

In my August 9 letter, I indicated that I did not believe that *involvement in hostilities was imminent. . . .* My view on these matters has not changed [emphasis added].

I appreciate the views you and other members of the congressional leadership have expressed throughout the past 3 months during our consultations. I look forward to continued consultation and cooperation with the Congress in pursuit of peace, stability, and security in the Gulf region.

Sincerely,

GEORGE BUSH

We observe that the language in the phrase "inherent right of individual and collective self-defense" has its basis in Chapter VII, Article 51, of the United Nations Charter, which states, "Nothing in the present Charter shall impair the inherent right of *individual or collective self-defense if an armed attack occurs* against a Member of the United Nations [emphasis added]."[2] We observe also that the second emphasized statement, "I indicated that I did not believe that involvement in hostilities was imminent," was designed to prevent triggering War Powers Resolution Section 4(a)(1), which requires the president to make a report to Congress within forty-eight hours of the deployment of United States armed forces "into hostilities or into situations where imminent involvement in hostilities is clearly indicated by the circumstances."[3]

UNITED NATIONS SECURITY COUNCIL RESOLUTION 678

November 29, 1990

This date was the turning point for the Persian Gulf crisis. Just nine days earlier a number of Democrats filed suit to have President Bush seek approval from Congress before he launched an all-out attack on Saddam Hussein. The number of war protests had been increasing steadily on the one hand, but there was a more determined movement to clamp down harder on Iraq on the other hand. The United Nations Security Council had just passed S.C. Resolution 677 the previous day. Now, amid all the emotion around the world over the atrocities already committed by Hussein, or announced to take place in the near future, the United Nations Security Council issued the most important of all resolutions—S.C. Resolution 678 (November 29, 1990). That resolution is stated verbatim in Exhibit 9.2 below:[4]

Exhibit 9.2
United Nations Security Council Resolution 678

Resolution 678 (Nov. 29, 1990)

The Security Council,

Recalling and reaffirming its resolutions 660 (1990), 661 (1990), 662 (1990), 664 (1990), 665 (1990), 666 (1990), 667 (1990), 669 (1990), 670 (1990), and 674 (1990),

Noting that, despite all efforts by the United Nations, Iraq refuses to comply with its obligation to implement resolution 660 (1990) and the above subsequent relevant resolutions, in flagrant contempt of the Council,

Mindful of its duties and responsibilities under the Charter of the United Nations for the maintenance and preservation of international peace and security,

Determined to secure full compliance with its decisions,

Acting under Chapter VII of the Charter of the United Nations,

1. Demands that Iraq comply fully with resolution 660 (1990) and all subsequent relevant resolutions and decides, while maintaining all its decisions, to allow Iraq one final opportunity, as a pause of good will, to do so;

2. Authorizes Member States cooperating with the Government of Kuwait, unless Iraq on or before 15 January 1991 fully implements, as set forth in paragraph 1 above, the foregoing resolutions, to use all necessary means to uphold and implement Security Council resolution 660 (1990) and all subsequent relevant resolutions and to restore international peace and security in the area;

3. Requests all States to provide appropriate support for the actions undertaken in pursuance of paragraph 2 of this resolution;

4. Requests the States concerned to keep the Council regularly informed on the progress of actions undertaken pursuant to paragraphs 2 and 3 of this resolution;

5. Decides to remain seized of the matter. VOTE: 12 for, 2 against (Cuba and Yemen), 1 abstention (China).

The resolution passed by the United Nations Security Council on this day was historic for a number of reasons. November 29, 1990, was the first time in history that a U.S. secretary of state had presided over a United Nations Security Council session. It was only the fourth time in the United Nations' forty-five-year history that all five of the permanent member foreign ministers had met together. (The five permanent members were the United States, China, France, the United Kingdom, and the Soviet Union.

The authorization in S.C. Resolution 678 for member states to "use all necessary means to uphold and implement Security Council resolution 660 (1990) and all subsequent relevant resolutions and to restore international peace and security in the area" was the strongest possible language, implying that parties to the Charter could deploy armed forces for offensive action. Notice, however, that there was a window from August 29, 1990, through January 14, 1991, at midnight, that was referred to as a "pause for peace"—the actual wording was "pause of good will"—during which Iraq could peacefully withdraw.

On November 30, President Bush held a news conference during which he outlined his assessment of the Gulf crisis and acknowledged the United Nations Security Council Resolution 678. In that news conference he was asked whether he would like Congress to pass a resolution similar to the one that the United Nations Security Council had passed. He answered that he would like to have one[5] (but he would later say that he thought that he actually did not need one to take offensive action against Iraq).[6] Marlin Fitzwater also released a statement regarding President Bush's telephone conversations with President Mubarak of Egypt, President Ozal of Turkey, King Fahd of Saudi Arabia, Prime Minister Major of the United Kingdom, and the amir of Kuwait regarding President Bush's role in the Gulf crisis.[7]

The communications listed above indicate that there was a desire on the part of the president to keep Congress and the American people apprized of the developments in the Persian Gulf crisis. What they also point out is the atmosphere of urgency and shared commitment to respond to the aggressive actions of one member of the United Nations against another and within the framework of the United Nations Charter.

Was there advice and consent from the U.S. Congress for the actions taken against Iraq up to this point? The verbatim correspondence and resolutions presented in the previous chapter are evidence that there was reporting and consultation during every phase of the deployment of troops. Perhaps the significant issue is whether this consultation took the form desired by Congress, that is, whether the president called on Congress for approval to proceed to the next phase.

By the end of 1990 and the beginning of 1991, it was obvious that the United States and the coalition forces were postured for a major hostile confrontation with Iraqi forces. On October 15, 1990, President Bush told the American people of the suffering endured by the Kuwaiti people, such as newborn babies thrown out of incubators and the incubators then shipped to Baghdad, dialysis patients ripped from their dialysis machines and the machines sent to Baghdad, children shot while their parents watched, women raped in order to propagate the Iraqi population and change the demographics of Kuwait, and other atrocities.[8] Descriptions of Iraqi destruction of this type and worse were repeated by all news media over and over again by the end of the year.

While the American public was concerned with the horror of the pain and suffering inflicted on the people of Kuwait by Saddam Hussein's army, the Congress was concerned with whether the president should seek its approval to take action against Iraq and satisfy the requirements of the War Powers Resolution. With eleven United Nations Security Council resolutions condemning Iraq's occupation of Kuwait, with fifty-four nations making economic or military contributions to the Gulf effort,[9] and with thirteen NATO allies already participating with the United States in naval blockades in the Persian Gulf,[10] would there not seem to be more than enough evidence that further armed force would be necessary to assist Kuwait and Saudi Arabia against the threat of further Iraqi hostilities? At issue was whether the explicit, inherent, implied, and/or aggregate powers of the president as commander in chief and chief executive under the U.S. Constitution were sufficient to permit further escalation of U.S. involvement in the Persian Gulf. Additionally, at issue was whether Congress had given its advice and consent, explicitly or implicitly, since August 2, 1990, to proceed.

PRESIDENT REQUESTS CONGRESSIONAL SUPPORT

January 8, 1991

On January 8, 1991, President Bush sent the following letter to Speaker of the House of Representatives Thomas Foley, Senate Majority Leader George Mitchell, Senate Republican Leader Robert Dole, and House of Representatives Republican Leader Robert Michel:[11]

Exhibit 9.3
Letter from President Bush to Congressional Leaders

January 8, 1991

Dear _____ :

   The current situation in the Persian Gulf, brought about by Iraq's unprovoked invasion and subsequent brutal occupation of Kuwait, threatens vital U.S. interests. The situation also threatens the peace. It would, however, greatly enhance the chances for peace if Congress were now to go on record supporting the position adopted by the UN Security Council on twelve separate occasions. Such an action would underline that the United States stands with the international community and on the side of law and decency; it also would help dispel any belief that may exist in the minds of Iraq's leaders that the United States lacks the necessary unity to act decisively in response to Iraq's continued aggression against Kuwait.

   Secretary of State Baker is meeting with Iraq's Foreign Minister on January 9. It would have been most constructive if he could have presented the Iraqi government a Resolution passed by both houses of Congress supporting the UN position and in particular Security Council Resolution 678. As you know, I have frequently stated my desire for such a Resolution. Nevertheless, there is still opportunity for Congress to act to strengthen the prospects for peace and safeguard this country's vital interests.

   I therefore request that the House of Representatives and the Senate adopt a Resolution stating that Congress supports the use of all necessary means to implement UN Security Council Resolution 678. Such action would send the clearest possible message to Saddam Hussein that he must withdraw without condition or delay from Kuwait. Anything less would only encourage Iraqi intransigence; anything else would risk detracting from the international coalition arrayed against Iraq's aggression.

   Mr. Speaker, I am determined to do whatever is necessary to protect America's security. I ask Congress to join with me in this task. I can think of no better way than for Congress to express its support for the President at this critical time. This truly is the last best chance for peace.

   Sincerely,

GEORGE BUSH

Source: "Letter to Congressional Leaders on the Persian Gulf Crisis—January 8, 1991," in *Public Papers of the Presidents of the United States: George Bush*, Vol. 2 (Washington, D.C.: U.S. Government Printing Office, 1992): 13–14.

   The letter from President Bush to the congressional leaders (1) provides a rationale for continued action, (2) requests action from both the Senate and the House of Representatives, and (3) requests specific support from Congress—"request[s] that the House of Representatives and the Senate adopt a Resolution stating that Congress supports the *use of all necessary means* to implement UN Security Council Resolution 678 [emphasis added]." The highlighted phrase is crucial since it could be interpreted as use of offensive armed force.

In his sixty-eighth news conference in the Briefing Room of the White House the following day, January 9, 1991, the following question-and-answer session reveals the position of the president on whether the request he made to Congress on January 8, 1991, and reproduced above was made pursuant to the War Powers Resolution and his authority in the Persian Gulf:[12]

Q. Can you tell us what your attitude now is about the use-of-force resolution that you asked for yesterday with the Congress?

THE PRESIDENT. . . . I am anxious to see and would certainly welcome a resolution that says we are going to implement the United Nations resolutions to a tee. . . .

Q. Do you think you need such a resolution? And if you lose it, would you be bound by that?

THE PRESIDENT. I don't think I need it. I think Secretary Cheney expressed it very well the other day. There are different opinions on either side of this question, but Saddam Hussein should be under no question on this: I feel that I have the authority to fully implement the United Nations resolutions.

Q. And the question of being bound—the second part of that?

THE PRESIDENT. I still feel that I have the constitutional authority—many attorneys having so advised me.

Q. If the Congress of the United States refuses to give you a resolution that—refuses to even give you a Gulf of Tonkin type resolution, how can you go to war?

THE PRESIDENT. I don't think they're going to refuse.

THE PRESIDENT. [Breaking in on a question] There have been 200—I'll just repeat for the record that there have been a lot of uses of force in our history and very few declarations of war. But I have tried. I have done more consultation with the Congress than any other President. . . .

Q. . . . We can't be rushing headlong into war this way. Can you tell us that there is nothing, that is what we appear to be getting—that Saddam isn't going to move and we're going to war?

THE PRESIDENT. I'm not going to use that phrase. I am going to say, if Saddam doesn't move, we are going to fully implement Resolution 678. And it will be fully complied with.

DECLARATION OF WAR OR ASSISTANCE

The excerpts from the news conference of January 9, 1991, just cited reveal President Bush's belief that he already had constitutional authority to proceed with conducting the operation in the Persian Gulf. Did he need the resolution that he requested of Congress? He thought that it would send a message to Saddam Hussein of unity of purpose on the part of the people of the United States, but not that the resolution was a prerequisite for continuing to implement the twelve United Nations Security Council resolutions, especially S.C. Resolution 678.

When the question was raised regarding whether the president would be bound by any such resolution, he replied with two answers: (1) that he had the authority to fully implement the United Nations resolutions, and (2) that he had the authority under the Constitution.[13] When asked whether he could go to war if the Congress did not give him a Gulf of Tonkin–type resolution, the president replied that he thought that the Congress would not refuse to give him such a resolution.[14] One of the reasons why he made this statement of confidence is that, by the time of this news conference, the public seemed to be solidly behind a use of force against Saddam Hussein. Graphic evidence of the rapes, pillage, and destruction of Kuwait by Iraq was seen daily on television newscasts and in the print media. Another reason was that on October 2, 1990, the U.S. Senate had passed Senate Concurrent Resolution No. 147 with a vote of ninety-six yeas, three nays, and one not voting (Rollcall Vote No. 258 Leg.). The Nays were Hatfield, Kennedy, and Kerry. Not voting was Wilson. This concurrent resolution stated in part,[15]

That (a) the Congress strongly approves the leadership of the President in successfully pursuing the passage of United Nations Security Council Resolutions . . . , which call for—(1) the immediate, complete, and unconditional withdrawal of all Iraqi forces from Kuwait . . . (b) The Congress approves the actions taken by the President in support of these goals, including the involvement of the United Nations and of the friendly governments. The Congress supports continued action by the President.

While not a "blank check" like the Gulf of Tonkin Resolution, this concurrent resolution, was a congressional approval of the president's actions that was virtually unanimous in the Senate. Since the situation had worsened for Kuwait since that time, the president could be confident that such support had not waned.

When asked point-blank whether Saddam was driving us into war, the president responded with an answer that would not trigger the War Powers Resolution—"I'm not going to use that phrase. I am going to say, if Saddam doesn't move, we are going to fully implement Resolution 678. And it will be fully complied with."[16]

The language and nuances of the questions and answers examined above are important from several aspects. The president did not want to give Congress the impression that this was a request for any "authorization" to use force. He also did not want to cause a confrontation with Congress by acknowledging that war was imminent. If he had done so, he would have had to confront Section 4(a)(1) of the War Powers Resolution, which states, "Sec. 4.(a) In the absence of a declaration of war, in any case in which the United States Armed Forces are introduced—(1) into hostilities or into situations where imminent involvement in hostilities is clearly indicated by the circumstances; . . . The President shall submit within 48 hours to the Speaker of the House of Representatives and to the President pro tempore of the Senate a report."[17]

AUTHORIZATION FOR USE OF MILITARY FORCE

Against the backdrop of a network of diplomatic activities among the coalition of some twenty-eight countries, after the failure of the Arab League to obtain a peaceful solution with Saddam Hussein, and after countless consultations between Congress and the executive, including news conferences and cabinet interviews, it became obvious to both Republicans and Democrats alike that sanctions were not working. Debate in Congress centered around two main issues: (1) would waiting for the sanctions to have the desired effect take an unacceptable toll in human lives and welfare in Kuwait and (2) should the president formally request authorization from Congress before commencing an all-out war against Iraq.

January 14, 1991

Some say that the congressional debates in the days just prior to January 14, 1991, depicted Congress in its finest hour. There was full and public debate regarding the costs and benefits of war with Iraq. While in Congress the word "war" was used in almost every argument by those debating the Persian Gulf issue, the president did not use that word (for reasons cited above). A common thread ran through the debates—the United Nations Security Council's Resolution 678 deadline of January 15, 1991. It was literally the midnight hour for that resolution and for the debates in Congress. After hours of debate, the Congress passed the joint resolution presented below in Exhibit 9.4.[18]

Exhibit 9.4
H.J. Res. 77—Authorization for Use of Military Force against Iraq

Joint Resolution to Authorize the Use of United States Armed Forces Pursuant to United Nations Security Council Resolution 678

Whereas the Government of Iraq without provocation invaded and occupied the territory of Kuwait on August 2, 1990;

Whereas both the House of Representatives (in H.J. Res. 658 of the 101st Congress) and the Senate (in S. Con. Res. 147 of the 101st Congress) have condemned Iraq's aggression;

Whereas, Iraq's conventional, chemical, biological, and nuclear weapons and ballistic missile programs and its demonstrated willingness to use weapons of mass destruction pose a grave threat to world peace;

Whereas the international community has demanded that Iraq withdraw unconditionally and immediately from Kuwait and that Kuwait's independence and legitimate government be restored;

Whereas the United Nations Security Council repeatedly affirmed the inherent right of individual or collective self-defense in response to the armed attack by Iraq against Kuwait in accordance with Article 51 of the United Nations Charter;

Whereas, in the absence of full compliance by Iraq with its resolutions, the United Nations Security Council in Resolution 678 has authorized member states of the United Nations to use all necessary means, after January 15, 1991, to uphold and implement all relevant Security Council resolutions and to restore international peace and security in the area; and

Whereas Iraq has persisted in its illegal occupation of, and brutal aggression against Kuwait: Now, therefore, be it

Resolved by the Senate and House of Representatives of the United States of American in Congress assembled,

SECTION 1. SHORT TITLE.

This joint resolution may be cited as the "Authorization for Use of Military Force Against Iraq Resolution."

SEC. 2. AUTHORIZATION FOR USE OF UNITED STATES ARMED FORCES.

(a) AUTHORIZATION.—The President is authorized, subject to subsection (b), to use United States Armed Forces pursuant to United Nations Security Council Resolution 678 (1990) in order to achieve implementation of Security Council Resolutions 660, 661, 662, 664, 665, 666, 667, 669, 670, 674, and 677.

(b) REQUIREMENT FOR DETERMINATION THAT USE OF MILITARY FORCE IS NECESSARY.—Before exercising the authority granted in subsection (a), the President shall make available to the Speaker of the House of Representatives and the President pro tempore of the Senate his determination that—(1) the United States has used all appropriate diplomatic and other peaceful means to obtain compliance by Iraq with the United Nations Security Council resolutions cited in subsection (a); and

(2) that those efforts have not been and would not be successful in obtaining such compliance.

(c) WAR POWERS RESOLUTION REQUIREMENTS.—

(1) SPECIFIC STATUTORY AUTHORIZATION.—Consistent with section 8(a)(1) of the War Powers Resolution, the Congress declares that this section is intended to constitute specific statutory authorization within the meaning of section 5(b) of the War Powers Resolution.

(2) APPLICABILITY OF OTHER REQUIREMENTS.—Nothing in this resolution supersedes any requirement of the War Powers Resolution.

SEC. 3. REPORTS TO CONGRESS.

At least once every 60 days, the President shall submit to the Congress a summary on the status of efforts to obtain compliance by Iraq with the resolutions adopted by the United Nations Security Council in response to Iraq's aggression.

Approved January 14, 1991.

Source: Public Law 102–1 (H.J. Res. 77): January 14, 1991.

Was this a declaration of war? If not, did Congress have to provide such a resolution as this one to the President? Did the resolution give the president authority that he did not have before it was approved? Recall from the January 8, 1991, letter from President Bush to the Speaker of the House of Representatives and to the president pro tempore of the Senate that he made the following request: "I therefore request that the House of Representatives and the Senate adopt a Resolution stating that Congress supports the use of all necessary means to implement UN Security Council Resolution 678."[19]

Observe that there was no reference to the War Powers Resolution in that request. The only reference to authority was to the UN Security Council Resolution 678.

Perhaps the clearest illustration of President Bush's perception of his constitutional authority is revealed in his statement to Congress and to the American people during the signing of House of Representatives Joint Resolution 77. That statement, reproduced in Exhibit 9.5, leaves no uncertainty regarding whether the joint resolution circumscribed his authority under the Constitution at all.[20]

Exhibit 9.5
President Bush's Statement on Signing H.J. Res. 77

Today I am signing H.J. Res. 77, the "Authorization for Use of Military Force Against Iraq Resolution." By passing H.J. Res. 77, the Congress of the United States has expressed its approval of the use of U.S. Armed Forces consistent with U.N. Security Council Resolution 678. I asked the Congress to support implementation of U.N. Security Council Resolution 678 because such action would send the clearest possible message to Saddam Hussein that he must withdraw from Kuwait without condition or delay. I am grateful to those of both political parties who joined in the expression of resolve embodied in this resolution. To all, I emphasize again my conviction that this resolution provides the best hope for peace.

The debate on H.J. Res. 77 reflects the profound strength of our constitutional democracy. In coming to grips with the issues at stake in the Gulf, both Houses of Congress acted in the finest traditions of our country. This resolution provides unmistakable support for the international community's determination that Iraq's ongoing aggression against, and occupation of, Kuwait shall not stand. As I made clear to congressional leaders at the outset, my request for congressional support did not, and my signing this resolution does not, constitute any change in the long-standing positions of the executive branch on either the *President's constitutional authority to use the Armed Forces to defend vital U.S. interests or the constitutionality of the War Powers Resolution* [emphasis added]. I am pleased, however, that differences on these issues between the President and many in the Congress have not prevented us from uniting in a common objective. I have had the benefit of extensive and meaningful consultations with the Congress throughout this crisis, and I shall continue to consult closely with the Congress in the days ahead.

GEORGE BUSH

The White House
January 14, 1991

The signing of House of Representatives Joint Resolution 77 ushered in the beginning of the end of Iraq's occupation of Kuwait. Recall that the deadline set in United Nations Security Council Resolution 678 was "on or before January 15, 1991."[21] Recall also the reference to that same deadline in the preamble to H.J. Res. 77.[22] With the support of the U.S. Congress now a public law—P.L. 102–1—the "line in the sand" that was drawn when

Iraq invaded Kuwait led to war against Iraq in an operation appropriately designated "Desert Storm."

OPERATION DESERT STORM

Had there been advice and consent of Congress before U.S. armed forces were deployed in the coalition war with Iraq? Documents and events relevant to the use of force in Kuwait and Iraq in this chapter and the previous chapter leave little doubt that there was advice and consent of Congress. It was common knowledge to the whole world, through the electronic and print media, what was going on in the Persian Gulf, who the players were, what they sought to achieve, and what might be the next moves by both sides.

Could anyone doubt that the coalition forces in Saudi Arabia and in other military facilities, including ships in and around the Persian Gulf, would launch a major assault on the Iraqi forces occupying Kuwait and in Iraq? Impossible. The television networks CNN and C-SPAN had on-the-spot television pictures of events in Iraq, in Kuwait, in Saudi Arabia, and on the various ships at sea. Additionally, military briefings had been provided at regular intervals during the day and night from the Pentagon and from the White House since August 2, 1990, when Iraq first invaded Kuwait.

January 16, 1991

Three major events developed during the hours of January 16, 1991, which had significant constitutional implications: (1) President Bush sent a letter to congressional leaders pursuant to H.J. Res. 77; (2) Marlin Fitzwater released a statement from the White House at 7:08 p.m. indicating the beginning of the liberation of Kuwait; (3) the president, at 9:01 p.m. from the Oval Office of the White House, announced the beginning of Desert Storm.

The letter from President Bush (identical letters) sent to Speaker of the House of Representatives Thomas Foley, to President Pro Tempore of the Senate Robert Byrd, to Senate Majority Leader George Mitchell, to Senate Republican Leader Robert Dole, and to House Republican Leader Robert Michel, outlined his authority for commencing the attack on Iraq in Desert storm. It also contained a statement of the rationale for use of force rather than the other measures called for in the twelve United Nations Security Council resolutions associated with the Iraqi invasion. The letter, mentioned in (1) above, is given below in Exhibit 9.6.[23]

Exhibit 9.6
Letter from President Bush to Congress Regarding H.J. Res. 77

January 16, 1991

Dear Mr. Speaker: (Dear Mr. President:)

Pursuant to section 2(b) of the Authorization for Use of Military Force Against Iraq Resolution (H.J. Res 77, Public Law 102–1), I have concluded that:

1. the United States has used all appropriate diplomatic and other peaceful means to obtain compliance by Iraq with U.N. Security Council Resolutions 660, 661, 662, 664, 665, 666, 667, 669, 670, 674, 677, and 678; and

2. that those efforts have not been and would not be successful in obtaining such compliance.

Enclosed is a report that supports my decision.

Sincerely,

GEORGE BUSH

Source: "Letter to Congressional Leaders Transmitting a Report Pursuant to the Resolution Authorizing the Use of Force against Iraq," in *Public Papers of the Presidents of the United States: George Bush,* Vol. 1 (Washington, D.C.: U.S. Government Printing Office, 1992): 42.

Whether the president wanted this letter to satisfy the spirit of Section 4(a)(1) of the War Powers Resolution or not, he did "submit within 48 hours to the Speaker of the House of Representatives and to the president pro tempore of the Senate a report, in writing."[24] The statement read to the reporters in the Briefing Room of the White House was also significant in that it set forth the time and code name of the operation liberating Kuwait from Iraqi occupation. It is presented in Exhibit 9.7 below:[25]

Exhibit 9.7
Press Secretary's Statement on Kuwaiti Liberation

January 16, 1991

I have a statement by the President of the United States.

The liberation of Kuwait has begun. In conjunction with the forces of our coalition partners, the United States has moved under the code name Operation Desert Storm to enforce the mandates of the United Nations Security Council. As of 7 p.m. Eastern Standard Time, Operation Desert Storm forces were engaging targets in Kuwait and Iraq.

President Bush will address the Nation at 9 p.m. tonight from the Oval Office. I'll try to get you more as soon as we can. Thank you very much.

Source: "Statement on Allied Military Action in the Persian Gulf—January 16, 1991," in *Public Papers of the Presidents of the United States: George Bush,* Vol. 1 (Washington, D.C.: U.S. Government Printing Office, 1991): 42.

At 9:01 p.m. the president announced from the Oval Office of the White House, "Just 2 hours ago, allied air forces began an attack on military targets in Iraq and Kuwait. These attacks continue as I speak."[26]

DESERT STORM: PRESIDENTIAL CONSULTATION

We observe a chronology of events in the preceding chapter and in the current one indicating that sufficient consultation between the Congress and the president did occur to a degree that more than satisfied the requirements of any interpretation of the War Powers Resolution. The chronology has also helped us to view the interaction of the Congress and the president with the United Nations Security Council. Having examined the most significant of the documents which communicate the authority to act on use of force, do we not have compelling evidence that, at least in the Persian Gulf operation, the Congress and the president did fulfill their respective constitutional responsibilities? What role did the War Powers Resolution play in the events leading up to and including Desert Storm?

The next chapter will provide an analysis of the War Powers Resolution and different views regarding its applicability, including some possible amendments to its language.

NOTES

1. George Bush, "Letter to Congressional Leaders on the Deployment of Additional United States Armed Forces to the Persian Gulf—November 16, 1990," in *Public Papers of the Presidents of the United States: George Bush,* Vol. 1 (Washington, D.C.: U.S. Government Printing Office, 1991): 1617–1618. (Hereafter in this chapter, the two-volume work will be referred to as *Public Papers: George Bush.*)

2. United Nations, *Charter of the United Nations*, Chapter VII, Article 51.

3. U.S. House of Representatives, "Joint Resolution concerning the War Powers of Congress and the President," November 7, 1973, P.L. 93–148, 87 Stat. 555 (1973), Sec. 4(a)(1).

4. U.S. Department of State, "UN Security Council Resolutions on Iraq," *U.S. Department of State Dispatch* 1:14 (December 3, 1990): 298.

5. "The President's News Conference—November 30, 1990," in *Public Papers: George Bush*, Vol. 1, pp. 1719–1721.

6. "The President's News Conference on the Persian Gulf Crisis—January 9, 1991," in *Public Papers: George Bush*, Vol. 2, pp. 19–20.

7. "The President's News Conference—November 30, 1990," in *Public Papers: George Bush*, Vol. 1, p. 1729.

8. "Iraqi Atrocities in Kuwait—Excerpts from Remarks by President Bush at the Hyatt Regency Hotel, Dallas, Texas, October 15, 1990," *U.S. Department of State Dispatch* 1:8 (October 22, 1990): 205.

9. James Baker, "Isolation Strategy toward Iraq," ibid., p. 204.

10. Raymond Seita, "The Persian Gulf Crisis and US-European Relations," *U.S. Department of State Dispatch* 1:6 (October 15, 1990): 186.

11. "Letter to Congressional Leaders on the Persian Gulf Crisis—January 8, 1991," in *Public Papers: George Bush*, Vol. 1, pp. 13–14.

12. "The President's News Conference on the Persian Gulf Crisis—January 9, 1991," ibid., pp. 17–23. President Bush was referring to the lists of uses of force presented in Appendices C and D. Notice that of the 215 uses of force from the year 1798 through 1989, only 5 were declared wars. See *Congressional Record—Senate* (January 10, 1991): S130–S135.

13. "The President's News Conference on the Persian Gulf Crisis—January 9, 1991," in *Public Papers: George Bush*, Vol. 1, p. 20. See also Vance, Cyrus. "Striking the Balance: Congress and the President under the War Powers Resolution," in Appendix 5, U.S. House of Representatives, *War Powers: Origins, Purposes, and Applications: Hearings before the Subcommittee on Arms Control, International Security and Science of the Committee on Foreign Affairs*, 100th Cong., 2nd Sess., August 4, 1988 and September 27, 1988 (Washington, D.C.: U.S. Government Printing Office, 1989): 288–304, and U.S. Senate, *The War Power after 200 Years: Congress and the President at a Constitutional Impasse: Hearings before the Special Subcommittee on War Powers of the Senate Committee on Foreign Relations*, 100th Cong., 2nd Sess. (Washington, D.C.: U.S. Government Printing Office, 1989).

14. "The President's News Conference on the Persian Gulf Crisis—January 9, 1991," in *Public Papers: George Bush*, Vol. 1, p. 20; James Benjamin, "Rhetoric and the Performative Act of Declaring War," *Presidential Studies Quarterly* 21:1 (Winter 1991): 73–84; James Bennet, "The Senate's Lame Doves: Why They Failed to Stop the War," *Washington Monthly* (March 1991): 43–46; Joan Biskupic, "Constitution's Conflicting Clauses Underscored by Iraq Crisis: Provisions on Waging War Leave a Basic Question Unanswered, Does Congress or the President Call the Shot?" *Congressional Quarterly Weekly Report* (January 5, 1991): 33–36; George Bush, "Letter to Congressional Leaders Reporting on the National Emergency with Respect to Iraq," in *Public Papers: George Bush*, Vol. 2, pp. 131–133; Arthur Blair, *At War in the Gulf: A Chronology* (College Station: Texas A&M University Press, 1992).

15. U.S. Senate, *Congressional Record—Senate,* October 2, 1990, S14338.

16. "The President's News Conference on the Persian Gulf Crisis—January 9, 1991," in *Public Papers: George Bush*, Vol. 1, p. 22. Even though President Bush's language skirted the issue, his actions up to this point and planned response to the Iraqi hostilities clearly would have placed U.S. armed forces "into hostilities or into situations where imminent involvement in hostilities is clearly indicated by the circumstances." See Section 4(a)(1), The War Powers Resolution 87 Stat. 555 (1973).

17. Section 4(a)(1), The War Powers Resolution 87 Stat. 555 (1973); U.S. House of Representatives, *The War Powers Resolution: A Special Study of the Committee on Foreign Affairs* (Committee Print), Committee on Foreign Affairs, (Washington, D.C.: U.S. Government Printing Office, 1982): 287–292; U.S. House of Representatives, *War Powers: Origins, Purposes, and Applications: Hearings before the Subcommittee on Arms Control, International Security and Science of the Committee on Foreign Affairs*, 100th Cong., 2nd Sess., August 4, 1988, and September 27, 1988 (Washington, D.C.: U.S. Government Printing Office, 1989); Robert Turner, "The War Powers Resolution: Its Origins and Purpose," in ibid., pp. 55–113.

18. U.S. Congress, "Authorization for Use of Military Force against Iraq Resolution," Public Law 102-1 (H.J. Res. 77), January 14, 1991. The irony of this resolution is that on January 9, 1991, in "The President's News Conference on the Persian Gulf Crisis," President Bush's sixty-eighth news conference in the Briefing Room of the White House, the president was asked the following question regarding a resolution from Congress authorizing military use of force against Iraq: "Do you think you need such a resolution? And if you lose it, would you be bound by that?" To which he replied, "I don't think I need it. I think Secretary Cheney expressed it very well the other day. There are different opinions on either side of the question, but Saddam Hussein should be under no question on this: I feel that I have the authority to fully implement the United Nations resolutions." See *Public Papers: George Bush*, Vol. 1, p. 20.

19. "Letter to Congressional Leaders on the Persian Gulf Crisis—January 8, 1991," in *Public Papers: George Bush,* Vol. 1, pp. 13–14.

20. "Statement on Signing the Resolution Authorizing the Use of Military Force against Iraq—January 14, 1991," in ibid., p. 40.

21. United Nations S.C. Res. 678 (November 29, 1990), presented verbatim in Exhibit 9.2.

22. H.J. Res. 77—"Authorization for Use of Military Force against Iraq Resolution," presented in Exhibit 9.4.

23. "Letter to Congressional Leaders Transmitting a Report Pursuant to the Resolution Authorizing the Use of Force against Iraq," in *Public Papers: George Bush*, Vol. 1, p. 42.

24. Section 4(a)(1), The War Powers Resolution 87 Stat. 555 (1973).

25. "Statement on Allied Military Action in the Persian Gulf—January 16, 1991," in *Public Papers: George Bush*, Vol. 1, p. 42.

26. "Address to the Nation Announcing Allied Military Action in the Persian Gulf—January 16, 1991," in ibid., pp. 42–45.

PART V

Necessity of Declaration of War and War Powers Resolution

Chapter 10

The Question of War

The correspondence presented in Chapter 7 between Dante B. Fascell, chairman of the House of Representatives Committee on Foreign Affairs and J. Edward Fox, assistant secretary, legislative affairs, Department of State, clearly illustrates the "standoff" between the Congress and the executive on the issue of complying with the provisions of the War Powers Resolution.[1] One must conclude from that exchange that Congress insists that the president must comply with the provisions of the War Powers Resolution. The president, however, provides reports "consistent with the War Powers Resolution" and not specifically and unequivocally specifying that any report is "pursuant to the provisions of the War Powers Resolution."[2] Another example of the type of wording used by recent presidents regarding complying with the War Powers Resolution is President Ronald Reagan's letter to Speaker of the House of Representatives Jim Wright, on September 21, 1987, regarding the U.S. engagement of of the Iranian mine-laying seacraft *Ajr* in the Persian Gulf. The last paragraph of that letter states:

These limited defensive actions have been taken by our Armed Forces in accordance with international law, and pursuant to my constitutional authority with respect to the conduct of foreign relations and as Commander-in-Chief. While being mindful of the historical differences between the legislative and executive branches of government, and the positions taken by all of my predecessors in office, with respect to the interpretation and constitutionality of certain of the provisions of the War Powers Resolution, I nonetheless am providing this report in a spirit of mutual cooperation toward a common goal.[3]

If the War Powers Resolution has done no more than be a constant reminder to the president and to Congress that they should keep each other informed regarding the status and progress of international political situations which might require the use of U.S. armed forces, it probably has achieved the spirit of its objectives. Additionally, is it not true that "compliance with reservations is compliance nevertheless"? Perhaps our preoccupation with the constitutional and legal issues inside the window of commitment of armed forces and the conflict between the president and Congress inside that same window clouds the more fundamental issues of whether (1) the concept of a "declaration of war" is irrelevant and perhaps meaningless now, (2) Congress has, in fact, been giving its advice and consent to the president incrementally over time, directly and indirectly, (3) Congress or the president could refine the War Powers Resolution in a manner such that neither would feel that the doctrine of separation of powers was compromised, (4) the roles of Congress, the president, mutual defense treaties, and humanitarian concepts have changed so drastically in the last half century that they call for a new structure of congressional-presidential relationships.

CONCEPT OF DECLARATION OF WAR

Between 1787 and 1994, the United States has been involved in five declared wars. Appendix D lists those wars as (1) the War of 1812 (1812–1815), (2) the Mexican War (1846–1848), (3) The Spanish-American War, (1898), (4) World War I (1917–1918), and (5) World War II (1941–1945). Half a century has passed since the last declaration of war. By contrast, there have been over 200 instances of the use of U.S. armed forces in hostilities abroad, usually associated with mutual defense agreements and treaties. Appendix C lists 210 instances of the use of U.S. armed forces abroad between 1798 and 1989 without a declaration of war.

One might argued that a declaration of war, in any of the "uses of force" listed in Appendix C, would not have made any difference in the military outcome. One would have to admit the possibility, however, that had there been a declaration of war in those instances, the political result might have been a coalescence against the United States by the allies of the enemies of those to whom we gave support.[4] Would any of the major conflicts since World War II qualify as a war? Yes, absolutely. The Korean and Vietnam conflicts had all the characteristics of wars. The potential scope of military activities in Korea and Vietnam was well known by everyone who had the remotest knowledge of events in the early stages of both of those conflicts.[5] Congressional hearings, CIA intelligence reports, press briefings, and reports from foreign governments and agencies were being funneled through Congress and the appropriate committees for months, and even years in some cases, before hostilities became imminent.

If the United States had joined in a declaration of war with South Korea or South Vietnam against North Korea and North Vietnam respectively, the whole focus of both conflicts would surely have been profoundly different. Just as America has mutual security agreements with other nations, so also do North Korea and North Vietnam. If one of the nations in a mutual security agreement is attacked by another nation not covered by the agreement, the attack is held to be an attack on all of the signatories to the agreement.[6] Joining either South Korea or South Vietnam in declared war would have meant that the United States was also declaring war against any one or all of the signatories to any mutual security agreements to which North Korea or North Vietnam might be parties. The threat of retaliatory nuclear war was always a possibility before the Cold War was over. For that and other reasons, the U.S. actions assisting South Korea and South Vietnam were treated only as defensive measures, "police action," to support a weaker state.[7]

Ely suggests that the Gulf of Tonkin Resolution was "a suitably specific combat authorization"—in other words, it could actually have been construed as a declaration of war.[8] It was not, however, viewed by either Congress or President Lyndon Johnson as a declaration of war. Congress and the president were of a single mind that the Gulf of Tonkin Resolution was just that—a resolution of support and assistance to South Vietnam against aggressors from North Vietnam. In fact, the actual language of the resolution was similar in form and format to that normally used by the United Nations when it "authorizes" the "use of all necessary means" to implement the provisions of Security Council resolutions.[9]

Given that the United States has formally declared war in only five cases since 1787 (the last being the declaration of war in World War II a half century ago), it would seem that the power to declare war is less relevant and important than the power, or obligation, to counsel the president in advance of implementation of use-of-force decisions.

SOMALIA AND BOSNIA-HERZEGOVINA

A persistent argument that is repeated in each hearing before congressional committees regarding the War Powers Resolution and the president's commitment of U.S. armed forces abroad is that the president did not consult with Congress before he sent forces into hostilities abroad. In the previous chapters, the events surrounding Desert Shield and Desert Storm

were carefully documented to illustrate continuing congressional-presidential consultation. The congressional hearings, correspondence to Congress,
press conferences, meetings between White House liaisons and congressional staff, and briefings by appropriate military representatives regarding
developments in Saudi Arabia, Kuwait, Iran, and Iraq prior to Iraq's
invasion of Kuwait filled the print and electronic media daily. In the whole
scenario of contact between the executive and Congress, there could have
been absolutely no doubt regarding the military risks involved, the national
interests at stake, and the political benefits and liabilities of assisting Kuwait
and Saudi Arabia in the event that Iraq might stage some form of aggression.

The long- and short-range intentions of Iraq regarding each of its neighboring states had been known for years, and the ultimate invasion of Kuwait
did not come as much of a political or military surprise to those who study
Middle Eastern political and military history. At any time, Congress could
have passed a "sense of Congress" resolution to give the president its advice
and an indication of whether or not it would consent to armed conflict there.

The more recent cases of Somalia and Bosnia-Herzegovina indicate that
Congress has become more inclined to signal the president early that it may
have reservations regarding increasing the scope of activities in situations
in which it appears that military assistance may turn into limited war.

Since the fall of Somalia's Siad Barre in January of 1991, the issue of
widespread starvation and violence in Somalia seized the attention of the
electronic and print news media. Pictures of emaciated Somalians were in
the newspapers and on television almost daily, accompanied by pleas for
the U.S. government to take some humanitarian action. Debates on the
floors of the House of Representatives and Senate during 1991 depicted
violence and starvation in Somalia as intolerable. On February 7, 1991, the
Senate passed Senate Resolution 258 regarding the situation in Somalia. By
August 3, 1992, the Senate was joined by the House of Representatives in
Senate Concurrent Resolution 132 regarding Somalia. By October 2, 1992,
the House of Representatives had passed House Concurrent Resolution 370
regarding Somalia.[10] These efforts resulted in the Horn of Africa Recovery
and Food Security Act, Public Law 102–274, an urgent plea for action in
Somalia.[11]

On December 3, 1992, the United Nations Security Council passed UN
Security Council Resolution 794 (1992) with a unanimous vote of fifteen
to zero.[12] On December 8, 1992, in response to United Nations Security
Council Resolution 794, the secretary of defense prepared a memorandum
outlining a contingency plan for Operation Restore Hope in Somalia.[13] On
December 8, 1992, President George Bush deployed U.S. armed forces to
Somalia in response to UN Security Council Resolution 794.[14] On Decem-

ber 10, 1992, the president outlined his activities in Somalia in a letter to Speaker of the House of Representatives Thomas Foley.[15]

During the first three weeks of October 1993, the Senate was considering the Department of Defense appropriations bill for 1994. After a series of amendments to the actual authorization bill, the Senate settled on a "sense of the Congress" resolution calling for restrictions on the Somalia operations. This resolution was made unnecessary when President Bill Clinton submitted a report to the Speaker of the House of Representatives and to the president pro tempore of the Senate, dated October 13, 1993, agreeing to withdraw troops from Somalia by March 31, 1994.

What is important to observe here is that there was almost a three-year history of congressional debates, hearings before Congress, consultation with congressional committees, high-level briefings by Pentagon staff, and public debate regarding hostilities within Somalia, yet in October 1993 there was a major concern regarding the applicability of the War Powers Resolution.

In the case of Bosnia-Herzegovina, the "Joint Chiefs of Staff Briefing on Current Military Operations in Somalia, Iraq, and Yugoslavia" indicated that hostilities in that area were not just imminent but ongoing. That briefing was dated January 29, 1993. As of February 1994 President Bill Clinton had not decided to deploy U.S. armed forces or use U.S. air power in the Bosnia-Herzegovina hostilities.

In both cases just cited, the Congress had many months' notice of impending hostilities and the actual involvement or planned involvement in these hostilities. Was there not a point at which Congress could have drafted a concurrent resolution or joint resolution indicating to the president that it was the "sense of the Congress and of the American people" that U.S. armed forces should be withdrawn or not deployed? It has been the case, without exception, that the president has notified congressional leaders hours before or hours after the actual engagement of troops in hostilities. In the absence of a declaration of war, one might ask what is the best time to draw Congress into the "engagement in hostilities" decisions, especially in view of all other types of consultation that might have taken place months or even years prior.

WAR POWER OR POLITICAL POWER

Amending the War Powers Resolution in such a manner that individuals would have augmented standing in court to start the Section 4(a)(1) clock would perhaps unnecessarily draw the judiciary into the process. There would still be some question regarding whether Congress could legislate and the Supreme Court could adjudicate what the Constitution did not allocate. A constitutional confrontation would serve no useful purpose, especially if such a confrontation would appear to the public as a power play on the part of Congress, the president, or the Court.

Those calling for an amendment of the War Powers Resolution would like to have more consultation between the president and the Congress *prior* to troop deployment. Such amendments would tighten the conditions under which the president would be "authorized" to use force. The House and Senate joint resolutions are entitled "Authorization for. . ." or "Authorizing . . . ," and so on. The executive is careful to implicitly ask, with each joint resolution presented to it, whether it really needed Congress to authorize what it already had authority to do. President George Bush said it clearly during the signing of the resolution authorizing use of force against Iraq:[16]

As I made clear to congressional leaders at the outset, my request for congressional support did not, and my signing this resolution does not, constitute any change in the long-standing positions of the executive branch on either the President's constitutional authority to use the Armed Forces to defend vital U.S. interests or the constitutionality of the War Powers Resolution. I am pleased, however, that differences on these issues between the President and many in Congress have not prevented us from uniting in a common objective. I have had the benefit of extensive and meaningful consultations with the Congress throughout this crisis, and I shall continue to consult closely with the Congress in the days ahead.

The consultation referred to in President Bush's letter was implemented through many channels of the executive with the Congress. Some have indicated, however, that the consultation section of the War Powers Resolution should be changed to require the president to consult with a permanent consultative body consisting of representatives such as the Speaker of the House of Representatives, the president pro tempore of the Senate, the majority party leader, the minority party leader, and the chairs of the Committee on Foreign Affairs and the Armed Services Committee of the House and Senate, respectively.[17] Others believe that even such a consultative body might not give the rest of Congress a voice in use-of-force decisions because the group just mentioned comprises only leadership positions and may not reflect the true "sense of the Congress."

Representative Dante Fascell made a subtle but important argument that within forty-eight hours after every major military incident in the Persian Gulf, the president actually did submit a war powers report to Congress.[18] The thrust of his observation was that the resolution is working, even if the president does not use phrases such as "pursuant to . . . War Powers Resolution." Fascell observed that the many legislative initiatives did not move Congress closer to explicit invocation of the War Powers Resolution.

Former Secretary of State Cyrus R. Vance and Representative Stephen Solarz provide yet another illustration of the congressional-presidential conflict over invocation of the War Powers Resolution or "triggering the sixty–day time clock" after notification under Section 4(a)(1) of the War Powers Resolution in the following exchange:[19]

MR. SOLARZ. So far as I can recall, no president in the last fifteen years has ever submitted a notification clearly and unequivocally triggering that requirement.

MR. VANCE. In a vast majority of cases, indeed in almost all of them you do get a report. That report speaks for itself, whether it is called a notification or not.

Perhaps the best single summary of the issue is presented in a U.S. House of Representatives Committee on Foreign Affairs staff report dated August 4, 1988:[20]

No president has ever submitted a report "pursuant to" Section 4 of the WPR. The usual terminology used is "taking note of" or "consistent with" either Section 4 or the WPR in general. With respect to a Section 4(a)(1) situation, the rationale is obvious: the President does not want to trigger the Section 5(b) 60–day time period by formally submitting a "war powers report" pursuant to the law. However, 19 reports have been submitted addressed to the appropriate Congressional leaders, and recording the facts about the introduction of U.S. Armed Forces, usually citing the constitutional authority of the President as commander-in-chief, and sometimes explicitly addressing the issue of scope and duration.

The recurring issue seems to be what would be accomplished by more explicit invocation of the War Powers Resolution. Would it give Congress more power? Would it cause the president to bring Congress into the decisions, inside the window of commitment of armed forces, more intimately? With several hundred bills facing Congress each week, can it make a meaningful contribution to military decisions, or is it at its best helping the president with the political decisions? Should the whole of Congress be involved in such consultation, or is it sufficient for selected members of the leadership of both parties to be involved?

In the court cases and congressional debates involving the War Powers Resolution and the authority of Congress versus the authority of the president, an implicit question is whether the president should or can commit troops in situations where the Congress does not agree with the president. The problem has been that Congress has answered with a mixed voice. The

535 voices in Congress do not speak as one on this complex issue for a number of reasons—members of Congress have special local political interests, regional interests, coalition interests, national political party interests, and, in general, constitute a spectrum of social and political heterogeneity.

With a concurrent resolution, Congress could send messages to the president indicating the "sense of Congress" at any time during the hearings-debate-consultation phases of a conflict, as was demonstrated above in the case of Somalia. The concurrent resolution would not require the president's signature, but it would indicate congressional approval or disapproval for a given course of action or plan involving U.S. armed forces. Another level of notice to the president that Congress approves or disapproves a given course of action in a given conflict situation would be a joint resolution from Congress. This resolution must be either signed or vetoed by the president. Either way, both the Congress and the president would be on record regarding their respective positions on use of force in a given situation.

As mentioned in the beginning of this chapter, "compliance with reservations is compliance nevertheless." Without exception, all presidents have complied with the reporting provision of the War Powers Resolution, even if the compliance is couched in executive caveats. The president's cabinet and executive staff members do consult with members of Congress on a continual basis formally and informally. From that perspective, the War Powers Resolution needs no further "fine-tuning." It works well from the perspective of the executive—which continues to maintain its constitutional autonomy—and from the perspective of Congress, which has been receiving reports and consultation, even if these are not in the format it would prefer.

If Congress were unanimous in its stand against the use of U.S. armed forces in a given conflict, a president would have to be a political fatalist to even consider going ahead in such a campaign, and it would be politically fatal. The problem is that partisanship and a genuine belief that the president does have prerogatives in war making act to split the Congress and leave the president to grasp the moment and, perhaps, the power.

REPEALING THE WAR POWERS RESOLUTION

In a March 21, 1995, news release, Senator Robert Dole (R-Kans.) released the text of testimony before the Senate Committee on Foreign Relations in which he discussed Senate 5—the Peace Powers Act of 1995.[21]

The major thrust of that act was to repeal the War Powers Resolution. In the news release, the senator stated,[22]

in the aftermath of the nation's most bitter and divisive war, I thought we needed to reassert the legitimate role of Congress in decisions of war and peace. On the Senate floor in October 1973, I said "the War Powers Resolution is a responsible and necessary attempt to serve the national interests by harmonizing the roles of the legislative and executive branches in the exercise of the war power." Unfortunately, 22 years later it is apparent the War Powers Resolution has failed.

The author received from Representative Henry J. Hyde copies of letters that President George Bush, President Jimmy Carter, and President Gerald Ford sent him in his efforts to repeal the War Powers Resolution (Amendment No. 47, H.R. 1561, Sec. 2707). The text of these letters was also published in the *Congressional Record* (June 17, 1995 at II5656). Since the texts of the letters are short, they are reproduced in part below.

From President George Bush: "Dear Henry, You are 100 percent correct in opposing the War Powers Resolution as an unconstitutional infringement on the authority of the President. I hope that you are successful in your effort to change the War Powers Resolution and restore proper balance between the Executive and Legislative Branches."[23]

From President Jimmy Carter: "To Congressman Henry Hyde [*sic*] I fully support your effort to repeal the War Powers Resolution. Best wishes in this good work."[24]

From President Gerald R. Ford: "Dear Henry: I share your views that the War Powers Resolution is an impractical, unconstitutional infringement on the authority of the President. I opposed the Resolution as a Member of the House. As President, I refused to recognize it as a Constitutional limitation on the power of the Commander-in-Chief."[25]

Just before the vote to repeal the War Powers Resolution, on June 7, 1995, Speaker of the House of Representatives Newt Gingrich (R-Ga.) made an impassioned speech to the House of Representatives, saying, "But this particular bill was wrong when it was passed. It has not worked in 20 years. And it is wrong now. And we should clean up the law, get it back to the constitutional framework and allow the President of the United States to lead in foreign policy with us deciding on key issues by our power of the purse."[26]

It is interesting to note that Speaker Gingrich's remarks were made by a Republican Speaker of the House of Representatives in support of a Democratic President, Bill Clinton. Remarkably, however, President Clinton did not join Presidents Bush, Carter, and Ford in their support of Speaker Newt

Gingrich's or Representative Henry Hyde's efforts to repeal the War Powers Resolution. The repeal attempt failed in the House by a vote of 201 ayes, 217 nays, and 17 not voting.

Representative David Funderburk (R-N.C.), on the floor of the House of Representatives, placed the War Powers Resolution in context in an interesting manner by stating,[27]

The conflict between congressional and Presidential war powers is as old as the Constitution. But, until the twin disasters of Watergate and Vietnam, the President's authority over the deployment of American troops had been relatively undisputed. The War Powers Act, passed over the veto of President Nixon in 1973, changed that. The act was the centerpiece of the activist, radical Vietnam/Watergate Congress.

Senate Majority Leader Robert Dole (R-Kans.) quotes Senator Joseph Biden (D-Del.) as saying, "The War Powers Resolution has failed to fulfill its intent, and has been . . . ineffective."[28] Senator Dole then added, "In my view, . . . we do not need to keep bad laws on the books while searching for a way to resolve the ongoing executive-legislative tension over the powers of war and peace."[29]

Perhaps the time is right for the War Powers Resolution, adopted out of protest during a time of national frustration and activism, to be replaced by some measure such as Senator Dole's Peace Powers Act, designed with deliberation during a time when the nation is at peace with its own soul and with its neighbors.

NOTES

1. U.S. House of Representatives, "Letter of September 21, 1987, to Secretary of State George P. Schultz from Hon. Dante B. Fascell, Chairman, Committee on Foreign Affairs, regarding Legal Advice in Connection with the U.S. Military Presence in the Persian Gulf and the War Powers Resolution," and "Letter to Chairman Fascell from Assistant Secretary of State J. Edward Fox Dated March 30, 1988 Responding to Chairman Fascell's September 21, 1987 Letter," in *The War Powers Resolution: Relevant Documents, Correspondence, Reports*, Committee Print, Subcommittee on Arms Control, International Security and Scientific Affairs of the House Committee on Foreign Affairs, 100th Cong., 2nd Sess., May 1988 ed. (Washington, D.C.: U.S. Government Printing Office, 1988): 93–99.

2. U.S. House of Representatives, *War Powers: Origins, Purposes, and Applications: Hearings before the Subcommittee on Arms Control, International Security and Science of the Committee on Foreign Affairs*, 100th Cong., 2nd Sess., August 4, 1988 and September 27, 1988 (Washington, D.C.: U.S. Government Printing Office, 1989): 219.

3. "Report Dated September 23, 1987 from President Ronald Reagan to Hon. Jim Wright, Speaker of the House of Representatives, regarding the U.S. Engagement of the Iranian Minelaying Craft, the Iran *Ajr*, in the Persian Gulf on September 21, 1987" in *The War Powers Resolution: Relevant Documents, Correspondence, Reports*, Committee Print, Subcommittee on Arms Control, International Security and Scientific Affairs of the House Committee on Foreign Affairs, 100th Cong., 2nd Sess., May 1988 ed. (Washington, D.C.: U.S. Government Printing Office, 1988): 100–101.

4. John Ely, *War and Responsibility: Constitutional Lessons of Vietnam and Its Aftermath* (Princeton, N.J.: Princeton University Press, 1993): 23–28.

5. Anthony Austin, *The President's War: The Story of the Tonkin Gulf Resolution and How the Nation Was Trapped in Vietnam* (Philadelphia: J. B. Lippincott, 1971); Scott Breckinridge, *The CIA and the U.S. Intelligence System* (Boulder, Colo.: Westview, 1986); Joseph Dawson, *Commanders in Chief: Presidential Leadership in Modern Wars* (Lawrence: University Press of Kansas, 1993), especially Chapter 5 on Harry Truman and Chapter 6 on Lyndon Johnson; Robert Donovan, *Conflict and Crisis: The Presidency of Harry S. Truman, 1945–1948* (New York: Praeger, 1977), and *Tumultuous Years: The Presidency of Harry S. Truman, 1949–1953* (New York: W. W. Norton, 1982); Burton Kaufman, *The Korean War: Challenges in Crisis, Credibility, and Command* (New York: Knopf, 1986); Glen Paige, *The Korean Decision, June 24–30, 1950* (New York: Free Press, 1968).

6. This is the language of, for example, SEATO, the United Nations Charter, NATO, and other mutual defense treaties. They all have in common the concept that "an attack upon one of the members is an attack upon all of the members." Thomas Franck, and Faiza Patel, "UN Police Action in Lieu of War: 'The Old Order Changeth,'" *American Journal of International Law* 81:1 (January 1991): 63–74; Michael Glennon, "The Constitution and Chapter VII of the United Nations Charter," *American Journal of International Law* 85:1 (January 1991): 74–88.

7. Michael Barnhart, ed., *Congress and United States Foreign Policy: Controlling the Use of Force in the Nuclear Age* (Albany: State University of New York Press, 1987); Thomas Franck, and Faiza Patel, "UN Police Action in Lieu of War: 'The Old Order Changeth,'" *American Journal of International Law*, 81:1 (January 1991): 74–88; Barry Blechman, *The Politics of National Defense: Congress and U.S. Defense Policy from Vietnam to the Persian Gulf* (Oxford: Oxford University Press, 1990); Larry Cable, *Conflict of Myths: The Development of American Counterinsurgency Doctrine and the Vietnam War* (New York: New York University Press, 1986); Dan Caldwell, "A Research Note on the Quarantine of Cuba, October 1962," *International Studies Quarterly* XXII (December 1978): 625–633; Ronald Elving, "America's Most Frequent Fight Has Been the Undeclared War," *Congressional Quarterly Weekly Report* 49:1 (January 5, 1991): 37–39.

8. John Ely, *War and Responsibility: Constitutional Lessons of Vietnam and Its Aftermath* (Princeton, N.J.: Princeton University Press, 1993): 26–27.

9. George Bush, "Letter to Congressional Leaders Transmitting a Report Pursuant to the Resolution Authorizing the Use of Force against Iraq—January 16, 1991," in *Public Papers of the Presidents of the United States: George Bush*, 2 Vols. (Washington, D.C.: U.S. Government Printing Office, 1992): 42 (hereafter in this chapter, this book will be referred to as *Papers: George Bush*); George Bush, "Statement on Signing the Resolution Authorizing the Use of Military Force against Iraq—January 14, 1991," in ibid., p. 40; Michael Glennon, "The Constitution and Chapter VII of the United Nations Charter," *American Journal of International Law* 85:1 (January 1991): 74–88; George Bush, "Letter to Congressional Leaders on the Persian Gulf Conflict—January 18, 1991," in *Public Papers: George Bush*, p. 52.

10. U.S. House of Representatives, *The Crisis in Somalia: MARKUP on S.J. Res. 45—Authorizing the Use of U.S. Armed Forces in Somalia,* Committee on Foreign Affairs, 102nd Cong., 2nd Sess., May 5, 1993 (Washington, D.C.: U.S. Government Printing Office, 1993), Appendix 5. Hereafter in this chapter, this work will be referred to as *The Crisis in Somalia.*

11. George Bush, "Letter to Thomas S. Foley, Speaker of the House of Representatives—December 10, 1992," in U.S. House of Representatives, *The Crisis in Somalia,* p. 113; U.S. Senate, Committee on Armed Services, *U.S. Military Operations in Somalia,* S. Hrg. 103–846, 103rd. Cong., 2nd Sess., May 12, 21, 1994 (Washington, D.C.: U.S. Government Printing Office, 1994); U.S. Senate, *Operation Restore Hope, the Military Operations in Somalia: Hearings before the Committee on Armed Services,* S. Hrg. 102–1100, 102nd Cong., 2nd Sess., December 9, 1992 (Washington, D.C.: U.S. Government Printing Office, 1993) (hereafter in this chapter, this work will be referred to as *Operation Restore Hope*); U.S. Senate, *Joint Chiefs of Staff Briefing on Current Military Operations in Somalia, Iraq, and Yugoslavia: Hearings before the Committee on Armed Services,* S. Hrg. 103–176, 103rd Cong., 1st Sess., January 29, 1993 (Washington, D.C.: U.S. Government Printing Office, 1993).

12. George Bush, "Letter to Thomas S. Foley, Speaker of the House of Representatives—December 10, 1992," in U.S. House of Representatives, *The Crisis in Somalia,* Appendix 3, pp. 116–119; U.S. Senate, *Operation Restore Hope.*

13. U.S. House of Representatives, *The Crisis in Somalia,* Appendix 2, p. 115; U.S. Senate, *Operation Restore Hope*; U.S. Senate, *Joint Chiefs of Staff Briefing on Current Military Operations in Somalia, Iraq, and Yugoslavia: Hearings before the Committee on Armed Services,* S. Hrg. 103–176, 103rd Cong., 1st Sess., January 29, 1993 (Washington, D.C.: U.S. Government Printing Office, 1993).

14. U.S. House of Representatives, *The Crisis in Somalia,* Article 6 of the Preamble to S.J. Res. 45, Appendix 4, p. 126; U.S. Senate, *Current Military Operations in Somalia: Hearings before the Committee on Armed Services,* S. Hrg. 103–220, 103rd Cong., 1st Sess., March 25, 1993 (Washington, D.C.: U.S. Government Printing Office, 1993); U.S. Senate Committee on Armed Services,

U.S. Military Operations in Somalia, S. Hrg. 103–846, 103rd Cong., 2nd Sess., May 12, 21, 1994 (Washington, D.C.: U.S. Government Printing Office, 1994).

15. U.S. House of Representatives, *The Crisis in Somalia,* Appendix 1, pp. 113–114; U.S. Senate, *Operation Restore Hope;* U.S. Senate, *Current Military Operations in Somalia: Hearings before the Committee on Armed Services,* S. Hrg. 103–220, 103rd Cong., 1st Sess., March 25, 1993 (Washington, D.C.: U.S. Government Printing Office, 1993).

16. George Bush, "Statement on Signing the Resolution Authorizing the Use of Force against Iraq—January 14, 1991," in *Public Papers: George Bush,* p. 40.

17. Leon Leighton, "The Enduring Vitality of the War Powers Resolution: The Inadequacy of H.J. Res. 601 and S.J. Res. 323," in U.S. House of Representatives, *War Powers: Origins, Purposes, and Applications: Hearings before the Subcommittee on Arms Control, International Security and Science of the Committee on Foreign Affairs,* 100th Cong., 2nd Sess., August 4, 1988, and September 27, 1988 (Washington, D.C.: U.S. Government Printing Office, 1989): 356, and "Statement of Hon. Cyrus R. Vance, Former Secretary of State" in the same source, p. 133.

18. Dante Fascell, "The Enduring Strength of the War Powers Resolution," *Congressional Record,* October 21, 1988, as presented in Appendix 7, ibid., p. 359. For examples confirming Fascell's observation, see George Bush, "Letter to Congressional Leaders Transmitting a Report Pursuant to the Resolution Authorizing the Use of Force against Iraq—January 16, 1991," in *Public Papers: George Bush,* p. 42; George Bush, "Statement on Signing the Resolution Authorizing the Use of Military Force against Iraq—January 14, 1991," in ibid., p. 40; George Bush, "Letter to Congressional Leaders on the Persian Gulf Conflict—January 18, 1991," in ibid., p. 52, and many others which are too numerous to cite here. They may be found in the *Public Papers* of President George Bush, Vol. 1.

19. U.S. House of Representatives, *War Powers: Origins, Purposes, and Applications: Hearings before the Subcommittee on Arms Control, International Security and Science of the Committee on Foreign Affairs,* 100th Cong., 2nd Sess., August 4, 1988, and September 27, 1988 (Washington, D.C.: U.S. Government Printing Office, 1989): 219, and Cyrus Vance, "Striking the Balance: Congress and the President under the War Powers Resolution," in Appendix 5, ibid., pp. 288–304.

20. Ibid., p. 232. It is instructive to also read Part II of this same committee staff report, pp. 236–239, for "Proposals to Amend the War Powers Resolution."

21. Robert Dole, "S.5: The Peace Powers Act of 1995—Testimony of Senate Majority Leader Bob Dole, Senate Committee on Foreign Relations," news release, March 21, 1995.

22. Ibid.

23. Copy of President George Bush's letter provided to the author by Representative Henry J. Hyde (R-Ill.) June 16, 1995.

24. Copy of President Jimmy Carter's letter provided to the author by Representative Henry J. Hyde (R-Ill.) June 16, 1995.

25. Copy of President Gerald Ford's letter provided to the author by Representative Henry J. Hyde (R-Ill.) June 16, 1995.

26. Speaker of the House of Representatives Newt Gingrich before the House of Representatives, June 7, 1995, *Congressional Record—House*, H5673.

27. Representative David Funderburk speech, U.S. House of Representatives, *Congressional Record—House*, June 7, 1995, H5662.

28. Robert Dole, "S.5: The Peace Powers Act of 1995—Testimony of Senate Majority Leader Bob Dole, Senate Committee on Foreign Relations," news release, March 21, 1995.

29. Ibid.

U.S. Presidents and Their Terms of Office

No.	President	Term
1	George Washington	1789–1797
2	John Adams	1797–1801
3	Thomas Jefferson	1801–1809
4	James Madison	1809–1817
5	James Monroe	1817–1825
6	John Quincy Adams	1825–1829
7	Andrew Jackson	1829–1837
8	Martin Van Buren	1837–1841
9	William Harrison	1841
10	John Tyler	1841–1845
11	James Polk	1845–1849
12	Zachary Taylor	1849–1850
13	Millard Fillmore	1850–1853
14	Franklin Pierce	1853–1857
15	James Buchanan	1857–1861
16	Abraham Lincoln	1861–1865
17	Andrew Johnson	1865–1869
18	Ulysses Grant	1869–1877
19	Rutherford Hayes	1877–1881
20	James Garfield	1881
21	Chester Arthur	1881–1885

22	Grover Cleveland	1885–1889
23	Benjamin Harrison	1889–1893
24	Grover Cleveland	1893–1897
25	William McKinley	1897–1901
26	Theodore Roosevelt	1901–1909
27	William Taft	1909–1913
28	Woodrow Wilson	1913–1921
29	Warren Harding	1921–1923
30	Calvin Coolidge	1923–1929
31	Herbert Hoover	1929–1933
32	Franklin Roosevelt	1933–1945
33	Harry Truman	1945–1953
34	Dwight Eisenhower	1953–1961
35	John Kennedy	1961–1963
36	Lyndon Johnson	1963–1969
37	Richard Nixon	1969–1974
38	Gerald Ford	1974–1977
39	Jimmy Carter	1977–1981
40	Ronald Reagan	1981–1989
41	George Bush	1989–1993
42	Bill Clinton	1993–

United Nations Security Council Resolutions Issued for Desert Shield and Desert Storm

660 (1990), 661 (1990), 662 (1990), 664 (1990), 665 (1990), 666 (1990), 667 (1990), 669 (1990), 670 (1990), 674 (1990), 677 (1990), 678 (1990)

Resolution 660 (August 2, 1990)

The Security Council,

Alarmed by the invasion of Kuwait on 2 August 1990 by the military forces of Iraq,

Determining that there exists a breach of international peace and security as regards the Iraqi invasion of Kuwait,

Acting under Articles 39 and 40 of the Charter of the United Nations,

1. *Condemns* the Iraqi invasion of Kuwait;

2. *Demands* that Iraq withdraw immediately and unconditionally all its forces to the positions in which they were located on 1 August 1990;

3. *Calls upon* Iraq and Kuwait to begin immediately intensive negotiations for the resolution of their differences and supports all efforts in this regard, and especially those of the League of Arab States;

4. *Decides* to meet again as necessary to consider further steps to ensure compliance with the present resolution.

VOTE: 14 for, 0 against, 1 abstention (Yemen)

Resolution 661 (August 6, 1990)

The Security Council,

Reffirming its resolution 660 (1990) of 2 August 1990,

Deeply concerned that that resolution has not been implemented and that the invasion by Iraq of Kuwait continues with further loss of human life and material destruction,

Determined to bring the invasion and occupation of Kuwait by Iraq to an end and to restore the sovereignty, independence and territorial integrity of Kuwait,

Noting that the legitimate Government of Kuwait has expressed its readiness to comply with resolution 660 (1990),

Mindful of its responsibilities under the Charter of the United Nations for the maintenance of international peace and security,

Affirming the inherent right of individual or collective self-defence, in re-sponse-to the armed attack by Iraq against Kuwait, in accordance with Article 51 of the Charter,

Acting under Chapter VII of the Charter of the United Nations,

1. *Determines* that Iraq so far has failed to comply with paragraph 2 of resolution 660 (1990) and has usurped the authority of the legitimate Government of Kuwait;

2. *Decides*, as a consequence, to take the following measures to secure compliance of Iraq with paragraph 2 of resolution 660 (1990) and to restore the authority of the legitimate Government of Kuwait;

3. *Decides* that all States shall prevent:

(a) The import into their territories of all commodities and products originating in Iraq or Kuwait exported therefrom after the date of the present resolution;

(b) Any activities by their nationals or in their territories which would promote or are calculated to promote the export or trans-shipment of any commodities or products from Iraq or Kuwait; and any dealings by their nationals or their flag vessels or in their territories in any commodities or products originating in Iraq or Kuwait and exported therefrom after the date of the present resolution, including in particular any transfer of funds to Iraq or Kuwait for the purposes of such activities or dealings;

(c) The sale or supply by their nationals or from their territories or using their flag vessels of any commodities or products, including weapons or any other military equipment, whether or not originating in their territories but not including supplies intended strictly for medical purposes, and, in humanitarian circumstances, foodstuffs, to any person or body in Iraq or Kuwait or to any person or body for the purposes of any business carried on in or operated from Iraq or Kuwait and any activities by their nationais or in their territories which promote or are calculated to promote such sale or supply of such commodities or products;

4. *Decides* that all States shall not make available to the Government of Iraq or to any commercial, industrial or public utility undertaking in Iraq or Kuwait, any funds or any other financial or economic resources and shall prevent their nationals and any persons within their territories from removing from their territories or otherwise making available to that Government or to any such undertaking any such funds or resources and from remitting any other funds to persons or bodies within Iraq or Kuwait, except payments exclusively for strictly medical or humanitarian purposes and, in humanitarian circumstances, foodstuffs;

5. *Calls upon* all States, including States non-members of the United Nations, to act strictly in accordance with the provisions of the present resolution notwith-

standing any contract entered into or license granted before the date of the present resolution;

6. *Decides* to establish, in accordance with rule 28 of the provisional rules of procedure of the Security Council, a Committee of the Security Council consisting of all the members of the Council, to undertake the following tasks and to report on its work to the Council with its observations and recommendations:

(a) To examine the reports on the progress of the implementation of the present resolution which will be submitted by the Secretary-General;

(b) To seek from all States further information regarding the action taken by them concerning the effective implementation of the provisions laid down in the present resolution;

7. *Calls upon* all States to cooperate fully with the Committee in the fulfillment of its task, including supplying such information as may be sought by the Committee in pursuance of the present resolution;

8. *Requests* the Secretary-General to provide all necessary assistance to the Committee and to make the necessary arrangements in the Secretariat for the purpose;

9. *Decides* that, notwithstanding paragraphs 4 through 8 above, nothing in the present resolution shall prohibit assistance to the legitimate government of Kuwait, and *calls upon* all States:

(a) To take appropriate measures to protect assets of the legitimate Government of Kuwait and its agences;

(b) Not to recognize any regime set up by the occupying Power;

10. *Requests* the Secretary-General to report to the Council on the progress of the implementation of the present resolution, the first report to be submitted within thirty days;

11. *Decides* to keep this item on its agenda and to continue its efforts to put an early end to the invasion by Iraq.

VOTE: 13 for, 0 against, 2 abstentions (Cuba and Yemen)

Resolution 662 (August 9, 1990)

The Security Council,

Recalling its resolutions 660 (1990) and 661 (1990),

Gravely alarmed by the declaration by Iraq of a "comprehensive and eternal merger" with Kuwait,

Demanding, once again, that Iraq withdraw immediately and unconditionally all its forces to the positions in which they were located on 1 August 1990,

Determined to bring the occupation of Kuwait by Iraq to an end and to restore the sovereignty, independence and territorial integrity of Kuwait,

Determined also to restore the authority of the legitimate Government of Kuwait,

1. *Decides* that annexation of Kuwait by Iraq under any form and whatever pretext has no legal validity, and is considered null and void;

2. *Calls upon* all States, international organizations and specialized agencies not to recognize that annexation and to refrain from any action or dealing that might be interpreted as an indirect recognition of the annexation;

3. *Further demands* that Iraq rescind its actions purporting to annex Kuwait;

4. *Decides* to keep this item on its agenda and to continue its efforts to put an early end to the occupation.

VOTE: Unanimous (15–0)

Resolution 664 (August 18, 1990)

The Security Council,

Recalling the Iraqi invasion and purported annexation of Kuwait and resolutions 660, 661 and 662,

Deeply concerned for the safety and well being of third state nationals in Iraq and Kuwait,

Recalling the obligations of Iraq in this regard under international law,

Welcoming the efforts of the Secretary-General to pursue urgent consultations with the Government of Iraq following the concern and anxiety expressed by the members of the Council on 17 August 1990,

Acting under Chapter VII of the United Nations Charter

1. *Demands* that Iraq permit and facilitate the immediate departure from Kuwait and Iraq of the nationals of third countries and grant immediate and continuing access of consular officials to such nationals;

2. *Further demands* that Iraq take no action to jeopardize the safety, security or health of such nationals;

3. *Reaffirms* its decision in resolution 662 (1990) that annexation of Kuwait by Iraq is null and void, and therefore, demands that the Government of Iraq rescind its orders for the closure of diplomatic and consular missions in Kuwait and the withdrawal of the immunity of their personnel, and refrain from any such actions in the future;

4. *Requests* the Secretary-General to report to the Council on compliance with this resolution at the earliest possible time.

VOTE: Unanimous (15–0)

Resolution 665 (August 25, 1990)

The Security Council,

Recalling its resolutions 660 (1990), 661 (1990), 662 (1990) and 664 (1990) and demanding their full and immediate implementation,

Having decided in resolution 661 (1990) to impose economic sanctions under Chapter VII of the Charter of the United Nations,

Determined to bring an end to the occupation of Kuwait by Iraq which imperils the existence of a Member State and to restore the legitimate authority, the sovereignty, independence and territorial integrity of Kuwait which requires the speedy implementation of the above resolutions,

Deploring the loss of innocent life stemming from the Iraqi invasion of Kuwait and determined to prevent further such losses,

Gravely alarmed that Iraq continues to refuse to comply with resolutions 660 (1990), 661 (1990), and 664 (1990) and in particular at the conduct of the Government of Iraq in using Iraqi flag vessels to export oil,

1. *Calling upon* those Member States cooperating with the Government of Kuwait which are deploying maritime forces to the area to use such measures commensurate to the specific circumstance as may be necessary under the authority of the Security Council to halt all inward and outward maritime shipping in order to inspect and verify their cargoes and destinations and to ensure strict implementation of the provisions related to such shipping laid down in resolution 661 (1990);

2. *Invites* Member States accordingly to co-operate as may be necessary to ensure compliance with the provisions of resolution 661(1990) with maximum use of political and diplomatic measures, in accordance with paragraph 1 above;

3. *Requests* all States to provide in accordance with the Charter such assistance as may be required by the States referred to in paragraph 1 of this resolution;

4. *Further requests* the States concerned to co-ordinate their actions in pursuit of the above paragraphs of this resolution using as appropriate mechanisms of the Military Staff Committee and after consultation with the Secretary-General to submit reports to the Security Council and its Committee established under resolution 661 (1990) to facilitate the monitoring of the implementation of this resolution;

5. *Decides* to remain actively seized of the matter.
VOTE: 13 for, 0 against, 2 abstentions (Cuba and Yemen)

Resolution 666 (September 13, 1990)

The Security Council,

Recalling its resolution 661 (1990), paragraphs 3 (c) and 4 of which apply, except in humanitarian circumstances, of foodstuffs,

Recognizing that circumstances may arise in which it will be necessary for foodstuffs to be supplied to the civilian population in Iraq or Kuwait in order to relieve human suffering,

Noting that in this respect the Committee established under paragraph 6 of that resolution has received communications from several Member States,

Emphasizing that it is for the Security Council, alone or acting through the Committee, to determine whether humanitarian circumstances have arisen,

Deeply concerned that Iraq has failed to comply with its obligations under Security Council resolution 664 (1990) in respect of the safety and well-being of third State nationals, and reaffirming that Iraq retains full responsibility in this regard under international humanitarian law including, where applicable, the Fourth Geneva Convention,

Acting under Chapter VII of the Charter of the United Nations,

1. *Decides* that in order to make the necessary determination whether or not for the purposes of paragraph 3 (c) and paragraph 4 of resolution 661 (1990) humanitarian circumstances have arisen, the Committee shall keep the situation regarding foodstuffs in Iraq and Kuwait under constant review;

2. *Expects* Iraq to comply with its obligations under Security Council resolution 664 (1990) in respect of third State nationals and reaffirms that Iraq remains fully responsible for their safety and well-being in accordance with international humanitarian law including, where applicable, the Fourth Geneva Convention;

3. *Requests*, for the purposes of paragraphs 1 and 2 of this resolution, that the Secretary-General seek urgently, and on a continuing basis, information from relevant United Nations and other appropriate humanitarian agencies and all other sources on the availability of food in Iraq and Kuwait, such information to be communicated by the Secretary-General to the Committee regularly;

4. *Requests* further that in seeking and supplying such information particular attention will be paid to such categories of persons who might suffer specially, such as children under 15 years of age, expectant mothers, maternity cases, the sick and the elderly;

5. *Decides* that if the Committee, after receiving the reports from the Secretary-General, determines that circumstances have arisen in which there is an urgent humanitarian need to supply foodstuffs to Iraq or Kuwait in order to relieve human suffering, it will report promptly to the Council its decision as to how such need should be met;

6. *Directs* the Committee that in formulating its decisions it should bear in mind that foodstuffs should be provided through the United Nations in co-operation with the International Committee of the Red Cross or other appropriate humanitarian agencies and distributed by them or under their supervision in order to ensure that they reach the intended beneficiaries;

7. *Requests* the Secretary-General to use his good offices to facilitate the delivery and distribution of foodstuffs to Kuwait and Iraq in accordance with the provisions of this and other relevant resolutions;

8. *Recalls* that resolution 661 (1990) does not apply to supplies intended strictly for medical purposes, but in this connection recommends that medical supplies should be exported under the strict supervision of the Government of the exporting State or by appropriate humanitarian agencies.

VOTE: 13 for, 0 against, 2 abstentions (Cuba and Yemen)

Resolution 667 (September 16, 1990)

The Security Council,

Reaffirming its resolutions 660 (1990), 661 (1990), 662 (1990), 664 (1990), 665 (1990) and 666 (1990),

Recalling the Vienna Conventions of 18 April 1961 on diplomatic relations and of 24 April 1963 on consular relations, to both of which Iraq is a party,

Considering that the decision of Iraq to order the closure of diplomatic and consular missions in Kuwait and to withdraw the immunity and privileges of these missions and their personnel is contrary to the decisions of the Security Council, the international Conventions mentioned above and international law,

Deeply concerned that Iraq, notwithstanding the decisions of the Security Council and the provisions of the Conventions mentioned above, has committed acts of violence against diplomatic missions and their personnel in Kuwait,

Outraged at recent violations by Iraq of diplomatic premises in Kuwait and at the abduction of personnel enjoying diplomatic immunity and foreign nationals who were present in these premises,

Considering that the above actions by Iraq constitute aggressive acts and a flagrant violation of its international obligations which strike at the root of the conduct of international relations in accordance with the Charter of the United Nations,

Recalling that Iraq is fully responsible for any use of violence against foreign nationals or against any diplomatic or consular mission in Kuwait or its personnel,

Determined to ensure respect for its decisions and for Article 25 of the Charter of the United Nations,

Further considering that the grave nature of Iraq's actions, which constitute a new escalation of its violations of international law, obliges the Council not only to express its immediate reaction but also to consult urgently to take further concrete measures to ensure Iraq's compliance with the Council's resolutions,

Acting under Chapter VII of the Charter of the United Nations,

1. *Strongly condemns* aggressive acts perpetrated by Iraq against diplomatic premises and personnel in Kuwait, including the abduction of foreign nationals who were present in those premises;

2. *Demands* the immediate release of those foreign nationals as well as all nationals mentioned in resolution 664 (1990);

3. *Further demands* that Iraq immediately and fully comply with its international obligations under resolutions 660 (1990), 662 (1990) and 664 (1990) of the Security Council, the Vienna Conventions on diplomatic and consular relations and international law;

4. *Further demands* that Iraq immediately protect the safety and well-being of diplomatic and consular personnel and premises in Kuwait and in Iraq and take no action to hinder the diplomatic and consular missions in the performance of their functions, including access to their nationals and the protection of their person and interests;

5. *Reminds* all States that they are obliged to observe strictly resolutions 661 (1990), 662 (1990), 664 (1990), 665 (1990) and 666 (1990);

6. *Decides* to consult urgently to take further concrete measures as soon as possible, under Chapter VII of the Charter, in response to Iraq's continued violation of the Charter, of resolutions of the Council and of international law.

VOTE: Unanimous (15–0)

Resolution 669 (September 24, 1990)

The Securty Council,

Recalling its resolution 661(1990) of 6 August 1990,

Recalling also Article 5O of the Charter of the United Nations,

Conscious of the fact that an increasing number of requests for assistance have been received under the provisions of Article 5O of the Charter of the United Nations,

Entrusts the Committee established under resolution 661 (1990) concerning the situation between Iraq and Kuwait with the task of examining requests for assistance under the provisions of Article 50 of the Charter of the United Nations and making recommendations to the President of the Security Council for appropriate action.

VOTE: Unanimous (15–0)

Resolution 670 (September 25, 1990)

The Security Council,

Reaffirming its resolutions 660 (1990), 661 (1990), 662 (1990), 664 (1990), 665 (1990), 666 (1990), and 667 (1990);

Condemning Iraq's continued occupation of Kuwait, its failure to rescind its actions and end its purported annexation and its holding of third State nationals against their will, in flagrant violation of resolutions 660 (1990), 662 (1990), 664 (1990) and 667 (1990) and of international humanitarian law;

Condemning further the treatment by Iraqi forces of Kuwaiti nationals, including measures to force them to leave their own country and mistreatment of persons and property in Kuwait in violation of international law;

Noting with grave concern the persistent attempts to evade the measures laid down in resolution 661 (1990);

Further noting that a number of States have limited the number of Iraqi diplomatic and consular officials in their countries and that others are planning to do so;

Determined to ensure by all necessary means the strict and complete application of the measures laid down in resolution 661 (1990);

Determined to ensure respect for its decisions and the provisions of Articles 25 and 48 of the Charter of the United Nations;

Affirming that any acts of the Government of Iraq which are contrary to the above-mentioned resolutions or to Articles 25 or 48 of the Charter of the United Nations, such as Decree No. 377 of the Revolution Command Council of Iraq of 16 September 1990, are null and void;

Reaffirming its determination to ensure compliance with Security Council resolutions by maximum use of political and diplomatic means;

Welcoming the Secretary-General's use of his good offices to advance a peaceful solution based on the relevant Security Council resolutions and noting with appreciation his continuing efforts to this end;

Underlining to the Government of Iraq that its continued failure to comply with the terms of resolutions 660 (1990), 661 (1990), 662 (1990), 664 (1990), 666 (1990) and 667 (1990) could lead to further serious action by the Council under the Charter of the United Nations, including under Chapter VII;

Recalling the provisions of Article 103 of the Charter of the United Nations;

Acting under Chapter VII of the Charter of the United Nations:

1. *Calls upon* all States to carry out their obligations to ensure strict and complete compliance with resolution 661 (1990) and in particular paragraphs 3, 4 and 5 thereof;

2. *Confirms* that resolution 661 (1990) applies to all means of transport, including aircraft;

3. *Decides* that all States, notwithstanding the existence of any rights or obligations conferred or imposed by any international agreement or any contract entered into or any licence or permit granted before the date of the present resolution, shall deny permission to any aircraft to take off from their territory if the aircraft would carry any cargo to or from Iraq or Kuwait other than food in humanitarian circumstances, subject to authorization by the Council or the Committee established by resolution 661 (1990) and in accordance with resolution 666 (1990), or supplies intended strictly for medical purposes or solely for UNIIMOG;

4. *Decides further* that all States shall deny permission to any aircraft destined to land in Iraq or Kuwait, whatever its State of registration, to overfly its territory unless:

(a) The aircraft lands at an airfield designated by that State outside Iraq or Kuwait in order to permit its inspection to ensure that there is no cargo on board in violation of resolution 661 (1990) or the present resolution, and for this purpose the aircraft may be detained for as long as necessary; or

(b) The particular flight has been approved by the Committee established by resolution 661 (1990); or

(c) The flight is certified by the United Nations as solely for the purposes of UNIIMOG;

5. *Decides* that each State shall take all necessary measures to ensure that any aircraft registered in its territory or operated by an operator who has his principal place of business or permanent residence in its territory complies with the provisions of resolution 661 (1990) and the present resolution;

6. *Decides* further that all States shall notify in a timely fashion the Committee established by resolution 661 (1990) of any flight between its territory and Iraq or Kuwait to which the requirement to land in paragraph 4 above does not apply, and the purpose for such a flight;

7. *Calls upon* all States to co-operate in taking such measures as may be necessary, consistent with international law, including the Chicago Convention, to ensure the effective implementation of the provisions of resolution 661 (1990) or the present resolution;

8. *Calls upon* all States to detain any ships of Iraqi registry which enter their ports and which are being or have been used in violation of resolution 661 (1990),

or to deny such ships entrance to their ports except in circumstances recognized under international law as necessary to safeguard human life;

9. *Reminds* all States of their obligations under resolution 661 (1990) with regard to the freezing of Iraqi assets, and the protection of the assets of the legitimate Government of Kuwait and its agencies, located within their territory and to report to the Committee established under resolution 661 (1990) regarding those assets;

10. *Calls upon* all States to provide to the Committee established by resolution 661 (1990) information regarding the action taken by them to implement the provisions laid down in the present resolution;

11. *Affirms* that the United Nations Organization, the specialized agencies and other international organizations in the United Nations system are required to take such measures as may be necessary to give effect to the terms of resolution 661 (1990) and this resolution;

12. *Decides* to consider, in the event of evasion of the provisions of resolution 661 (1990) or of the present resolution by a State or its nationals or through its territory, measures directed at the State in question to prevent such evasion;

13. *Reaffirms* that the Fourth Geneva Convention applies to Kuwait and that as a High Contracting Part to the Convention Iraq is bound to comply fully with all its terms and in particular is liable under the Convention in respect of the grave breaches committed by it, as are individuals who commit or order the commission of grave breaches.

VOTE: 14 for, 1 against (Cuba)

Resolution 674 (October 29, 1990)

The Security Council,

Recalling its resolutions 660 (1990), 661 (1990), 662 (1990), 664 (1990), 665 (1990), 666 (1990), 667 (1990) and 670 (1990),

Stressing the urgent need for the immediate and unconditional withdrawal of all Iraqi forces from Kuwait, for the restoration of Kuwait's sovereignty, independence and territorial integrity, and of the authority of its legitimate government,

Condemning the actions by the Iraqi authorities and occupying forces to take third State nationals hostage and to mistreat and oppress Kuwaiti and third State nationals, and the other actions reported to the Council such as the destruction of Kuwaiti demographic records, forced departure of Kuwaitis, and relocation of population in Kuwait and the unlawful destruction and seizure of public and private property in Kuwait including hospital supplies and equipment, in violation of the decisions of this Council, the Charter of the United Nations, the Fourth Geneva Convention, the Vienna Conventions on Diplomatic and Consular Relations and international law,

Expressing grave alarm over the situation of nationals of third States in Kuwait and Iraq, including the personnel of the diplomatic and consular missions of such States,

Reaffirming that the Fourth Geneva Convention applies to Kuwait and that as a High Contracting Party to the Convention Iraq is bound to comply fully with all its terms and in particular is liable under the Convention in respect of the grave breaches committed by it, as are individuals who commit or order the commission of grave breaches,

Recalling the efforts of the Secretary-General concerning the safety and well-being of third State nationals in Iraq and Kuwait,

Deeply concerned at the economic cost, and at the loss and suffering caused to individuals in Kuwait and Iraq as a result of the invasion and occupation of Kuwait by Iraq,

Acting under Chapter VII of the United Nations Charter,

Reaffirming the goal of the international community of maintaining international peace and security by seeking to resolve international disputes and conflicts through peaceful means,

Recalling also the important role that the United Nations and its Secretary-General have played in the peaceful solution of disputes and conflicts in conformity with the provisions of the United Nations Charter,

Alarmed by the dangers of the present crisis caused by the Iraqi invasion and occupation of Kuwait, directly threatening international peace and security, and seeking to avoid any further worsening of the situation,

Calling upon Iraq to comply with the relevant resolutions of the Security Council, in particular resolutions 660 (1990), 662 (1990) and 664 (1990),

Reaffirming its determination to ensure compliance by Iraq with the Security Council resolutions by maximum use of political and diplomatic means,

A

1. *Demands* that the Iraqi authorities and occupying forces immediately cease and desist from taking third State nationals hostage, and mistreating and oppressing Kuwaiti and third State nationals, and from any other actions such as those reported to the Council and described above, violating the decisions of this Council, the Charter of the United Nations, the Fourth Geneva Convention, the Vienna Conventions on Diplomatic and Consular Relations and international law;

2. *Invites* States to collate substantiated information in their possession or submitted to them on the grave breaches by Iraq as per paragraph 1 above and to make this information available to the Council;

3. *Reaffirms* its demand that Iraq immediately fulfill its obligations to third State nationals in Kuwait and Iraq, including the personnel of diplomatic and consular missions, under the Charter, the Fourth Geneva Convention, the Vienna Conventions on Diplomatic and Consular relations, general principles of international law and the relevant resolutions of the Council;

4. *Reaffirms further* its demand that Iraq permit and facilitate the immediate departure from Kuwait and Iraq of those third State nationals, including diplomatic and consular personnel, who wish to leave;

5. *Demands* that Iraq ensure the immediate access to food, water and basic services necessary to the protection and well-being of Kuwaiti nationals and of nationals of third States in Kuwait and Iraq, including the personnel of diplomatic and consular missions in Kuwait;

6. *Reaffirms* its demand that Iraq immediately protect the safety and well-being of diplomatic and consular personnel and premises in Kuwait and in Iraq, take no action to hinder these diplomatic and consular missions in the performance of their functions, including access to their nationals and the protection of their person and interests and rescind its orders for the closure of diplomatic and consular missions in Kuwait and the withdrawal of the immunity of their personnel;

7. *Requests* the Secretary-General, in the context of the continued exercise of his good offices concerning the safety and well-being of third State nationals in Iraq and Kuwait, to seek to achieve the objectives of paragraphs 4, 5 and 6 and in particular the provision of food, water and basic services to Kuwaiti nationals and to the diplomatic and consular missions in Kuwait and the evacuation of third State nationals;

8. *Reminds* Iraq that under international law it is liable for any loss, damage or injury arising in regard to Kuwait and third States, and their nationals and corporations, as a result of the invasion and illegal occupation of Kuwait by Iraq;

9. *Invites* States to collect relevant information regarding their claims, and those of their nationals and corporations, for restitution or financial compensation by Iraq with a view to such arrangements as may be established in accordance with international law;

10. *Requires* that Iraq comply with the provisions of the present resolution and its previous resolutions, failing which the Council will need to take further measures under the Charter,

11. *Decides* to remain actively and permanently seized of the matter until Kuwait has regained its independence and peace has been restored in conformity with the relevant resolutions of the Security Council.

B

12. *Reposes* its trust in the Secretary-General to make available his good offices and, as he considers appropriate, to pursue them and undertake diplomatic efforts in order to reach a peaceful solution to the crisis caused by the Iraqi invasion and occupation of Kuwait on the basis of Security Council resolutions 660 (1990), 662 (1990) and 664 (1990), and calls on all States, both those in the region and others, to pursue on this basis their efforts to this end, in conformity with the Charter, in order to improve the situation and restore peace, security and stability;

13. *Requests* the Secretary-General to report to the Security Council on the results of his good offices and diplomatic efforts.

VOTE: 13 for, 0 against, 2 abstentions (Cuba and Yemen)

Resolution 677 (November 28, 1990)

The Security Council,

Recalling its resolutions 660 (1990) of 2 August 1990, 662 (1990) of 9 August 1990, and 674 (1990) of 29 October 1990,

Reiterating its concern for the suffering caused to individuals in Kuwait as a result of the invasion and occupation of Kuwait by Iraq,

Gravely concerned at the ongoing attempt by Iraq to alter the demographic composition of the population of Kuwait and to destroy the civil records maintained by the legitimate Government of Kuwait,

Acting under Chapter VII of the Charter of the United Nations,

1. *Condemns* the attempts by Iraq to alter the demographic composition of the population of Kuwait and to destroy the civil records maintained by the legitimate Government of Kuwait;

2. *Mandates* the Secretary-General to take custody of a copy of the population register of Kuwait, the authenticity of which has been certified by the legitimate Government of Kuwait and which covers the registration of population up to 1 August 1990;

3. *Requests* the Secretary-General to establish, in co-operation with the legitimate Government of Kuwait, an Order of Rules and Regulations governing access to and use of the said copy of the population register.

VOTE: Unanimous (15–0)

Resolution 678 (November 29, 1990)

The Security Council,

Recalling and reaffirming its resolutions 660 (1990), 661 (1990), 662 (1990), 664 (1990), 665 (1990), 666 (1990), 667 (1990), 669 (1990), 670 (1990) and 674 (1990),

Noting that, despite all efforts by the United Nations, Iraq refuses to comply with its obligation to implement resolution 660 (1990) and the above subsequent relevant resolutions, in flagrant contempt of the Council,

Mindful of its duties and responsibilities under the Charter of the United Nations for the maintenance and preservation of international peace and security,

Determined to secure full compliance with its decisions, *Acting* under Chapter VII of the Charter of the United Nations,

1. *Demands* that Iraq comply fully with resolution 660 (1990) and all subsequent relevant resolutions and decides, while maintaining all its decisions, to allow Iraq one final opportunity, as a pause of goodwill, to do so;

2. *Authorizes* Member States co-operating with the Government of Kuwait, unless Iraq on or before 15 January 1991 fully implements, as set forth in paragraph 1 above, the foregoing resolutions, to use all necessary means to uphold and implement Security Council resolution 660 (1990) and all subsequent relevant resolutions and to restore international peace and security in the area;

3. *Requests* all States to provide appropriate support for the actions undertaken in pursuance of paragraph 2 of this resolution;

4. *Requests* the States concerned to keep the Council regularly informed on the progress of actions undertaken pursuant to paragraphs 2 and 3 of this resolution;

5. *Decides* to remain seized of the matter.

VOTE: 12 for, 2 against (Cuba and Yemen), 1 abstention (China)

Two Hundred and Eight Instances of United States "Use of Force" Abroad without a Declaration of War, 1798–1989

(See Appendix D for Declared Wars)

1798–1800	Undeclared naval war with France.
1801–1805	Tripoli. The First Barbary War.
1806	Mexico (Spanish territory). Capt. Z. M. Pike's invasion of Rio Grande.
1806–1810	Gulf of Mexico. American gunboats off Mississippi delta against Spanish and French.
1810	West Florida (Spanish territory). Gov. Claiborne with troops east of Mississippi.
1812	Amelia Island and other parts of East Florida, then under Spain. Occupation by Gen. George Matthews.
1813	West Florida (Spanish territory). Gen. Wilkinson seizes Mobile Bay.
1813–14	Marquesas Islands. Fort built on Nukahiva Island.
1814	Spanish Florida. Gen. Andrew Jackson takes Pensacola.
1814–1825	Caribbean. Fighting in Cuba, Puerto Rico, Santo Domingo, and Yucatán.
1815	Algiers. The Second Barbary War.
1815	Tripoli. Decatur's squadron at Tunis and Tripoli.
1816	Spanish Florida. United States destroys Nicholis Fort.
1816–1818	Spanish Florida. First Seminole War.
1817	Amelia Island (Spanish territory off Florida). United States lands and fights smugglers.

1818	Oregon. USS *Ontario* tales Columbia River.
1820–1823	Africa. United States raids slave traffic.
1822	Cuba. U.S. Navy lands and burns pirate station.
1823	Cuba. U.S. Navy landings in Escondido, Cayo Bianco, Siquapa Bay, Cape Cruz, and Camrioca.
1824	Cuba. USS *Porpoise* pursues pirates.
1824	Puerto Rico (Spanish territory). Com. David Porter attacks pirates at Fajarado.
1825	Cuba. United States and Britain capture pirates at Sagua La Grande.
1827	Greece. Pirates hunted at Argenteire, Miconi, and Androse.
1831–1832	Falkland Islands. Capture of three American ships investigated.
1832	Sumatra. Retaliation to village of Quallah Battoo for attacks on American ships.
1833	Argentina. U.S. interests in Buenos Aires protested during insurrection.
1835–1836	Peru. U.S. interests protected during revolution in Callao and Lima.
1836	Mexico. Gen. Gaines occupies Nacogdoches (Texas).
1838–1839	Sumatra. Retaliation to villages of Quallah Battoo and Muckie (Mukki) for attacks on U.S. shipping.
1840	Fiji Islands. Retaliation for attacks on U.S. ships.
1841	Drummond Island, Kingsmill group. Murder of U.S. seaman avenged.
1841	Samoa. Murder of seaman on Upolu Island avenged.
1842	Mexico. Com. T. A. C. Jones occupies Monterrey and later San Diego, California.
1843	China. *St. Louis* lands after dispute at Canton.
1843	Africa. Four U.S. ships land to punish attacks on U.S. shipping.
1844	Mexico. U.S. forces protect Texas against Mexico.
1849	Smyrna. U.S. forces gain release of seized American.
1851	Turkey. Demonstration along Turkish Levantine coast after massacre at Jaffa.
1851	Johanns Island (east of Africa). Retaliation for imprisonment of American ship captain.
1852–1853	Argentina. Marines protect American interests.

1853	Nicaragua. United States protects American interests.
1853–1854	Japan. Perry expedition.
1853–1854	Ryukyu and Bonin Islands. Com. Perry lands to open up commerce.
1854	China. U.S. interests protected during Shanghai civil strife.
1854	Nicaragua. San Juan del Norte (Greytown) destroyed to avenge American minister to Nicaragua.
1855	China. U.S. interests protected against pirates.
1855	Fiji Islands. Reparation sought for attacks on Americans.
1855	Uruguay. U.S. interests protected during revolution in Montevideo.
1856	Panama, Republic of New Granada. U.S. interests protected during insurrection.
1856	China. Attack on U.S. boat avenged.
1857	Nicaragua. William Walker's attempt to get control of the country opposed.
1858	Uruguay. Two U.S. ships land to protect U.S. interests during revolution in Montevideo.
1858	Fiji Islands. Retaliation for murder of two U.S. citizens.
1859	Turkey. Naval retaliation for massacre of Americans at Jaffa.
1859	Paraguay. Navy retaliates for attack on naval vessel in Paraná River.
1859	Mexico. U.S. forces pursue Cortina across Mexican border.
1859	China. U.S. interests in Shanghai protected.
1860	Angola, Portuguese West Africa. U.S. interests at Kissembo protected during civil unrest.
1860	Colombia, Bay of Panama. U.S. interests protected during revolution.
1863	Japan. Retaliation for firing on U.S. ship at Shimonoseki.
1864	Japan. U.S. minister to Japan protected.
1865	Panama. U.S. lives and property protected during revolution.
1866	Mexico. Gen. Sedgwick captures Matamoras to protect U.S. interests.
1866	China. Retaliation for assault on U.S. consul at Newchwang (Yingkow).
1867	Nicaragua. Marines occupy Managua and León.
1867	Island of Formosa. Retaliation for murder of crew of American vessel.

1868	Japan (Osaka, Hiolo, Nagasaki, Yokohama, and Negata). U.S. interests protected during civil war.
1868	Uruguay. U.S. interests protected during insurrection at Montevideo.
1868	Colombia. U.S. interests protected at Aspinwall.
1870	Mexico. Pirate ship *Forward* destroyed.
1870	Hawaiian Islands. American flag placed at half-mast upon death of Queen Kalama.
1871	Korea. Retaliation for murder of crew of *General Sherman*.
1873	Colombia (Bay of Panama). U.S. interests protected during civil insurrection.
1873	Mexico. Border crossed to pursue cattle thieves.
1874	Hawaiian Islands. U.S. interests protected during coronation of new king.
1876	Mexico. Town of Matamoras policed temporarily.
1882	Egypt. U.S. interests protected during looting of city of Alexandria by Arabs.
1885	Panama (Colón). Transit protected and established during revolution.
1888	Korea. U.S. interests in Seoul protected during political unrest.
1888	Haiti. American steamer retaken.
1888–1889	Samoa. U.S. citizens and consulate protected during civil war.
1889	Hawaiian Islands. U.S. interests protected during revolution.
1890	Argentina. U.S. consulate and legation in Buenos Aires protected.
1891	Haiti. U.S. interests on Navassa Island protected.
1891	Bering Strait. Seal poaching stopped.
1891	Chile. U.S. Consulate and refugees protected during revolution in Valparaiso.
1893	Hawaii. Provisional government under Sanford B. Dole protected.
1894	Brazil. U.S. shipping at Rio de Janeiro protected during Brazilian civil war.
1894	Nicaragua. U.S. interests at Bluefields protected following revolution.
1894–1895	China. Marines move to Peking for protection during Sino-Japanese War.
1894–1895	China. U.S. nationals at Newchwang (Yingkow) protected.

1894–1896	Korea. U.S. interests protected during Sino-Japanese War.
1895	Colombia. U.S. interests protected during bandit attack on town of Bocas del Toro.
1896	Nicaragua. U.S. interests protected in Corinto.
1898	Nicaragua. U.S. interests protected in San Juan del Sur.
1898–1899	China. Legation at Peking and consulate at Tientsin guarded during civil unrest.
1899	Nicaragua. U.S. interests in San Juan del Norte and Bluefields protected from Gen. Juan P. Reyes.
1899	Samoa. U.S. interests protected during civil unrest.
1899–1901	Philippine Islands. U.S. interests protected and islands taken during Filipino war for independence.
1900	China. Lives protected during Boxer uprising.
1901	Colombia (state of Panama). Transit on isthmus protected during revolution.
1902	Colombia. U.S. interests at Bocas del Toro protected during civil war.
1902	Colombia (state of Panama). Transit crossing the isthmus protected during civil war.
1903	Honduras. U.S. Consulate at Puerto Cortés protected during revolution.
1903	Dominican Republic. U.S. interests at Santo Domingo protected during revolution.
1903	Syria. U.S. Consulate at Beirut protected during feared Moslem uprising.
1903–1904	Abyssinia. U.S. consul general protected while he is negotiating treaty.
1903–1914	Panama. U.S. interests protected during construction of isthmus canal.
1904	Dominican Republic. Protect U.S. interests in Puerto Plata, Sosua, and Santo Domingo City during revolution.
1904	Tangier, Morocco. Demonstration by U.S. troops for release of kidnapped American.
1904	Panama. U.S. lives protected at Ancón during feared insurrection.
1904–1905	Korea. U.S. Legation at Seoul guarded.
1904–1905	Korea. Marine guard sent to Seoul for protection during Russo-Japanese War.
1906–1909	Cuba. Protect U.S. interests protected during revolution.

1907	Honduras. U.S. interests protected during war between Honduras and Nicaragua.
1910	Nicaragua. Information obtained and U.S. interests protected in Corinto and Bluefields.
1911	Honduras. U.S. interests protected during civil war.
1911	China. Several instanceofo protection of U.S. interests during nationalist revolution.
1912	Honduras. U.S. forces protect American-owned railroad at Puerto Cortés.
1912	Panama. U.S. troops supervise elections outside Canal Zone.
1912	Cuba. U.S. interests protected in Province of Oriente and in Havana.
1912	China. U.S. interests on Kentucky Island and Camp Nicholson protected during revolution.
1912	Turkey. U.S. Legation at Constantinople guarded during Balkan War.
1912–1925	Nicaragua. U.S. interests protected during attempted revolution. Small force remains until 1925.
1912–1941	China. U.S. interests protected in several instances covered by treaties with China ranging from 1858 to 1901.
1913	Mexico. U.S. Marines help evacuate U.S. citizens from Yaqui valley during civil strife.
1914	Haiti. U.S. interests protected during civil unrest.
1914	Dominican Republic. U.S. Navy assists Puerto Plata during internal revoution.
1914–1917	Mexico. U.S. activity during Dolphin affair and Villa's raids. Pershing's expedition.
1915–1934	Haiti. United States helps maintain order during periods of chronic and threatened insurrection.
1916	China. U.S. interests at Nanking protected during riot.
1916–1924	Dominican Republic. United States helps maintain order during periods of chronic and threatened insurrection.
1917	China. U.S. interests protected during civil unrest at Chungking.
1917–1922	Cuba. U.S. interests protected during insurrection. Two companies remain at Camaguey.
1918–1919	Mexico. Bandits pursued across border. Battle at Nogales.
1918–1920	Panama. Police duty during elections at Chiriqui.

1918–1920	Soviet Russia. Troops in Vladivostok to protect U.S. interests during battle between Bolsheviki and Czech legion.
1919	Dalmatia. Order maintained between Italians and Serbs at request of Italian authorities.
1919	Turkey. USS *Arizona* protects U.S. Consulate during Greek occupation of Constantinople.
1919	Honduras. Order maintained in neutral zone.
1920	China. Lives protected at Kiukiang.
1920	Guatemala. U.S. interests protected during fight between Unionists and the government of Guatemala.
1920–1922	Russia (Siberia). Radio station on Russian Island, Bay of Vladivostok, protected.
1921	Panama–Costa Rica. Naval squadron helps prevent war in isthmus.
1922	Turkey. U.S. lives protected when Turkish Nationalists enter Smyrna.
1922–1923	China. U.S. lives protected during civil unrest.
1924	Honduras. U.S. lives and interests protected during election hostilities.
1924	China. Lives protected in Shanghai during Chinese factional hostilities.
1925	China. Lives protected in International Settlement.
1925	Honduras. Foreigners protected at La Ceiba during civil unrest.
1925	Panama. U.S. interests protected during strikes and rent riots.
1926	China. U.S. lives protected at Hankow and Kiukiang.
1926–1933	Nicaragua. U.S. lives and interests protected upon coup d'état of General Chamorro.
1927	China. U.S. lives protected during hostilities in Nanking, Shanghai, and Tientsin.
1932	China. U.S. lives protected during Japanese occupation of Shanghai.
1933	Cuba. Naval forces demonstrate during revolution against President Gerardo Machada.
1940	Newfoundland, Bermuda, St. Lucia, Bahamas, Jamaica, Antigua, Trinidad, and British Guiana. Lend-lease air and naval bases protected.
1941	Greenland. Taken under protection by United States.

1941	Netherlands (Dutch) Guiana. Troops occupy Dutch Guiana to protect aluminum ore supply.
1941	Iceland. Taken under protection by United States.
1941	Germany. Navy protection of ship lanes to Europe.
1945	China. U.S. troops help Chinese Nationalists disarm and repatriate Japanese in China.
1946	Trieste. Troops sent because Yugoslav forces shot down U.S. plane over Venezia Giulia.
1948	Palestine. Consular guard protects U.S. consul general.
1948–1949	China. U.S. Embassy in Nanking and U.S. lives in Shanghai protected.
1950–1953	Korean War. Assistance to South Korea under United Nations Security Council resolutions.
1950–1955	Formosa (Taiwan). U.S. Seventh Fleet protects Formosa and Chinese Nationalists against Chinese Communists.
1954–1955	China. U.S. Navy evacuates U.S. personnel from Tachen Islands.
1956	Egypt. Marines evacuate U.S. nationals during Suez crisis.
1958	Lebanon. Assistance given to Lebanon during insurrection from outside.
1959–1960	The Caribbean. Second Marine Ground Task Force protects U.S. nationals during Cuban crisis.
1962	Cuba. President Kennedy "quarantines" shipping of missiles to Cuba by Soviet Union.
1962	Thailand. Third Marine Expeditionary Unit protects Thailand from Communist threat.
1962–1975	Laos. U.S. military support to Laos.
1964	Congo. Airlift of Congolese troops and Belgian paratroopers to rescue foreigners.
1964–1973	Vietnam War. United States supports South Vietnam against Communist attacks. Congress issues Gulf of Tonkin Resolution.
1965	Dominican Republic. U.S. interests protected during Dominican revolt.
1967	Congo. United States provides logistic support to Congo central government.
1970	Cambodia. United States helps South Vietnam against Viet Cong and North Vietnamese.

1974	Evacuation from Cyprus. United States helps in evacuation during hostilities between Turkish and Greek Cypriot forces.
1975	Evacuation from Vietnam. United States helps evacuate U.S. nationals from Vietnam.
1975	Evacuation from Cambodia. United States helps evacuate U.S. nationals from Cambodia.
1975	South Vietnam. United States helps evacuate U.S. and South Vietnamese nationals from U.S. Embassy in Saigon and Tan Son Nhut Airfield.
1975	*Mayaguez* incident. U.S. forces ordered to retake SS *Mayaguez* from Cambodian forces.
1976	Lebanon. United Staytes helps evacuate U.S. nationals and Europeans from Lebanon after hostilities there.
1976	Korea. Troops reinforced after U.S. personnel killed in demilitarized zone.
1978	Zaire. Support provided to Belgian and French rescue operations in Zaire.
1980	Iran. Attempt to rescue American hostages held in Iran. Six transports and eight helicopters.
1981	El Salvador. Military advisors assist in training government forces in counterinsurgency.
1981	Libya. Nimitz planes shoot down two Libyan jets over Gulf of Sidra after heat-seeking missile fired by Libyan jets.
1982	Sinai. Participation in multinational force and observers in Sinai under P.L. 97–132.
1982	Lebanon. Marines help withdrawal of members of Palestine Liberation Organization force from Beirut.
1982	Lebanon. United States aids in restoration of Lebanese government sovereignty under P.L. 98–119.
1983	Egypt. U.S. AWACS planes assist Sudan and Egypt after Libyan bombing.
1983–1989	Honduras. United States ferries Honduran troops to Nicaraguan border to repel Nicaraguan troops.
1983	Chad. United States sends two AWACS planes and eight F-15s to assist Chad against Libyan forces.
1983	Grenada. U.S. troops help restore law and order at request of Organization of Eastern Caribbean States.
1984	Persian Gulf. Saudi Arabian jets, aided by U.S. AWACS planes and a KC-10 tanker, shoot down two Iranian fighter planes over Persian Gulf.

1985	Italy. Navy pilots force Egyptian airliner with hijackers of Achille Lauro to land in Sicily.
1986	Libya. U.S. forces conduct freedom of navigation exercises around Gulf of Sidra. Hostile exchange of Libyan and U.S. missiles ensue.
1986	Libya. United States conducts bombing strikes on terrorist and military installations in Libya.
1986	Bolivia. U.S. forces and aircraft assist Bolivia in antidrug operations.
1987–1988	Persian Gulf. After Iran-Iraq War, United States assists reflagging operations with Kuwait.
1988	Panama. United States increases troops during instability associated with the Noriega regime.
1989	Libya. Two U.S. Navy F-14s from USS *John Kennedy* shoot down two hostile Libyan jets over Mediterranean Sea.
1989	Panama. President Bush sends U.S. troops in response to General Noriega's disregard of Panamanian election results.
1989	Andean Initiative in War on Drugs. President Bush sends troops to help Colombia, Bolivia, and Peru combat drug producers and traffickers.
1989	Philippines. U.S. fighter planes help Aquino government repel a coup attempt. Marines sent to protect U.S. Embassy in Manila.

Source: Adapted from *Congressional Record—Senate* (January 10, 1991): S130–S135.

Five Declared Wars between 1787 and 1993

1812–1815	War of 1812. On June 18, 1812, the United States declared war against the United Kingdom of Great Britain and Ireland.
1846–1848	Mexican War. On May 13, 1846, the United States declared war against Mexico.
1898	The Spanish-American War. On April 25, 1898, the United States declared war against Spain.
1917–1918	World War I. On April 6, 1917, the United States declared war against Germany and on December 7, 1917, against Austria-Hungary.
1941–1945	World War II. On December 8, 1941, the United States declared war against Japan, on December 11 against Germany and Italy, and on June 5, 1942, against Bulgaria, Hungary, and Romania.

Appendix E

Excerpts from the United Nations Charter

CHAPTER I. PURPOSES AND PRINCIPLES

Article 1

The Purposes of the United Nations are:

1. To maintain international peace and security, and to that end: to take effective collective measures for the prevention and removal of threats to the peace, and for the suppression of acts of aggression or other breaches of the peace, and to bring about by peaceful means, and in conformity with the principles of justice and international law, adjustment or settlement of international disputes or situations which might lead to a breach of the peace:

2. To develop friendly relations among nations based on respect for the principle of equal rights and self-determination of peoples, and to take other appropriate measures to strengthen universal peace:

3. To achieve international cooperation in solving international problems of an economic, social, cultural, or humanitarian character, and in promoting and encouraging respect for human rights and for fundamental freedoms for all without distinction as to race, sex, language, or religion: . . .

Article 2

The Organization and its Members, in pursuit of the Purposes stated in Article 1, shall act in accordance with the following Principles:

1. The Organization is based on the principle of the sovereign equality of all its Members.

2. All Members, in order to ensure to all of them the rights and benefits resulting from membership, shall fulfil in good faith the obligations assumed by them in accordance with the present Charter.

3. All Members shall settle their international disputes by peaceful means in such a manner that international peace and security, and justice, are not endangered.

4. All Members shall refrain in their international relations from the threat or use of force against the territorial integrity or political independence of any state, or in any other manner inconsistent with the Purposes of the United Nations.

5. All Members shall give the United Nations every assistance in any action it takes in accordance with the present Charter, and shall refrain from giving assistance to any state against which the United Nations is taking preventive or enforcement action.

7. Nothing contained in the present Charter shall authorize the United Nations to intervene in matters which are essentially within the domestic jurisdiction of any state or shall require the Members to submit such matters to settlement under the present Charter; but this principle shall not prejudice the application of enforcement measures under Chapter VII.

CHAPTER IV. THE GENERAL ASSEMBLY

FUNCTIONS AND POWERS

Article 11

2. The General Assembly may discuss any questions relating to the maintenance of international peace and security brought before it by any Member of the United Nations, or by the Security Council, or by a state which is not a Member of the United Nations in accordance with Article 35, paragraph 2, and, except as provided in Article 12, may make recommendations with regard to any such questions to the state or states concerned or to the Security Council or to both. Any such question on which action is necessary shall be referred to the Security Council by the General Assembly either before or after discussion.

Article 12

1. While the Security Council is exercising in respect of any dispute or situation the functions assigned to it in the present Charter, the General Assembly shall not make any recommendation with regard to that dispute or situation unless the Security Council so requests.

CHAPTER VI. PACIFIC SETTLEMENT OF DISPUTES

Article 33

1. The parties to any dispute, the continuance of which is likely to endanger the maintenance of international peace and security, shall, first of all, seek a solution by negotiation, enquiry, mediation, conciliation, arbitration, judicial settlement,

resort to regional agencies or arrangements, or other peaceful means of their own choice.

Article 36

1. The Security Council may, at any stage of a dispute of the nature referred to in Article 33 or of a situation of like nature, recommend appropriate procedures or methods of adjustment.

Article 37

1. Should the parties to a dispute of the nature referred to in Article 33 fail to settle it by the means indicated in that Article, they shall refer it to the Security Council.

Article 38

Without prejudice to the provisions of Articles 33 to 37, the Security Council may, if all the parties to any dispute so request, make recommendations to the parties with a view to a pacific settlement of the dispute.

CHAPTER VII. ACTION WITH RESPECT TO THREATS TO THE PEACE, BREACHES OF THE PEACE AND ACTS OF AGGRESSION

Article 39

The Security Council shall determine the existence of any threat to the peace, breach of the peace, or act of aggression and shall make recommendations, or decide what measures shall be taken in accordance with Articles 41 and 42, to maintain or restore international peace and security.

Article 40

In order to prevent an aggravation of the situation, the Security Council may, before making the recommendations or deciding upon the measures provided for in Article 39, call upon the parties concerned to comply with such provisional measures as it deems necessary or desirable. Such provisional measures shall be without prejudice to the rights, claims, or position of the parties concerned. The Security Council shall duly take account of failure to comply with such provisional measures.

Article 41

The Security Council may decide what measures not involving the use of armed force are to be employed to give effect to its decisions, and it may call upon the

Members of the United Nations to apply such measures. These may include complete or partial interruption of economic relations and of rail, sea, air, postal, telegraphic, radio, and other means of communication, and the severance of diplomatic relations.

Article 42

Should the Security Council consider that measures provided for in Article 41 would be inadequate or have proved to be inadequate, it may take such action by air, sea, or land forces as may be necessary to maintain or restore international peace and security. Such action may include demonstrations, blockade, and other operations by air, sea, or land forces of Members of the United Nations.

Article 43

1. All Members of the United Nations, in order to contribute to the maintenance of international peace and security, undertake to make available to the Security Council, on its call and in accordance with a special agreement or agreements, armed forces assistance, and facilities, including rights of passage, necessary for the purpose of maintaining international peace and security.

2. Such agreement or agreements shall govern the numbers and types of forces, their degree of readiness and general location, and the nature of the facilities and assistance to be provided.

3. The agreement or agreements shall be negotiated as soon as possible on the initiative of the Security Council. They shall be concluded between the Security Council and Members or between the Security Council and groups of Members and shall be subject to ratification by the signatory states in accordance with their respective constitutional processes.

Article 44

When the Security Council has decided to use force it shall, before calling upon a Member not represented on it to provide armed forces in fulfillment of the obligations assumed under Article 43, invite that Member, if the Member so desires, to participate in the decisions of the Security Council concerning the employment of contingents of that Member's armed forces.

Article 45

In order to enable the United Nations to take urgent military measures, Members shall hold immediately available national air-force contingents for combined international enforcement action. The strength and degree of readiness of these contingents and plans for their combined action shall be determined, within the limits laid down in the special agreement or agreements referred to in Article 43, by the Security Council with the assistance of the Military Staff Committee.

Article 46

Plans for the application of armed force shall be made by the Security Council with the assistance of the Military Staff Committee.

Article 47

1. There shall be established a Military Staff Committee to advise and assist the Security Council on all questions relating to the Security Council's military requirements for the maintenance of international peace and security, the employment and command of forces placed at its disposal, the regulation of armaments, and possible disarmament.

2. The Military Staff Committee shall consist of the Chiefs of Staff of the permanent members of the Security Council or their representatives. Any Member of the United Nations not permanently represented on the Committee shall be invited by the Committee to be associated with it when the efficient discharge of the Committee's responsibilities requires the participation of that Member in its work.

3. The Military Staff Committee shall be responsible under the Security Council for the strategic direction of any armed forces placed at the disposal of the Security Council. Questions relating to the command of such forces shall be worked out subsequently.

Article 48

1. The action required to carry out the decisions of the Security Council for the maintenance of international peace and security shall be taken by all the Members of the United Nations or by some of them, as the Security Council may determine.

2. Such decisions shall be carried out by the Members of the United Nations directly and through their action in the appropriate international agencies of which they are members.

Article 49

The Members of the United Nations shall join in affording mutual assistance in carrying out the measures decided upon by the Security Council.

Article 51

Nothing in the present Charter shall impair the inherent right of individual or collective self-defense if an armed attack occurs against a Member of the United Nations, until the Security Council has taken the measures necessary to maintain international peace and security.

CHAPTER VIII. REGIONAL ARRANGEMENTS

1. Nothing in the present Charter precludes the existence of regional arrangements or agencies for dealing with such matters relating to the maintenance of international peace and security as are appropriate for regional action, provided that such arrangements or agencies and their activities are consistent with the Purposes and Principles of the United Nations.

CHAPTER IX. INTERNATIONAL ECONOMIC AND SOCIAL COOPERATION

Article 55

With a view to the creation of conditions of stability and well-being which are necessary for peaceful and friendly relations among nations based on respect for the principle of equal rights and self-determination of peoples, the United Nations shall promote:

a. higher standards of living, full employment, and conditions of economic and social progress and development;

b. solutions of international economic, social, health, and related problems; . . .

c. universal respect for, and observance of human rights and fundamental freedoms for all without distinction as to race, sex, language, or religion.

Article 56

All Members pledge themselves to take joint and separate action in cooperation with the Organization for the achievement of the purposes set forth in Article 55.

Article 106

Pending the coming into force of such special agreements referred to in Article 43 as in the opinion of the Security Council enable it to begin the exercise of its responsibilities under Article 42, . . .

Bibliography

Abel, Elie. *The Cuban Missile Crisis*. Philadelphia: J. B. Lippincott, 1966.

Acheson, Dean. "Dean Acheson's Version of Robert Kennedy's Version of the Cuban Missile Crisis: Homage to Plain Dumb Luck." *Esquire* LXXI (February 1969) 76 *et seq.*

Adams, Charles, ed. *The Works of John Adams*. 10 vols. Boston: Little, Brown, 1850–1856.

Adler, David. "The Constitution and Presidential Warmaking: The Enduring Debate." *Political Science Quarterly* 103 (Spring 1988): 1–36.

Allison, Graham. *Essence of Decision: Explaining the Cuban Missile Crisis*. Boston: Little, Brown, 1971.

Austin, Anthony. *The President's War: The Story of the Tonkin Gulf Resolution and How the Nation Was Trapped in Vietnam*. Philadelphia: J. B. Lippincott, 1971.

Bailey, Thomas. *Presidential Greatness*. New York: Appleton-Century-Crofts, 1968.

Ball, George. *The Past Has Another Pattern: Memoirs*. New York: W. W. Norton, 1982.

———. "Top Secret: The Prophecy the President Rejected." *Atlantic Monthly* 230 (July 1972): 35–49.

"Ballots and Bloodshed." *The New Republic* 194 (October 19, 1987): 4–5.

Barber, James. "Empire of the Son: How George Bush Rewrote the Book on the Imperial Presidency." *Washington Monthly* 23:10 (October 1991): 25–29.

Barnet, Richard. *Roots of War*. New York: Atheneum Publishers, 1971.

Barnhart, Michael, ed. *Congress and United States Foreign Policy: Controlling the Use of Force in the Nuclear Age*. Albany: State University of New York Press, 1987.

Barone, Michael. "A Question of Going to War." *U.S. News & World Report* (November 1, 1993): 49.

Bartlett, Ruhl, ed. *The Record of American Diplomacy*. 3rd ed. New York: Alfred A. Knopf, 1954.

Basler, Roy, et al., eds. *The Collected Works of Abraham Lincoln*. Vol. 1. New Brunswick, N.J.: Rutgers University Press, 1953.

Bassette, Joseph, and Jeffrey Tullis, eds. *The Presidency in the Constitutional Order*. Baton Rouge: Louisiana State University Press, 1981.

Benjamin, James. "Rhetoric and the Performative Act of Declaring War." *Presidential Studies Quarterly* 21:1 (Winter 1991): 73–84.

Bennet, James. "The Senate's Lame Doves: Why They Failed to Stop the War." *Washington Monthly* (March 1991): 43–46.

Berman, Larry. *Lyndon Johnson's War: The Road to Stalemate in Vietnam*. New York: Norton, 1989.

Bestor, Arthur. "'Advice' from the Very Beginning, 'Consent' When the End Is Achieved." *American Journal of International Law* 83:4 (October 1989): 750–757.

———. "Separation of Powers in the Domain of Foreign Affairs: The Original Intent of the Constitution Historically Examined." *Seton Hall Law Review* 5 (1974): 529.

Bickel, Alexander. "The Constitution and the War." *Commentary* 54 (July 1972): 49–55.

Bickel, Alexander, et al. "Indochina: The Constitutional Crisis." *Congressional Record* (daily ed.) 116 (May 13, 1970): S7117–S7123. Part II, *Congressional Record* (daily ed.) 116 (May 20, 1970): S7538–S7541.

Binkley, Wilfred. *President and Congress*. New York: Alfred A. Knopf, 1947.

Biskupic, Joan. "Constitutional Questions Remain." *Congressional Quarterly Weekly Report* 49:2 (January 12, 1991): 70.

———. "Constitution's Conflicting Clauses Underscored by Iraq Crisis: Provisions on Waging War Leave a Basic Question Unanswered, Does Congress or the President Call the Shot?" *Congressional Quarterly Weekly Report* (January 5, 1991): 33–36.

Blair, Arthur. *At War in the Gulf: A Chronology*. College Station: Texas A&M University Press, 1992.

Blechman, Barry. *The Politics of National Defense: Congress and U.S. Defense Policy from Vietnam to the Persian Gulf*. Oxford: Oxford University Press, 1990.

Blum, Andrew. "Litigation Bombards Courts." *The National Law Journal* 13:21 (January 28, 1991): 28.

Bondy, William. "The Separation of Governmental Powers in History, in Theory, and in Constitution." *Studies in History, Economics, and Public Law* 5:2 (Columbia University, 1896).

Bowen, Catherine. *Miracle at Philadelphia*. Boston: Little, Brown, 1966.

Bowens, Gregory. "House Backs Measure Allowing U.S. Role in U.N. Operation." *Congressional Quarterly Weekly Report* (May 29, 1993): 1373.

Bowens, Gregory, and Carroll Doherty. "Bombing, Widely Backed on Hill, Reopens War Powers Debate." *Congressional Quarterly Weekly Report* 51:27 (July 3, 1993): 1750–1751.

Boyd, Julian, ed. *The Papers of Thomas Jefferson.* 17 vols. Princeton, N.J.: Princeton University Press, 1950–1965.

Braestrup, Peter. *Big Story: How the American Press and Television Reported and Interpreted the Crisis of Tet 1968.* 2 vols. Boulder, Colo.: Westview, 1977.

Brant, Irving. *James Madison: Father of the Constitution, 1787–1800.* Indianapolis: Bobbs-Merrill, 1950.

Breckinridge, Scott. *The CIA and the U.S. Intelligence System.* Boulder, Colo.: Westview, 1986.

"Broken Clock." *The New Republic* (September 10, 1990): 12–13.

Brown, Seyom. *The Faces of Power: Constancy and Change in United States Foreign Policy from Truman to Reagan.* New York: Columbia University Press, 1983.

Brownlow, Louis. *The President and the Presidency.* Chicago: University of Chicago Press, 1949.

Brzezinski, Zbigniew. *Power and Principle: Memoirs of the National Security Advisor.* New York: Farrar, Strauss & Giroux, 1983.

Buckley, William, Jr. "The Constitutional Question." *National Review* 43:1 (January 28, 1991): 70.

_____. "Top Secret." *National Review* (September 25, 1987): 64.

"The Burden of Decisions: Will Circumstances Make War Inevitable? How the President Will Weigh His Options." *Newsweek* (October 29, 1990): 32–33.

Burnett, Edmund, ed. *Letters of Members of the Continental Congress, 1774–1789.* 8 vols. Washington, D.C.: Carnegie Institution of Washington, 1921–1936.

Burns, James. *The Deadlock of Democracy.* Englewood Cliffs, N.J.: Prentice-Hall, 1963.

_____. *Presidential Government: The Crucible of Leadership.* Boston: Houghton Mifflin, 1966.

Bush, George. "Letter to Congressional Leaders Reporting on the National Emergency with Respect to Iraq." *Public Papers of the Presidents of the United States: George Bush.* Washington, D.C.: U.S. Government Printing Office, 1992: 131–133.

_____. "Statement on Allied Military Action in the Persian Gulf, January 16, 1991." *Public Papers of the Presidents of the United States: George Bush.* Washington, D.C.: U.S. Government Printing Office, 1992: 42.

Byrd, Robert, Bob Dole, David Durenberger, and Brock Adams. "Should the Byrd-Warner Amendment Be Adopted?" *Congressional Digest* 66:12 (December 1987): 304–313.

Cable, Larry. *Conflict of Myths: The Development of American Counterinsurgency Doctrine and the Vietnam War.* New York: New York University Press, 1986.

Caldwell, Dan. "A Research Note on the Quarantine of Cuba, October 1962." *International Studies Quarterly* XXII (December 1978): 625–633.

Campbell, Colin. *Managing the Presidency: Carter, Reagan, and the Search for Executive Harmony.* Pittsburgh: University of Pittsburgh Press, 1986.

Caraley, Demetrios, ed. *The President's War Powers: From the Federalists to Reagan.* New York: Academy of Political Science, 1984.

Carmody, Cris, and Marcia Coyle. "Somalia Operation Poses Legal Issues." *The National Law Journal* 15:16 (December 21, 1992): 5.

Carpenter, William. "The Separation of Powers in the Eighteenth Century." *American Political Science Review* 22 (1928): 22.

Carter, Jimmy. "First Steps toward Peace: The Former President Calls for 'Flexibility'" *Newsweek* (December 17, 1990): 25.

———. *Keeping Faith: Memoirs of a President.* New York: Bantam Books, 1982.

Chamberlain, Laurence. *The President, Congress and Legislation.* New York: Columbia University Press, 1946.

Cheever, Daniel, and Field Haviland, Jr. *American Foreign Policy and the Separation of Powers.* Cambridge, Mass.: Harvard University Press, 1952.

Cheney, Dick. "Congressional Overreaching in Foreign Policy." In Robert Goldwin, and Robert Licht, eds., *Foreign Policy and the Constitution.* Washington, D.C.: American Enterprise Institute for Public Policy Research, 1990.

———. "Legislative-Executive Relations in National Security: Work Together to Govern." *Vital Speeches* 56:11 (March 15, 1990): 334–336.

Church, George. "Trip Wires to War: What Would It Take for the U.S. to Attack Iraq, and How Would Bush Square the Decision with the U.N. and Congress?" *Time* (October 29, 1990): 48–51.

Clark, Jeffrey. *Advice and Support: The Final Years, 1965–1973.* Washington, D.C.: U.S. Government Printing Office, 1988.

Clodfelter, Mark. *The Limits of Airpower: The American Bombing of North Vietnam.* New York: Free Press, 1989.

Clymer, Adam. "Democrats Study Amending War Powers Act." *New York Times* (October 24, 1993): 5N.

———. "Foreign Policy Tug-of-War: Latest in a Long String of Battles." *New York Times* (October 19, 1993): A4, A18.

Cohen, Richard. "Self-Executing Executive Agreements: A Separation of Powers Problem." *Buffalo Law Review* 24 (1974): 137.

Collidge, Francis, and Joel Sharrow. "The War-Making Powers: The Intentions of the Framers in Light of Parliamentary History." *Boston University Law Review* 50 (1970): 4–18.

Collins, James, Jr. *The Development and Training of the South Vietnamese Army, 1950–1972.* Washington, D.C.: U.S. Government Printing Office, 1975.

"Congress Approves Resolution Authorizing Use of Force." *Congressional Quarterly Weekly Report* 49:2 (January 12, 1991): 131.

"Congress, the President, and the Power to Commit Forces to Combat." Note. *Harvard Law Review* 81 (June 1968): 1771–1805.

Congressional Research Service. *The Constitution of the United States of America: Analysis and Interpretation.* Doc. No. 92–82. Washington, D.C.: U.S Government Printing Office, 1973.

Cook, Jacob, ed. *The Federalist.* Middletown, Conn.: Wesleyan University Press, 1961.

Cooper, Joseph, and Ann Cooper. "The Legislative Veto and the Constitution." *George Washington Law Review* 30 (1962): 467.

Corwin, Edward. *The President: Office and Powers.* 5th ed. New York: New York University Press, 1984.

——. *The President: Office and Powers.* New York: New York University Press, 1940.

——. *The President: Office and Powers 1787–1957.* New York: New York University Press, 1957.

Cotter, Cornelius, and Malcolm Smith. "Administrative Accountability to Congress: The Concurrent Resolution." *Western Political Quarterly* 9 (1956): 955.

Crabb, Cecil, Jr. *The Doctrines of American Foreign Policy: Their Meaning, Role, and Future.* Baton Rouge: Louisiana State University Press, 1982.

Crabb, Cecil, Jr., and Pat Holt. *Invitation to Struggle: Congress, the President, and Foreign Policy.* Washington, D.C.: Congressional Quarterly Press, 1989.

Crabb, Cecil, Jr., and Kevin Mulcahy. *Presidents and Foreign Policy Making: From FDR to Reagan.* Baton Rouge: Louisiana State University Press, 1986.

Cronin, Thomas. *The State of the Presidency.* 2nd ed. Boston: Little, Brown, 1975.

Crovitz, Gordon, and Jeremy Rabkin, eds. *The Fettered Presidency: Legal Constraints on the Executive Branch.* Washington, D.C.: American Enterprise Institute for Public Policy Research, 1989.

Curtis, Thomas, and Donald Westerfield. *Congressional Intent.* New York: Praeger, 1992.

Damrosch, Lori. "Constitutional Control of Military Actions: A Comparative Dimension." *American Journal of International Law* 85:1 (January 1991): 74–88.

"Dangerous, but Not Hostile." *Time* (September 7, 1987): 23.

Davies, Susan. "Congressional Encroachment on Executive Branch Communications." *University of Chicago Law Review* 57:4 (Fall 1990): 1297–1321.

Dawson, Joseph. *Commanders in Chief: Presidential Leadership in Modern Wars.* Lawrence: University Press of Kansas, 1993.

"Declare Yourselves." *National Review* (January 28, 1991): 16–17.

Destler, I. M. "Executive-Congressional Conflict in Foreign Policy: Explaining It, Coping with It." In Lawrence Dodd and Bruce Oppenheimer, eds., *Congress Reconsidered*, 3rd ed. Washington, D.C.: Congressional Quarterly Press, 1985.

Detzer, David. *The Brink: Cuban Missile Crisis, 1962.* New York: Thomas Y. Crowell, 1979.

Doherty, Carroll. "Bombing, Widely Backed on Hill, Reopens War Powers Debate." *Congressional Quarterly Weekly Report* (July 3, 1993): 1750–1751.

_____ . "Congress Faces Grave Choices As Clock Ticks toward War: Institutional Pride and Constitutional Authority at Stake As Capitol Hill Searches for Role in Gulf Crisis." *Congressional Quarterly Weekly Report* (January 5, 1991): 7–9.

_____ . "The Reluctant Warriors." *Congressional Quarterly Weekly Report* (February 13, 1993): 323.

_____ . "Senate Edges into Gulf Debate." *Congressional Quarterly Weekly Report* (January 5, 1991): 8.

_____ . "Uncertain Congress Confronts President's Gulf Strategy." *Congressional Quarterly Weekly Report* 48:46 (November 17, 1990): 3879–3882.

Doherty, Carroll, and Joan Biskupic. "Administration Makes Its Case but Fails to Sway Skeptics." *Congressional Quarterly Weekly Report* 48:49 (December 8, 1990): 4082–4085.

Donovan, Robert. *Conflict and Crisis: The Presidency of Harry S. Truman, 1945–1948.* New York: Praeger, 1977.

_____ . *Tumultuous Years: The Presidency of Harry S. Truman, 1949–1953.* New York: W. W. Norton, 1982.

Draper, Theodore. "The Constitution in Danger." *New York Review of Books* (March 1, 1990): 41–47.

_____ . "Presidential Wars." *New York Review of Books* (September 26, 1991): 64–74.

Dugger, Ronnie. *On Reagan: The Man and His Presidency.* New York: McGraw-Hill, 1983.

Dverin, Eugene, ed. *The Senate's War Powers: Debate on Cambodia from the Congressional Record.* Chicago: Markham Publishing Company, 1971.

Eagleton, Thomas. "The August 15 Compromise and the War Powers of Congress." *St. Louis University Law Journal* 18 (Fall 1973): 1–11.

_____ . "Congress and War Powers." *Missouri Law Review* 37 (Winter 1972): 1–32.

_____ . *War and Presidential Power: A Chronicle of Congressional Surrender.* New York: Liveright, 1974.

_____ . "Whose Power Is War Power?" *Foreign Policy* 8 (Fall 1972): 23–32.

Edwards, George. "The Two Presidencies: A Reevaluation." *American Politics Quarterly* 14 (July 1986): 247–263.

Edwards, George, et al. *The Presidency and Policy Making.* Pittsburgh: University of Pittsburgh Press, 1985.

Eisenhower, Dwight D. *Mandate for Change, 1953–56.* New York: New American Library, 1963.

———. *Waging Peace.* Garden City, N.Y.: Doubleday, 1965.

Elliot, Donald. "*INS v. Chadha*: The Administrative Constitution, the Constitution, and the Legislative Veto." *Supreme Court Review* 125 (1983): 125–176.

Elliot, Jonathan, ed. *The Debates in the Several State Conventions, on the Adoption of the Federal Constitution.* 5 vols. Washington, D.C.: Carnegie Institution of Washington, 1836–1845.

Ellsberg, Daniel. "Present Danger." *The Nation* (November 26, 1990): 1.

Elving, Ronald. "America's Most Frequent Fight Has Been the Undeclared War." *Congressional Quarterly Weekly Report* 49:1 (January 5, 1991): 37–39.

Ely, John. *On Taking Up Arms and Taking Responsibility: Constitutional Lessons of Vietnam and Its Aftermath.* Princeton, NJ: Princeton University Press, 1993.

———. "Suppose Congress Wanted a War Powers Act That Worked." *Columbia Law Review* 88:7 (November 1988): 1379–1431.

———. "The (Troubled) Constitutionality of the War They Told Us About." *Stanford Law Review* (Part 1 of 2 parts) 42:4 (April 1990): 876–926.

———. "The Unconstitutionality of the War They Didn't Tell Us About." *Stanford Law Review* 42:5 (May 1990): 1111–1148.

———. "Whose War Is It, Anyway? The Gulf and the War Powers Act." *The New Republic* 198:21 (May 23, 1988): 22–23.

Emerson, John. "War Powers Legislation." *West Virginia Law Review* 74 (November-January 1971–1972): 53–119.

Evans, Richard, and Robert Novak. *Lyndon B. Johnson: The Exercise of Power.* New York: The New American Library, 1966.

———. *Nixon in the White House: The Frustration of Power.* New York: Random House, 1971.

"Excerpts: The Great Debate on War Powers." *The National Law Journal* 13:20 (January 21, 1991): 26.

Farrand, Max, ed., *The Records of the Federal Convention of 1787.* 4 vols. New Haven, Conn.: Yale University Press, 1937.

Faulkner, Stanley. "War in Vietnam: Is It Constitutional?" *Georgetown Law Journal* 56 (June 1968): 1132–1143.

Fessler, Pamela. "Members Solemn over Crucial Choice . . . with Uncertain Outcome." *Congressional Quarterly Weekly Report* 49:2 (January 12, 1991): 66–67.

Filch, Richard, ed. *The Vietnam War and International Law.* Princeton, N.J.: Princeton University Press, 1969.

Finer, Herman. *The Presidency: Crisis and Regeneration.* Chicago: University of Chicago Press, 1960.

Firmage, Edwin. *To Chain the Dog of War: The War Power of Congress in History and Law.* Urbana: University of Illinois Press, 1989.

Fisher, Louis. "Congressional Participation in the Treaty Process." *University of Pennsylvania Law Review* 137 (1989): 1511.

_____ . *The Constitution between Friends: Congress, the President, and the Law.* New York: St. Martin's Press, 1978.

_____ . *Constitutional Conflicts between Congress and the President.* 3rd ed. Lawrence: University Press of Kansas, 1991.

_____ . "Delegating Power to the President." *Journal of Public Law* 19 (1970): 251.

_____ . *The Politics of Shared Power: Congress and the Executive.* Washington, D.C.: Congressional Quarterly Press, 1981.

_____ . *The President and Congress: Power and Policy.* New York: The Free Press, 1972.

Fitzpatrick, John, ed. *The Diaries of George Washington.* 4 vols. Boston: Houghton Mifflin, 1925.

_____ , ed. *The Writings of George Washington.* 39 vols. Washington, D.C.: U.S. Government Printing Office, 1931–1944.

Flynn, John. *The Roosevelt Myth.* New York: Devin-Adair, 1948.

Ford, Gerald. *A Time to Heal.* New York: Harper & Row, 1979.

Ford, Paul. *The Works of Thomas Jefferson.* Federal edition. 12 vols. New York: G. P. Putnam's Sons, 1904–1905.

Franck, Thomas. "Courts and Foreign Policy." *Foreign Policy* (Summer 1991): 66–86.

Franck, Thomas, and Faiza Patel. "UN Police Action in Lieu of War: 'The Old Order Changeth.'" *American Journal of International Law* 81:1 (January 1991): 63–74.

Franck, Thomas, and Edward Weisband. *Foreign Policy by Congress.* Oxford: Oxford University Press, 1979.

Freedman, Lawrence. *U.S. Intelligence and the Soviet Strategic Threat.* Boulder, Colo.: Westview, 1977.

Friedman, Norman. *Desert Victory: The War for Kuwait.* Annapolis, Md.: Naval Institute Press, 1991.

Friedrich, Carl. *Constitutional Government and Democracy.* New York: Ginn and Co., 1946.

Galloway, Joseph. "Shoot-Out in the Gulf, Echoes on Capitol Hill." *U.S. News & World Report* (October 19, 1987): 8.

Garthoff, Raymond. *Policy Versus Law: The Reinterpretation of the ABM Treaty.* Washington, D.C.: Brookings Institution, 1987.

George, Alexander. *Managing U.S.-Soviet Rivalry: Problems of Crisis Prevention.* Boulder, Colo.: Westview, 1983.

Gibbs, George. *Memoirs of the Administrations of Washington and John Adams, Edited from the Papers of Oliver Wolcott, Secretary of the Treasury.* 2 vols. New York: W. Van Norden, 1846.

Gibson, Rankin. "Congressional Concurrent Resolution: An Aid to Statutory Interpretation?" *American Bar Association Journal* 37 (1951): 421.

Glazer, Sarah. "Making Foreign Policy." *Editorial Research Reports* 1:24 (June 26, 1987): 314–326.

Glennon, Michael. "Mr. Sofaer's War Powers 'Partnership.'" *American Journal of International Law* 80:3 (July 1986): 584–586.

_____. "The Constitution and Chapter VII of the United Nations Charter." *American Journal of International Law* 85:1 (January 1991): 74–88.

_____. "The Gulf War and the Constitution." *Foreign Affairs* (Spring 1991): 84–101.

_____. "The Use of Custom in Resolving Separation of Powers Disputes." *Boston University Law Review* 64 (1984): 109.

Goldwater, Barry. "President's Ability to Protect America's Freedoms—the War-making Power." *Law and Social Order* 2 (1971): 423–449.

Goldwin, Robert, and Art Kaufman. *Separation of Powers: Does It Still Work?* Lanham, Md.: American Enterprise Institute, 1986.

Goldwin, Robert, and Robert Licht. *Foreign Policy and the Constitution.* Washington, D.C.: American Enterprise Institute for Public Policy Research, 1990.

Goodman, Allan. *The Lost Peace: America's Search for a Negotiated Settlement of the Vietnam War.* Stanford, Calif.: Hoover Institution, 1978.

Graebner, Norman. "The President as Commander in Chief: A Study in Power." *Journal of Military History* 57:1 (January 1993): 111–132.

Halperin, Morton. "Lawful Wars." *Foreign Policy* 72 (Fall 1988): 173–195.

Hamilton, Alexander, John Jay, and James Madison. *The Federalist: A Commentary on THE CONSTITUTION OF THE UNITED STATES Being a Collection of Essays Written in Support of the Constitution Agreed Upon September 17, 1787, by the Federal Convention.* Washington, D.C.: Robert B. Luce, Inc., 1976.

Hartmann, Robert. *Palace Politics: An Inside Account of the Ford Years.* New York: McGraw-Hill, 1980.

Haynes, George. *The Senate of the United States: Its History and Practice.* 2 vols. Boston: Houghton Mifflin, 1938.

Hebe, William. "Executive Orders and the Development of Presidential Power." *Villanova Law Review* 17 (1972): 688.

Henkin, Louis. *Foreign Affairs and the Constitution.* Mineola, N.Y.: The Foundation Press, 1972.

Hitchens, Christopher. "Minority Report." *The Nation* (October 15, 1990): 406.

Holland, Kenneth. "The War Powers Resolution: An Infringement on the President's Constitutional and Prerogative Powers." In Gordon Hoxie, ed.,

The Presidency and National Security Policy: 378–400. New York: Center for the Study of the Presidency, 1984.

Holt, Pat. *The War Powers Resolution: The Role of Congress in U.S. Armed Intervention.* Washington, D.C.: American Enterprise Institute, 1978.

"House and Senate Debate on Joint Resolution." *Congressional Quarterly Weekly Report* 49:2 (January 12, 1991): 132–134.

Hoxie, Gordon, ed. *The Presidency and National Security Policy.* New York: Center for the Study of the Presidency, 1984.

Hunt, Gaillard, ed. *The Writings of James Madison.* New York: Putnam, 1900–1910.

Hutchison, William, and William Rachal, eds. *The Papers of James Madison.* 6 vols. Chicago: University of Chicago Press, 1962–1969.

"Into Battle." *National Review* 3:2 (February 11, 1991): 13–15.

Israel, Fred, ed. *The State of the Union Messages of the Presidents 1790–1966.* 3 vols. New York: Chelsea House-Hector, 1966.

James, Patrick, and John Oneal. "The Influence of Domestic and International Politics on the President's Use of Force." *Journal of Conflict Resolution* 35:2 (June 1991): 307–332.

Javits, Jacob. "The War Powers Resolution and the Constitution: A Special Introduction." In Demetrios Caraley, ed., *The President's War Powers: From the Federalists to Reagan.* New York: Academy of Political Science, 1984.

———. *Who Makes War.* New York: William Morrow and Company, 1973.

Jayson, Lester, et al., eds. *The Constitution of the United States of America: Analysis and Interpretation* U.S. Senate Doc. No. 92–82. Washington, D.C.: U.S. Government Printing Office, 1973.

John, Ludwell III. "Abraham Lindoln and the Development of Presidential War-Making Powers: Prize Cases." *Civil War History* (September 1989): 208–224.

Johnson, Loch. *America's Secret Power: The CIA in a Democratic Society.* Oxford: Oxford University Press, 1989.

Johnson, Lyndon. *The Vantage Point: Perspectives on the Presidency, 1963–1969.* New York: Holt, Rinehart & Winston, 1971.

Johnston, Henry, ed. *The Correspondence and Public Papers of John Jay.* 4 vols. New York: G.P. Putnam's Sons, 1890–1893.

Jones, Gordon, and John Marini, eds. *The Imperial Congress: Crisis in the Separation of Powers.* Washington, D.C.: Heritage Foundation and Claremont Institute, 1988.

Kaiser, Frederick. "Congressional Control of Executive Actions in the Aftermath of the *Chadha* Decision." *Administrative Law Review* 36 (1984): 239.

Katzenbach, Nicholas. "Comparative Roles of the President and the Congress in Foreign Affairs." *Department of State Bulletin* 47 (September 11, 1967): 333–336.

Kaufman, Burton. *The Korean War: Challenges in Crisis, Credibility, and Command.* New York: Knopf, 1986.

Kennedy, Robert. *Thirteen Days: A Memoir of the Cuban Missile Crisis.* New York: W. W. Norton, 1969.

Keown, Stuart. "The President, the Congress, and the Power to Declare War." *University of Kansas Law Review* 16 (November 1967): 82–97.

Kinsley, Michael. "War and Powers." *The New Republic* (November 8, 1993): 6.

———. "The War Powers War." *The New Republic* (December 31, 1990): 4.

Kissinger, Henry. *White House Years.* Boston: Little, Brown, 1979.

———. *Years of Upheaval.* Boston: Little, Brown, 1982.

Koh, Harold. "Why the President (Almost) Always Wins in Foreign Affairs: Lessons of the Iran-Contra Affair." *Yale Law Journal* 97 (June 1988): 1292–1297.

Lacayo, Richard. "On the Fence: The President Says He Can Take America to War without Asking Congress. The Lawmakers Disagree—But Most Would Rather Not Take a Public Stand At All." *Time* (January 14, 1991): 12–14.

———. "A Reluctant Go-Ahead: As Hopes for Peace Fade, a Divided Congress Authorizes the President to Lead the United States into Battle." *Time* (January 21, 1991): 32–33.

Lea, James. "The President's Military Power under the Constitution." *USA Today* (Magazine) 116 (September 1987): 12–15.

Leckie, Robert. *The Wars of America.* New York: Harper & Row, 1968.

Lehman, John. *The Executive, Congress, and Foreign Policy: Studies of the Nixon Administration.* New York: Praeger, 1976.

Leich, Marian. "War Powers." *American Journal of International Law* 85:2 (April 1991): 340–341.

Leighton, Leon. "The Enduring Vitality of the War Powers Resolution: The Inadequacy of H.J. Res. 601 and S.J. Res. 323." In Appendix 6 of U.S. House of Representatives, *War Powers: Origins, Purposes, and Applications: Hearings before the Subcommittee on Arms Control, International Security and Science of the Committee on Foreign Affairs*: 305–358, 100th Cong., 2nd Sess., August 4, 1988 and September 27, 1988. Washington, D.C.: U.S. Government Printing Office, 1989.

Leiken, Robert, ed. *Central America: Anatomy of a Conflict.* New York: Pergamon, 1984.

Lodge, Henry Cabot. *The Works of Alexander Hamilton.* 2nd ed. 12 vols. New York: G. P. Putnam's Sons, 1903.

Lofgren, Charles. "*United States v. Curtiss-Wright Export Corporation*: An Historical Reassessment." *Yale Law Journal* 83 (November 1973): 21–32.

———. "War-Making under the Constitution: The Original Understanding." *Yale Law Journal* 81 (March 1972): 672–702.

Lomax, Louis. *Thailand: The War That Is, The War That Will Be.* New York: Random House, 1967.

Lowi, Theodore. *The Personal President: Power Invested, Promise Unfulfilled.* Ithaca, N.Y.: Cornell University Press, 1985.

Lowry, Mike. "War Powers Action." *The New Republic* 198:25 (June 20, 1988): 2.

Lowry v. Reagan. C.A. No. 87–2196 (December 18, 1987), slip opinion at 13.

McDougal, Myres, and Asher Lans. "Treaties and Congressional-Executive or Presidential Agreements: Interchangeable Instruments of National Policy." *Yale Law Journal* 54 (1945): 181, 534.

Madison, James. *Notes of Debates in the Federal Convention of 1787 Reported by James Madison.* Athens, Ohio: Ohio University Press, 1966. Reprint of House Document No. 398, *Documents Illustrative of the Formation of the Union of the American States.* Washington, D.C.: Government Printing Office, 1927.

"Main Provisions of the Senate-Passed Measure." *Congressional Digest* 66:12 (December 1987): 295–296.

Mandelbaum, Michael. *The Nuclear Question: The United States and Nuclear Weapons, 1946–1976.* Cambridge, England: Cambridge University Press, 1979.

Mann, Thomas, ed. *A Question of Balance: The President, the Congress, and Foreign Policy.* Washington, D.C.: The Brookings Institution, 1990.

Mathews, Craig. "The Constitutional Power of the President to Conclude International Agreements." *Yale Law Journal* 64 (1955): 345.

May, Ernest. *"Lessons" of the Past: The Use and Misuse of History in American Foreign Policy.* New York: Oxford University Press, 1973.

———. *The Ultimate Decision: The President as Commander in Chief.* New York: George Braziller, 1960.

Meeker, Leonard. "The Legality of United States Participation in the Defense of Viet-Nam." *Department of State Bulletin* 54 (April 28, 1966): 474–489.

Merrill, Maurice. "Standards—A Safeguard for the Exercise of Delegated Power," *Nebraska Law Review* 47 (1968): 469.

Merry, Robert. "President, Congress and War Powers." *Congressional Quarterly Weekly Report* (August 25, 1990): 2754.

Miller, Judith, and Laurie Mylroie. *Saddam Hussein and the Crisis in the Gulf.* New York: Times Books, 1990.

Mitchell, Broadus. *Alexander Hamilton.* New York: Macmillan, 1962.

Moore, Mike. "How George Bush Won His Spurs." *Bulletin of the Atomic Scientists* 47:8 (October 1991): 26–33.

———. "Imperial Thoughts: Crisis in the Middle East, a Half-Told Story." *The Quill* 78:8 (October 1990): 16–21.

Morgan, Clifton, and Kenneth Bickers. "Domestic Discontent and the External Use of Force." *Journal of Conflict Resolution* 36:1 (March 1992):25–52.

Morgan, Donald. *Congress and the Constitution: A Study of Responsibility.* Cambridge, Mass.: Harvard University Press, 1966.

Morris, Richard. *Great Presidential Decisions.* Philadelphia: J. B. Lippincott, 1960.

"Mr. Dole's Bad Idea." *New York Times* (October 19, 1993): A16.

Mueller, John. *War, Presidents and Public Opinion.* New York: John Wiley, 1973.

Murphy, John. "Knowledge Is Power: Foreign Policy and Information Interchange among Congress, the Executive Branch, and the Public." 49 *Tulane Law Review* 505 (1975).

———. "Treaties and International Agreements Other Than Treaties: Constitutional Allocation of Power and Responsibility among the President, the House of Representatives, and the Senate." 23 *University of Kansas Law Review* 23 (1975): 221.

Muskie, Edmund, et al., eds. *The President, Congress, and Foreign Policy.* Lanham, Md.: University Press of America, 1986.

Nathan, James. "Revising the War Powers Act." *Armed Forces & Society: An Interdisciplinary Journal* (Summer 1991): 513–543.

———. "Salvaging the War Powers Resolution." *Presidential Studies Quarterly* 23:2 (Spring 1993): 235–268.

Neustadt, Richard. *Presidential Power: The Politics of Leadership.* (New York: The New American Library, 1964.

———. *Presidential Power: The Politics of Leadership from FDR to Carter.* Rev. ed. New York: John Wiley, 1980.

Neustadt, Richard, and Ernest May. *Thinking in Time: The Uses of History for Decision-Makers.* New York: The Free Press, 1986.

Nixon, Richard M. *The Memoirs of Richard Nixon.* New York: Grosset & Dunlap, 1978.

———. *Six Crises.* New York: Pyramid Books, 1968.

———. "U.S. Foreign Policy for the 1970's: A New Strategy for Peace." *Message from the President of the United States Transmitting a Report on Foreign Relations.* House Document No. 91–258 (Feburary 18, 1970).

———. "Veto of War Powers Bill." *Congressional Quarterly Almanac, 1973* 29 (1974): 90–A–91–A.

Noah, Timothy. "War Powers Inaction." *The New Republic* 197 (July 6, 1987): 11–12.

Offutt, Milton. *The Protection of Citizens Abroad by the Armed Forces of the United States.* Baltimore: Johns Hopkins Press, 1928.

Paige, Glen. *The Korean Decision, June 24–30, 1950.* New York: Free Press, 1968.

Palmer, Bruce, Jr. *The 25-Year War: America's Role in Vietnam.* Lexington: University of Kentucky Press, 1984.

Palmer, Gregory. *The McNamara Strategy and the Vietnam War.* Westport, Conn.: Greenwood Press, 1978.

Peters, Richard. *The Public Statutes at Large of the United States of America.* Vol. 1. Boston: Charles Little and James Brown, 1845.

Pious, Richard. "Prerogative Power and the Reagan Presidency: A Review Essay."
    Political Science Quarterly 106:3 (Fall 1991): 499–510.
"Presidential Reports" Congressional Digest. 66:12 (December 1987): 292–293.
Public Papers of the Presidents of the United States: George Bush 1991. 2 vols.
    Washington, D.C.: U.S. Government Printing Office, 1992.
*Public Papers of the Presidents of the United States: Lyndon B. Johnson, 1963–
    1964.* 2 vols. Washington, D.C.: U.S. Government Printing Office, 1965.
Pusey, Merlo. *Big Government: Can We Control It?* New York: Harper & Broth-
    ers, 1945.
_____ . *Eisenhower the President.* New York: Macmillan, 1956.
_____ . *The Way We Go to War.* Boston: Houghton Mifflin, 1969.
Rauch, Basil. *Roosevelt from Munich to Pearl Harbor.* New York: Creative Age
    Press, 1950.
"Realism, Liberalism, and the War Powers Resolution." *Harvard Law Review*
    102:3 (January 1989): 637–657.
"Recent Action in Congress." *Congressional Digest* 66:12 (December 1987):
    294–295.
Rehnquist, William. "The Constitutional Issues—Administration Position." *New
    York University Law Review* 45 (June 1970): 628–639.
_____ . "Statement by William H. Rehnquist, Assistant Attorney General Office
    of Legal Counsel, on the President's Constitutional Authority to Order
    the Attack on the Cambodian Sanctuaries." In U.S. Senate, *Documents
    Relating to the War Power of Congress, The President's Authority as
    Commander-in-Chief and the War in Indochina:* 182–185. 91st Cong.,
    2nd Sess. Washington, D.C.: U.S. Government Printing Office, 1970.
Reisman, Michael. "War Powers: The Operational Code of Competence." *Ameri-
    can Journal of International Law* 83:4 (October 1989): 777–785.
Reveley, Taylor III. "Prepared Statement." In *The War Power after 200 Years:
    Congress and the President at a Constitutional Impasse.* Hearings before
    the Special Subcommittee on War Powers of the Senate Committee on
    Foreign Relations, 100th Cong., 2nd Sess. Washington, D.C.: U.S. Gov-
    ernment Printing Office, 1989.
_____ . *War Powers of the President and Congress: Who Holds the Arrows and
    Olive Branch?* Charlottesville: University Press of Virginia, 1981.
Richardson, Elliot. "The War Powers Resolution: Conflicting Constitutional Pow-
    ers, the War Powers and U.S. Foreign Policy." Testimony in U.S. House
    of Representatives, *War Powers: Origins, Purposes, and Applications:
    Hearings before the Subcommittee on Arms Control, International Secu-
    rity and Science of the Committee on Foreign Affairs:* 138–206. 100th
    Cong., 2nd Sess., August 4, 1988 and September 27, 1988. Washington,
    D.C.: U.S. Government Printing Office, 1989.
Richardson, James, ed. *Compilation of Messages and Papers of the Presidents.*
    Vol. 1 Washington, D.C.: U.S.Government Printing Office, 1896.

Robinson, Edgar, et al. *Powers of the President in Foreign Affairs.* San Francisco: Commonwealth Club, 1966.

Rockman, Bert. "Mobilizing Political Support for U.S. National Security." *Armed Forces and Society* 14 (Fall 1987): 17–41.

Rogers, James Grafton. *World Policing and the Constitution.* Boston: World Peace Foundation, 1945.

Rogers, William D. "The Constitutionality of the Cambodian Incursion." *American Journal of International Law* 65 (January 1971): 26–37.

Rogers, William P. "Congress, the President, and the War Powers." *California Law Review* 59 (September 1971): 1194–1214.

Rosenberg, David. "The Origins of Overkill: Nuclear Weapons and American Strategy, 1945–1960." *International Security* 8 (Spring 1983): 3–71.

Rosenberg, Douglas. "Delegation and Regulatory Reform: Letting the President Change the Rules." *Yale Law Journal* 89 (1980): 561.

Rosenman, Samuel, ed. *The Public Papers and Addresses of Franklin D. Roosevelt.* New York: Harper & Brothers, 1950.

Rostow, Eugene. "Great Cases Make Bad Law: The War Powers Act." *Texas Law Review* 50 (May 1972): 833–900.

———. "Once More unto the Breach: The War Powers Resolution Revisited." *Valparaiso University Law Review* 21 (Fall 1986): 1–52.

———. *Peace in the Balance: The Future of American Foreign Policy.* New York: Simon & Schuster, 1972.

———. "President, Prime Minister or Constitutional Monarch?" *American Journal of International Law* 83:4 (October 1989): 740–749.

Rovine, Arthur. "Separation of Powers and International Executive Agreements." *Indiana Law Review* 52 (1977): 397.

Rubinstein, Alvin. "New World Order or Hollow Victory?" *Foreign Affairs* 70 (Fall 1991): 53–65.

Rubner, Michael. "The Reagan Administration, the 1973 War Powers Resolution, and the Invasion of Grenada." *Political Science Quarterly* 100 (Winter 1985–1986): 627–647.

Savoy, Paul. "Peacekeepers for the Gulf." *The Nation* (November 26, 1990): 642–644.

Schachter, Oscar. "United Nations Law in the Gulf Conflict." *American Journal of International Law* 85:3 (July 1991): 452–473.

Scheffer, David. "National Guard Training Missions outside United States—Federal Control over National Guard—'Militia' Clauses of U.S. Constitution—'Montgomery Amendment.'" *American Journal of International Law* 84:4 (October 1990): 914–921.

Schlesinger, Arthur, Jr. *The Imperial Presidency.* Boston: Houghton Mifflin, 1973.

———. *A Thousand Days: John F. Kennedy in the White House.* Boston: Houghton Mifflin, 1965.

Schwartz, Bernard. *A Commentary on the Constitution of the United States*. Part 1: *The Powers of Government*. Vol. 2: *Powers of the President*. New York: Macmillan, 1936.

Scigliano, Robert. "The War Powers Resolution and the War Powers." in Joseph Bessette and Jeffery Tullis, eds., *The Presidency in the Constitutional Order*. Baton Rouge: Louisiana State University Press, 1981.

Sharp, U.S.G. *Strategy for Defeat: Vietnam in Retrospect*. Novato, Calif.: Presidio Press, 1978.

"Ship of Fools." *The Progressive* 54:3 (March 1989): 7–8.

Sidak, Gregory. "War, Liberty and Enemy Aliens." *New York University Law Review* 67:6 (December 1992): 1402–1431.

Slonin, Solomon. "Congressional-Executive Agreements." *Columbia Journal of Transnational Law* 14 (1975): 434.

Small, Norman. *Some Presidential Interpretations of the Presidency*. Baltimore: Johns Hopkins Press, 1932.

Smith, Jean. *George Bush's War*. New York: Holt, 1992.

Smoler, Fredric. "What Does History Have to Say about the Persian Gulf?" *American Heritage* 41 (November 1990): 100–107.

Smyrl, Marc. *Conflict or Codetermination? Congress, the President, and the Power to Make War*. Cambridge, Mass.: Ballinger, 1988.

Sofaer, Abraham. *War, Foreign Affairs and Constitutional Power: The Origins*. Cambridge, Mass.: Ballinger 1976.

"Somalia Operation Poses Novel Issues." *The National Law Journal* 15:16 (December 21, 1992): 5.

Sorensen, Theodore. *Decision-Making in the White House*. New York: Columbia University Press, 1963.

———. *Kennedy*. New York: Harper & Row, 1965.

Stennis, John, and William Fulbright. *The Role of Congress in Foreign Policy*. Washington, D.C.: American Enterprise Institute, 1971.

Stevenson, Adlai. Address at Harvard, 1954, as quoted in Louis Heren, *The New American Commonwealth*. New York: Harper & Row, 1968.

Strasser, Fred, and Marcia Coyle. "Law Professors Join the Debate on War Powers." *The National Law Journal* 13:14 (December 10, 1990): 5.

Stueck, William, Jr. *The Road to Confrontation: American Policy toward China and Korea, 1947–1950*. Chapel Hill: University of North Carolina Press, 1981.

Summers, Harry, Jr. *On Strategy: A Critical Analysis of the Vietnam War*. Novato, Calif.: Presidio Press, 1982.

———. *On Strategy II: A Critical Analysis of the Gulf War*. New York: Dell Books, 1992.

Sundquist, James. *Politics and Policy: The Eisenhower, Kennedy, and Johnson Years*. Washington, D.C.: The Brookings Institution, 1968.

Syrett, Harold, ed. *The Papers of Alexander Hamilton*. 15 vols. New York: Columbia University Press, 1961–1969.

Szulc, Tad. *The Illusion of Peace: Foreign Policy in the Nixon Years.* New York: Viking Press, 1978.

Taft, William. *The President and His Powers.* New York: Columbia University Press, 1967. Originally published in 1916.

Tomain, Joseph. "Executive Agreements and the Bypassing of Congress." *Journal of International Law and Economics* 8 (1973): 129.

"Tonkin Gulf Redux." *The Nation* 245:16 (November 14, 1987): 541.

Towell, Pat. "Clock Set for Senate Vote on Gulf, War Powers." *Congressional Quarterly Weekly Report* 46:18 (April 30, 1988): 1148.

Treverton, Gregory. *Covert Action: The Limits of Intervention in the Postwar World.* New York: Basic Books, 1987.

Truman, Harry S. *Memoirs.* Vol. 2. Garden City, N.Y.: Doubleday, 1956.

———. *Year of Decisions, 1945.* New York: New American Library, 1955.

———. *Years of Trial and Hope, 1946–1952.* New York: New American Library, 1956.

Truman, Margaret. *Harry S. Truman.* New York: William Morrow, 1973.

"Tug of War: Foreign Policy." *The Economist* (October 23, 1993): A30–31.

Tugwell, Rexford. *The Enlargement of the Presidency.* New York: Doubleday, 1960.

Turner, Robert. *The War Powers Resolution: Its Implementation in Theory and Practice.* (Philadelphia: Philadelphia Foreign Policy Research Institute, 1983.

———. "The War Powers Resolution: Its Origins and Purpose." In U.S. House of Representatives, *War Powers: Origins, Purposes, and Applications: Hearings before the Subcommittee on Arms Control, International Security and Science of the Committee on Foreign Affairs.* 100th Cong., 2nd Sess., August 4, 1988 and September 27, 1988. Washington, D.C.: U.S. Government Printing Office, 1989.

———. "The War Powers Resolution: Unconstitutional, Unnecessary and Unhelpful." *Loyola Los Angeles Law Review* 17 (1984): 683.

Turnsill, Charles, ed. *Formation of the Union of the American States.* Washington, D.C.: U.S. Government Printing Office, 1927.

United Nations. *Provisional Records of the Security Council.* U.N. Doc. S/PV.3046. New York: United Nations, January 31, 1992.

U.S. Department of Defense. *The Pentagon Papers: The Defense Department History of United States Decision Making on Vietnam.* 4 vols. Edited by Senator Gavel. Boston: Beacon Press, 1971.

U.S. Department of State. "The Gulf Crisis: UN Security Council Actions." *U.S. Department of State Dispatch* 1:14 (December 3, 1990): 296.

———. "The Legality of United States Participation in the Defense of Viet-Nam." *Department of State Bulletin* (March 28, 1966): 474–489.

U.S. Department of State, Historical Studies Division. *Armed Actions Taken by the United States without a Declaration of War, 1789–1967.* Res. Proj. No. 806A. Washington, D.C.: U.S. Government Printing Office, 1967.

U.S. Government Printing Office. *Journals of the Continental Congress, 1774–1789*. 34 vols. Washington, D.C.: U.S. Government Printing Office, 1904–1937.

————. *Weekly Compilation of Presidential Documents*. Washington, D.C.: U.S. Government Printing Office, weekly since 1965.

U.S. House of Representatives. *Congress, the President, and the War Powers*. Hearings before the House Subcommittee on National Security Policy and Scientific Developments of the Committee on Foreign Affairs, 91st Cong., 2nd Sess. Washington, D.C.: U.S. Government Printing Office, 1970.

————. *Intelligence Oversight Act of 1988*. H. Rept. 100–705, 100th Cong., 2nd Sess. Washington, D.C.: U.S. Government Printing Office, 1988.

————. *Report of the Congressional Committees Investigating the Iran-Contra Affair with Supplemental, Minority, and Additional Views*. H. Rept. 100–433, S. Rept. 100–216, 100th Cong., 1st Sess. Washington, D.C.: U.S. Government Printing Office, 1987.

————. *U.S. Intelligence Performance on Central America: Achievements and Selected Instances of Concern*. Committee Print. Subcommittee on Oversight and Evaluation of the House Permanent Select Committee on Intelligence, 97th Cong., 2nd Sess. Washington, D.C.: U.S. Government Printing Office, 1982.

————. *War Powers, Libya, and State-Sponsored Terrorism: Hearings before the Subcommittee on Arms Control, International Security and Science of the House Committee on Foreign Affairs*. 99th Cong., 2nd Sess. Washington, D.C.: U.S. Government Printing Office, 1986.

————. *War Powers: Origins, Purposes, and Applications: Hearings before the Subcommittee on Arms Control, International Security and Science of the Committee on Foreign Affairs*. 100th Cong., 2nd Sess., August 4, 1988, and September 27, 1988. Washington, D.C.: U.S. Government Printing Office, 1989.

————. *The War Powers Resolution: A Special Study of the Committee on Foreign Affairs*. Committee Print. Committee on Foreign Affairs. Washington, D.C.: U.S. Government Printing Office, 1982.

————. *The War Powers Resolution: Relevant Documents, Correspondence, Reports*. Committee Print. Subcommittee on International Security and Scientific Affairs of the House Committee on Foreign Affairs, 98th Cong., 1st Sess. Washington, D.C.: U.S. Government Printing Office, 1983.

U.S. House of Representatives Committee on Foreign Affairs. *The Crisis in Somalia: Markup on S.J. Res. 45 Authorizing the Use of U.S. Armed Forces in Somalia*. 103rd Cong., 1st Sess. May 5, 1993. Washington, D.C.: U.S. Government Printing Office, 1993.

————. *War Powers Legislation: Hearings*. 93rd Cong., 1st Sess., March 7–8, 13–15, 20. Washington, D.C.: U.S. Government Printing Office, 1973.

U.S. House of Representatives Committee on International Relations. "Hearings: Seizure of the *Mayaguez*." 94th Cong., 2nd Sess. Washington, D.C.: U.S. Government Printing Office, 1976.

U.S. House of Representatives Committee on Rules. *Studies on the Legislative Veto*. Committee Print. February 1980.

U.S. House of Representatives Select Committee to Investigate Covert Arms Transactions with Iran and Senate Select Committee on Secret Military Assistance to Iran and the Nicaraguan Opposition. *Report of the Congressional Committees Investigating the Iran-Contra Affair with Supplemental, Minority, and Additional Views*. 100th Cong., 1st Sess. H. Rept. 100–433, S. Rept. 100–216. Washington, D.C.: U.S. Government Printing Office, 1987.

U.S. Senate. *Alleged Assassination Plots Involving Foreign Leaders: An Interim Report of the Senate Select Committee to Study Government Operations with Respect to Intelligence Activities*. S. Rept. 94–465, 94th Cong., 1st Sess. Washington, D.C.: U.S. Government Printing Office, 1975.

———. *Assignment of Ground Forces of the United States to Duty in the European Area: Hearings before the Senate Foreign Relations and Armed Services Committees*. 82nd Cong., 1st Sess. Washington, D.C.: U.S. Government Printing Office, 1951.

———. *The Constitution of the United States of America: Analysis and Interpretations*. 92nd Cong., 2nd Sess., Document No. 92–82. Washington, D. C.: U.S. Government Printing Office, 1973.

———. *Current Military Operations: Hearings before the Committee on Armed Services*. 103rd Cong., 1st Sess., August 6, October 4, 7, 12, 13, 1993. Washington, D.C.: U.S. Government Printing Office, 1994.

———. *Current Military Operations in Somalia: Hearings before the Committee on Armed Services*. S. Hrg. 103–220, 103rd Cong., 1st Sess. March 25, 1993. Washington, D.C.: U.S. Government Printing Office, 1993.

———. *Department of Defense Response to the Persian Gulf Illness: Hearings before the Committee on Armed Services*. S. Hrg. 103–867, 103rd Cong., 2nd Sess., September 29, 1994. (Washington, D.C.: U.S. Government Printing Office, 1994.

———. *Documents Relating to the War Power of Congress, the President's Authority as Commander-in-Chief and the War in Indochina*. Committee on Foreign Relations, 91st Cong., 2nd Sess. Washington, D.C.: U.S. Government Printing Office, 1970.

———. "Executive Orders in Times of War and National Emergency." Senate Special Committee on National Emergencies and Delegated Powers, 93rd Cong., 2nd Sess., Committee Print. Washington, D.C.: U.S. Government Printing Office, June 1974.

———. *The INF Treaty Monitoring and Verification Capabilities*. S. Rept. 100–318, Senate Select Committee on Intelligence, 100th Cong., 2nd Sess. Washington, D.C.: U.S. Government Printing Office, 1988.

———. *Joint Chiefs of Staff Briefing on Current Military Operations in Somalia, Iraq, and Yugoslavia: Hearings before the Committee on Armed Services*. S. Hrg. 103–176, 103rd Cong., 1st Sess., January 29, 1993. Washington, D.C.: U.S. Government Printing Office, 1993.

———. *Meeting the Espionage Challenge: A Review of United States Counterintelligence and Security Programs*. S. Rept. 99–522, Senate Select Committee on Intelligence, 99th Cong., 2nd Sess. Washington, D.C.: U.S. Government Printing Office, 1986.

———. *Multinational Force in Lebanon*. S. Rept. 98–242, 98th Cong., 1st Sess. Washington, D.C.: U.S. Government Printing Office, 1983.

———. *Operation Restore Hope, the Military Operations in Somalia: Hearings before the Committee on Armed Services*. S. Hrg. 102–1100, 102nd Cong., 2nd Sess., December 9, 1992. Washington, D.C.: U.S. Government Printing Office, 1993.

———. *Principal Findings on the Capabilities of the U.S. to Monitor the SALT II Treaty*. Committee Print, Senate Select Committee on Intelligence, 96th Cong., 1st Sess. Washington, D.C.: U.S. Government Printing Office, 1979.

———. *Report of the Select Committee on Intelligence, U.S. Senate, Jan. 1, 1983 to Dec. 31, 1984*. S. Rept. 98–665, 98th Cong., 2nd Sess. Washington, D.C.: U.S. Government Printing Office, 1984.

———. *Situation in Cuba: Hearing before the Committee on Armed Services*. 103rd Cong., 2nd Sess., August 25, 1994. Washington, D.C.: U.S. Government Printing Office, 1994.

———. *Situation in Haiti: Hearing before the Committee on Armed Services*. 103rd Cong., 2nd Sess., September 28, 1994. Washington, D.C.: U.S. Government Printing Office, 1994.

———. *The Situation in Iran: Hearings before the Senate Committee on Foreign Relations*. 96th Cong., 2nd Sess. Washington, D.C.: U.S. Government Printing Office, 1980.

———. *Supplementary Detailed Staff Reports on Foreign and Military Intelligence—bk. 4—Final Report*. S. Rept. 94–755, Senate Select Committee to Study Governmental Operations with Respect to Intelligence Activities, 94th Cong., 2nd Sess. Washington, D.C.: U.S. Government Printing Office, 1976.

———. *The War Power after 200 Years: Congress and the President at a Constitutional Impasse: Hearings before the Special Subcommittee on War Powers of the Senate Committee on Foreign Relations*. 100th Cong., 2nd Sess. Washington, D.C.: U.S. Government Printing Office, 1989.

———. *War Powers*. S. Rept. 93–220, 93rd Cong., 1st Sess. Washington, D.C.: U.S. Government Printing Office, 1973.

———. *War Powers Legislation: Hearings before the Senate Foreign Relations Committee*. 92nd Cong., 1st Sess. Washington, D.C.: U.S. Government Printing Office, 1971.

U.S. Senate Committee on Armed Services. *U.S. Military Operations in Somalia.* S. Hrg. 103–846, 103 Cong., 2nd Sess., May 12, 21, 1994. Washington, D.C.: U.S. Government Printing Office, 1994.

U.S. Senate Committee on Foreign Relations. "Treaties and Other International Agreements: The Role of the United States Senate." 98th Cong., 2nd Sess. Committee Print. Washington, D.C.: U.S. Government Printing Office, June 1984.

U.S. Senate Committee on Foreign Relations and Committee on the Judiciary. *The ABM Treaty and the Constitution, Joint Hearings.* 100th Cong., 1st Sess. Washington, D.C.: U.S. Government Printing Office, 1987.

U.S. Senate Foreign Relations Committee. "Hearings on the Gulf of Tonkin, the 1964 Incidents." 90th Cong., 2nd Sess., February 20, 1968. Washington, D.C.: U.S. Government Printing Office, 1968.

———. "Hearings on the Southeast Asia Collective Defense Treaty." 83rd Cong., 2nd Sess., November 11, 1954. Washington, D.C.: U.S. Government Printing Office, 1954.

———. "Hearings on U.S. Commitments to Foreign Powers." 90th Cong., 1st Sess., August 16–September 19, 1967. Washington, D.C.: U.S. Government Printing Office, 1967.

———. "National Commitments." Senate Report No. 797, 90th Cong., 1st Sess., November 20, 1967. Washington, D.C.: U.S. Government Printing Office, 1967.

Vance, Cyrus. *Hard Choices: Critical Years in American Foreign Policy.* New York: Simon & Schuster, 1983.

———. "Striking the Balance: Congress and the President under the War Powers Resolution." In U.S. House of Representatives, *War Powers: Origins, Purposes, and Applications: Hearings before the Subcommittee on Arms Control, International Security and Science of the Committee on Foreign Affairs,* Appendix 5: 288–304. 100th Cong., 2nd Sess., August 4, 1988 and September 27, 1988. Washington, D.C.: U.S. Government Printing Office, 1989..

Vandenberg, Arthur, Jr., ed. *The Private Papers of Senator Vandenberg.* Boston: Houghton Mifflin, 1952.

Vandiver, Frank. "Lyndon Johnson: A Reluctant Hawk." In Joseph Dawson, *Commanders in Chief: Presidential Leadership in Modern Wars*: 127–143. Lawrence: University Press of Kansas, 1993.

Vyzhutovich, Valery. "Playing on People's Nerves: Both the Radical-Democrats and the Communist-Patriots Are Summoning the Specter of a State of Emergency to the Political Stage." *The Current Digest of the Post-Soviet Press* 44:45 (December 9, 1992): 5.

"The Waiting Game." *Commonweal* (November 23, 1990): 675–676.

"War Is Declared." *The Progressive* 51:11 (November 1987): 7.

"War Powerless." *The Nation* (October 22, 1990): 440–441.

"War Powers" *National Review* (November 19, 1990): 15.

"The War Powers Act." *Congressional Digest* 66:12 (December 1987): 290–291.
"War Powers Act and the Persian Gulf." *Congressional Digest* 66:12 (December 1987): 289.
"War Powers Resolution—RIP." *National Review* (August 23, 1993): 17.
"War Powers Time." *The New Republic* (May 17, 1993): 8.
Warren, Charles. *The Making of the Constitution.* Boston: Little, Brown, 1928.
Weeks, Douglas. "Legislative Power versus Delegated Legislative Power." *Georgetown Law Journal* 25 (1937): 314.
Weicker, Lowell, John Warner, Frank Murkowski, and John McCain. "Should Congress Move to Invoke the War Powers Resolution?" *Congressional Digest* 66:12 (December 1987): 296–303.
Weinberger, Caspar. "The War Powers Resolution—An Invitation to Disaster." *Forbes* (September 17, 1990): 29.
Westin, Alan. *The Anatomy of a Constitutional Law Case: Youngstown Sheet and Tube Co. v. Sawyer.* New York: Macmillan, 1958.
Westmoreland, William. "Vietnam in Perspective." *Military Review* 59 (January 1979): 34–43.
Weston, Burns. "Security Council Resolution 678 and Persian Gulf Decision Making: Precarious Legitimacy." *American Journal of International Law* 85:3 (July 1991): 516–535.
"Where Congress Fears to Float." *The Economist* 304 (August 15, 1987): 20.
Wilcox, Francis. *Congress, the Executive and Foreign Policy.* New York: Harper & Row, 1971.
Wilcox, Francis, and Richard Frank, eds. *The Constitution and the Conduct of Foreign Policy: An Inquiry by a Panel of the American Society of International Law.* New York: Praeger, 1976.
Wildavsky, Aaron, ed. *Perspectives on the Presidency.* Boston: Little, Brown, 1975.
———, ed. *The Presidency.* Boston: Little, Brown, 1969.
Will, George. "America's Inoculation by Somalia." *Newsweek* (September 6, 1993): 62.
Woodward, Bob. *The Commanders*: 306–307. New York: Simon & Schuster, 1991.
Wormuth, Francis. *The Vietnam War: The President versus the Constitution.* Santa Barbara, Calif.: Center for the Study of Democratic Institutions, 1968.
Wormuth, Francis, and Edwin Firmage. *To Chain the Dog of War: The War Power of Congress in History and Law.* 2nd ed. Urbana: University of Illinois Press, 1989.
Younger, Irving. "Congressional Investigations and Executive Secrecy: A Study in the Separation of Powers." *University of Pittsburgh Law Review 20* (1959): 755.

Index

Abel, Elie, 29, 215
Abramowitz, Morton, 105
Acheson, Dean, 215
Adams, Brock, 218
Adams, Charles, 27, 215
Adams, John, 28
Adler, David, 215
Advice and consent, 16, 33, 45, 46, 48, 55, 57, 58, 79, 81, 101, 105, 112, 113, 120, 138, 141, 142, 150, 159, 168
Africa Recovery and Food Security Act, 170
Aggregate powers, 26, 35, 37, 38, 39, 151
Agree to disagree, 5
Ajr, 167, 177
Albert, Carl, 103–4, 106, 112, 113
Allison, Graham, 215
All necessary means (measures), 3, 24, 53, 81, 83, 125, 133, 136–37, 147, 152–53
American Enterprise Institute, 40, 96, 112
Ange v. Bush, 35
Annexation of Kuwait (eternal merger), 125–26, 137

Armed conflict, 68
Austin, Anthony, 27, 59, 60, 93–94, 96, 177, 215
Authorized, Authorization, 113, 120, 127, 140, 156–58, 172

Baghdad, 134, 136, 151
Bailey, Stephen, 41
Bailey, Thomas, 215
Baker, James, 72, 140, 152, 162
Baldridge, Holmes, 37
Ball, George, 27, 215
Barber, James, 215
Barnet, Richard, 215
Barnhart, Michael, 177, 215
Barone, Michael, 216
Bartlett, Ruhl, 216
Basler, Roy, 216
Bass v. Tingy, 39
Benjamin, James, 162, 216
Bennet, James, 162, 216
Berman, Larry, 7, 27, 42, 59, 60, 216
Bessette, Joseph, 9, 27
Bestor, Arthur, 59, 97, 112, 113, 216
Bickel, Alexander, 59, 60, 74, 94, 216
Bickers, Kenneth, 226
Biden, Joseph, 141–42, 176

Binkley, Wilfred, 216
Biskupic, Joan, 60, 74, 143, 162, 216
Blair, Arthur, 162, 216
Blechman, Barry, 7, 177, 216
Blockade, 22, 26, 123–25, 127–30,
    132, 137, 143
Blum, Andrew, 216
Bondy, William, 41, 216
Bosnia-Hercegovina, 169–71
Bowen, Catherine, 27, 28, 216
Bowens, Gregory, 61, 72, 217
Boyd, Julian, 27, 29, 30, 217
Braestrup, Peter, 9, 217
Brant, Irving, 27, 39, 217
Braziller, George, 8
Breckinridge, Scott, 177, 217
Brewster, Daniel, 94, 96
Brown, Seyom, 217
Brownlow, Louis, 217
Brzezinski, Zbigniew, 72, 114, 217
Buckley, William, Jr., 217
Burnett, Edmund, 27, 29, 39, 217
Burns, James, 92, 217
Bush, George, vii, 4, 7, 34, 56, 60,
    64–65, 67, 70, 72, 74–75, 81, 83,
    94, 108, 112, 121–29, 131–34,
    138, 142–45, 147, 150–53, 157–
    58, 160–62, 170, 172, 175, 178,
    179, 217
Butler, Pierce, 18, 19
Byrd, Robert, 64, 102, 147, 159, 218

Cable, Larry, 7, 8, 60, 177, 218
Caldwell, Dan, 29, 108, 177, 218
Cambodia, 1, 8, 29, 51, 54, 55, 59,
    70, 73–74, 91, 97, 99, 103, 111
Campbell, Colin, 218
Caraley, Demetrios, 28, 40
Carmody, Cris, 218
Carpenter, William, 218
Carter, Jimmy, 102, 108, 110, 112,
    175, 179, 218
Chamberlain, Laurence, 218

Charter of the United Nations, 6, 53,
    63, 65–66, 69, 72, 82–83, 88, 148
Cheever, Daniel, 218
Cheney, Dick, 4, 61, 73, 153, 218
Chief Executive, 47, 133, 151
Church, Frank, 106
Church, George, 61, 71, 73, 108, 114,
    218
CIA, 168, 177
Clark, Jeffrey, 218
Clinton, William "Bill," 4, 108, 112,
    171, 175
Clodfelter, Mark, 7, 218
Clymer, Adam, 218
Coalition, 18, 147, 151–52, 159, 174;
    Forces, 130, 136, 142, 144
Cohen, Richard, 59, 218
Collective self-defense, 148, 156
Collidge, Francis, 219
Collins, James, Jr., 219
Colm, Gerhart, 41
Commander-in-Chief, 7, 9, 17, 26,
    27, 29, 31, 33, 40, 46, 49, 53, 56,
    59, 73, 83, 84, 86, 89, 92–93, 95,
    104, 113, 114, 120, 131, 133, 143,
    151, 167, 173, 177
Compliance with reservations, 119,
    168, 174
Concurrent resolution, 3, 7, 14, 83,
    88, 91, 98, 138–39, 154, 171, 174
Congressional consent (support,
    authority), 81–82, 121, 140, 151,
    154–55, 157, 174
Congressional Prerogative(s), 81
Consistent with War Powers (Resolu-
    tion), 107, 112, 114, 167, 173
Constitution(al), 6, 15, 16, 47, 143;
    Article I, 19, 20, 46, 53, 57; Arti-
    cle II, 16, 17, 27, 37, 46, 49; Arti-
    cle III, 25; Article VI, 46, 57;
    Article VII, 19; Article X, 19;
    Authority, 19, 29, 80, 92, 95, 98,

127, 139, 153, 172–73; Confrontation, 55, 172
Consultation, 6, 18, 23, 45, 48, 55, 57, 86, 101–8, 110–14, 119, 121, 141–42, 148, 150, 153, 155, 158, 161, 170, 172, 174
Conventional warfare, 5
Cook, Jacob, 28, 39, 219
Cooper, Ann, 219
Cooper, Joseph, 98, 219
Cooper-Church restrictions, 106, 114
Corwin, Edward, 16, 17, 27, 29, 57, 58, 219
Cotter, Cornelius, 98, 219
Covert action, 110
Coyle, Marcia, 218
Crabb, Cecil, Jr., 219
Cronin, Thomas, 219
Crovitz, Gordon, 219
C. Turner Joy, 2
Cuba, 29, 52, 124, 132, 149; Cuban Missile Crisis, 21, 22, 29, 70, 108
Curtis, Thomas, 219

Dames and Moore v. Regan, 41
Damrosch, Lori, 71, 92, 219
Davies, Susan, 219
Dawson, Joseph, 10, 177, 220
Declaration of war, 23, 26, 30, 59, 83, 94, 128, 130, 142, 153–54, 157, 168–69, 171
Declare(d) war, 17, 19, 20, 21, 22, 23, 24, 53, 69–70, 89, 143–44, 168–69
Defining moment, 56
Delegated: Authority, 68–70, 74; War, 6
Dellums v. Bush, 35, 40
Desert Shield/Desert Storm, 7, 34–35, 56, 65, 80, 108, 119–20, 142, 159–60, 169
Destler, I. M., 220
Detzer, David, 29, 220

Doherty, Carroll, 61, 73, 92, 220
Dole, Robert, xviii, 64, 141, 151, 159, 174, 176, 179–80, 216
Donovan, Robert, 8, 41, 59, 177, 220
Draper, Theodore, 220
Dugger, Ronnie, 220
Dumbarton Oaks, 63
Durenberger, David, 218
Dverin, Eugene, 59, 220

Eagleton, Thomas, xviii, 9, 10, 40, 60, 92–95, 97, 220
Economic Sanctions, 56, 123–24, 126–28, 133, 138–39
Edwards, George, 221
Eisenhower, Dwight D., 2, 8, 50–52, 70, 80, 82, 221
Elliot, Donald, 98, 221
Elliot, Jonathan, 29, 39, 221
Ellsberg, Daniel, 221
Elseworth, Oliver, 18, 19, 28
Elving, Ronald, 40, 108–9, 177, 221
Ely, John, 7, 8, 60–61, 74, 96, 98, 169, 177–78, 221
Embargo, 67, 124, 126, 128, 136
Emerson, John, 221
Ervin, Sam, 84, 94
Espionage, 109
Evans, Richard, 42, 59, 92, 98, 221
Executive, 172; Agreements, 40, 45, 49, 50, 52, 55–59, 61; Authority, 15, 111; Order, 41, 121, 127, 131; Power, 16, 33, 37, 38, 46, 49

Farrand, Max, 27, 29, 30, 57, 221
Fascell, Dante, xviii, 102, 107, 114, 167, 172–73, 176, 179
Faulkner, Stanley, 221
Federalist, 26, 28, 31, 39, 40
Fessler, Pamela, 221
Filch, Richard, 221
Finer, Herman, 222
Firmage, Edwin, 9, 222

Fisher, Louis, 28, 41, 47, 49, 58, 74,
     93, 97–98, 143, 222
Fitzpatrick, John, 58, 222
Fitzwater, Marlin, 132, 147, 150
Flynn, John, 222
Foley, Thomas S., 64, 70, 122, 147,
     151, 159, 171, 178
Ford, Gerald R., 102–4, 110–14, 175,
     180, 222
Ford, Paul, 27, 28, 29, 30, 39, 222
Foster v. Neilson, 58
*Fourteen Diamond Rings v. United
     States*, 58
Fourth Geneva Convention, 138
Fox, Edward, 107, 114, 167, 176
Franck, Thomas, 10, 71, 74, 109,
     115, 177, 222
Freedman, Lawrence, 222
Friedman, Norman, 222
Friedrich, Carl, 222
Fulbright, William, 53–55, 82–84,
     94–96, 113
Funderburk, David, xviii, 176, 180

Galloway, Joseph, 222
Garthoff, Raymond, 222
George, Alexander, 222
Gephardt, Richard, xviii
Gerry, Elbridge, 18, 19
Gibbs, George, 223
Gibson, Rankin, 98, 223
Gingrich, Newt, xviii, 175, 180
Glazer, Sarah, 223
Glennon, Michael, 10, 40, 60, 72,
     177–78, 223
Goldsmith, William, 58
Goldwater, Barry, 223
Goldwin, Robert, 40, 223
Goodman, Allan, 223
Gorbachev, Mikhail, 132–33, 145
Gore, Vice Albert, xviii
Graebner, Norman, 27, 40, 57, 223
Grenada, 102, 111

Gruening, Ernest, 94
Gulf Cooperation Council, 125
Gulf Crisis, 72–73, 138, 143
Gulf of Oman, 130
Gulf of Tonkin, 8, 70, 82, 92–93, 96;
     Resolution, 2, 27, 51, 53, 60, 79,
     82–85, 92, 95, 154, 169
Gulf War (conflict), 72, 91, 93, 132,
     138, 150

Haig v. Agee, 41
Halperin, Mortin, 223
Hamilton, Alexander, 17, 26, 27, 30,
     31, 36, 37, 39, 40, 58, 223
Hartmann, Robert, 112, 223
Haviland, Field, Jr., 218
Haynes, George, 223
Hebe, William, 41, 223
Helsinki Agreement, 132
Henkin, Louis, 223
Hitchens, Christopher, 223
Holland, Kenneth, 28, 112, 223
Holt, Pat, 112, 224
Holtzman, Elizabeth, 114
Holtzman v. Schlesinger, 98
Horn of Africa Recovery and Food
     Security Act, 170
Hostilities, 5, 38, 86–90, 101, 113,
     140, 142, 144, 148, 151, 163, 168,
     171
House Joint Resolution No. 77, 156–
     60, 163
Hoxie, Gordon, 28, 112, 224
Humanitarian aid, 120, 136
Human Shields, 130
Hunt, Gaillard, 27, 28, 30, 39, 224
Hussein, Saddam, 56, 75, 121, 129,
     133–34, 136–38, 143, 148, 151,
     152–53, 158
Hutchison, William, 28, 39, 224
Hyde, Henry, xviii, 175–76, 179

Imminent hostilities, 85–86, 88–89, 147–48, 155, 163, 169
Implied power, 49, 151
In accordance with, 112
Indochina, 92–93, 95, 97, 114
INS v. Chadha, 70, 74, 91, 98–99, 114
Intelligence Oversight Act of, 109
International Emergency Economic Powers Act, 122
Invasion of Kuwait, 17, 24, 70–71, 121–22, 129, 133, 136, 141, 145–46, 152, 159, 170
Invisible handshake, 5
Iran, 109, 111, 115, 170
Iraq, 4, 7, 51, 60, 65, 67, 69–70, 108–9, 114, 119–21, 122–23, 125, 133–34, 137, 139–40, 143, 161–62, 170; Invasion, 74, 121–22, 129, 133, 136, 141, 143–44
Israel, Fred, 224

James, Patrick, 94, 224
Javits, Jacob, 7, 26, 54, 82, 96, 224
Jay, John, 31, 36, 39, 58
Jayson, Lester, 39, 58, 224
Jefferson, Thomas, 23, 24, 27–30, 39
John, Ludwell, III, 30, 57, 74, 224
Johnson, Loch, 224
Johnson, Lyndon B., 2, 3, 7, 8, 27, 29, 38, 42, 52–54, 56, 59, 60, 73, 80–82, 85, 90, 92, 95, 96, 169, 177, 224
Johnston, Henry, 224
Joint resolution, 51, 53, 82–83, 87–91, 94, 120, 155, 157–58, 171, 174
Jones, Gordon, 224
Jordan, 129, 134, 136, 144
Judicial Branch (Judiciary), 6, 25, 26

Kaiser, Frederick, 98, 115, 224
Katzenback, Nicholas, 14, 15, 27, 39, 115, 224
Kaufman, Burton, 8, 177, 225

Kennedy, John F., 2, 8, 21, 22, 50, 51, 82
Kennedy, Robert, 225
Keown, Stuart, 97, 225
Kerry, John, 141, 154
Khmer Communist government, 103
Kimball, Warren, 59
Kinsley, Michael, 10, 225
Kissinger, Henry A., 9, 105, 113, 225
Koh, Harold, 39, 115, 225
Koh Tang Island, 103
Korea, 1, 8, 168
Korean Conflict, 1, 38, 177
Kuwait, 4, 7, 34, 56, 65, 68–70, 119–21, 123, 125, 132–33, 137, 139, 141, 143, 158, 161, 162, 171

Lacayo, Richard, 10, 74, 225
Lans, Asher, 40, 61
Laos, 1, 54, 80–81, 91
Lea, James, 225
League of Nations, 64
Lebanon, 112
Leckie, Robert, 225
Legislative veto, 98–99, 114
Lehman, John, 40, 98, 225
Leich, Marian, 141, 225
Leighton, Leon, 110, 179, 225
Leiken, Robert, 225
Liberation of Kuwait, 159–60
Libya, 103, 109, 111
Licht, Robert, 40
Lichter v. United States, 70, 74
Lincoln, Abraham, 26, 30, 57, 74
Line in the sand, 158
Lodge, Henry Cabot, 28, 30
Lofgren, Charles, 26, 30, 40–41, 225
Lomax, Louis, 225
Lowi, Theodore, 226
Lowry, Mike, 111, 226
Lowry v. Reagan, 111, 226
Luce, Robert, 58

McCain, John, xviii, 111
Maclay, William, 48, 58
McDougal, Myres, 40, 61
McGee, Gale, 57, 61
McNamara, Robert, 7, 95
Maddox, 2
Madison, James, 18, 19, 28, 30, 31, 36–39, 41, 58, 226
Major, John, 150
Make war, 23–25, 46
Mandelbaum, Michael, 226
Mann, Thomas, 40, 226
March, Carl, 58
Marini, John, 224
Mason, George, 18, 19
Mathews, Craig, 58, 226
May, Ernest, 8, 226
Mayaguez, 72, 102–6, 111–14
Meeker, Leonard, 95–96, 226
Merrill, Maurice, 74, 226
Merry, Robert, 226
Michel, Robert, 64, 94, 105, 151, 159
Miller, Judith, 226
Miller, Robert, 82–84
Mitchell, Broadus, 28, 30, 226
Mitchell, George, 64, 151, 159
Monroe Doctrine, 50, 57
Moore, Mike, 143, 226
Morgan, Clifton, 226
Morgan, Donald, 226
Morgan, Thomas E., 95, 113
Morris, Richard, 227
Morse, Wayne, 53, 82, 94, 96
Mueller, John, 227
Mulcahy, Kevin, 219
Murkowski, Frank, 111
Murphy, John, 58, 110, 227
Muskie, Edmund, 27, 40, 227
Mutual defense, 101; Agreements, 55, 168–69; Treaties, 51, 168
Myers v. United States, 39
Mylroie, Laurie, 226

Nathan, James, 61, 227
National Commitments Resolution, 13, 14, 15, 22, 27, 28, 51, 60
National Emergencies Act, 122–23, 127, 143
National emergency, 121–23, 143–44
NATO, xv, 15, 18, 68–69, 73, 147, 151, 177
Nelson, Gaylord, 82, 94
Neustadt, Richard, 10, 227
New York Times Co. v. United States, 41
Nixon, Richard M., xvi, 3, 4, 7, 9, 56, 70, 85, 89, 91, 97, 98, 107, 176, 227
Noah, Timothy, 227
Notification, 173
Novak, Robert, 42, 59, 92, 98, 221
Nunn, Sam, xviii

Oath of Office, 16, 46
Offutt, Milton, 227
Oneal, John, 93, 224
O'Neill, Thomas P., 112
One-third plus one vote, 91
Operation Restore Hope (Somalia), 170, 178
Ozal of Turkey, 150

Paige, Glen, 8, 177, 227
Palmer, Bruce, Jr., 7, 227
Palmer, Dave, 8
Palmer, Gregory, 7, 227
Patel, Faiza, 10, 71, 177, 222
Pause of good will, 149–50
Peace Powers Act of 1995, 174, 179
Permanent member, U.N. Security Council, 150
Persian Gulf, 60, 75, 92, 130, 139, 143, 147–48, 151–52, 154, 158–59, 161, 172, 176–77; Crisis, 72, 145, 148, 150, 162–63, 178
Peters, Richard, 227

Pickering, Thomas, 140
Pinkney, Charles, 18
Pious, Richard, 228
Prerogatives, 89, 112, 141. *See also*
 Congressional Prerogatives
Presidential Consultation, 89, 127,
 141, 153. *See also* Consultation
Presidential veto, 89
Prize Cases, 17, 24–26, 28, 30, 57, 74
Publis, 31
Pursuant to, 46, 86–88, 107, 122–23,
 141, 149, 167, 173, 178. *See also*
 Consistent with War Powers
Pusey, Merlo, 29, 59, 228

Quarantine, 21, 29, 108, 177
Quayle, Dan, 71, 122, 130

Rabkin, Jeremy, 219
Rachal, William, 28, 39, 224
Rauch, Basil, 228
Reagan, Ronald, 28, 102, 108, 110–
 12, 167, 177
Regan v. Wald, 41
Rehnquist, William H., 22, 29, 69–
 70, 73–74, 93, 228
Reisman, Michael, 228
Repeal War Powers Resolution, 174–
 75
Reporting, 86–89, 107
Reveley, Taylor, III, 40, 58, 228
Richards, Lois, 109
Richardson, Elliot L., 97, 103, 111,
 228
Richardson, James, 229
Ripened, 35, 40
Robinson, Edgar, 8, 229
Rockman, Bert, 229
Rogers, James Grafton, 229
Rogers, William D., 97–98, 111, 229
Rogers, William P., 97, 229
Roosevelt, Franklin, 20, 35, 50, 51,
 57, 59

Rosenberg, David, 229
Rosenberg, Douglas, 229
Rosenman, Samuel, 229
Rostow, Eugene, 42, 95, 229
Roth, Toby, 108
Rovine, Arthur, 229
Rubinstein, Alvin, 229
Rubner, Michael, 111, 229
Rumsfeld, Donald H., xv, xviii
Rusk, Dean, 51, 95
Russell, Richard, 3, 21, 22
Rutlidge, John, 19

Sanctions, 123–24, 126–28, 133, 138,
 144, 155
Saudi Arabia, 34, 51, 56, 120–21,
 125–27, 140–41, 145, 170
Savoy, Paul, 94, 229
Sawyer, Charles, 36, 37
Schachter, Oscar, 72, 93–94, 229
*Schechter Poultry Corp. v. United
 States*, 70
Scheffer, David, 229
Schlesinger, Arthur, Jr., 8, 96, 99, 229
Schultz, George P., 102, 107, 114
Schwartz, Bernard, 27, 230
Schwarzkopf, Norman, 4, 71
Scigliano, Robert, 9, 230
Scott, High, 111
SEATO, 18, 54–55, 83, 92, 177;
 Treaty, 8, 52–53, 73, 79, 81, 93
Security agreement, 126
Seiberling, John, 114
Seita, Raymond, 162
Senate Concurrent Resolution No.
 132, 170
Senate Concurrent Resolution No.
 147, 138, 141–42, 145–46, 154,
 156
Sense of Congress, 89–90, 170–72,
 174
Sense of the Senate, 13
Separability Clause, 89

Separation of Powers, 41, 103, 110, 115, 168

Sharp, U.S.G., 9, 230

Sheik Jabir al-Ahmad al-Jabir Al Sabah, 128

Sherman, Roger, 18, 19, 28

Shevardnadze, Eduard, 123, 132–33

Sidak, Gregory, 230

Sixty-day period (clock), 87, 90–91, 111, 157, 173

Slonin, Solomon, 58–59, 230

Small, Norman, 24, 28–30, 230

Smith, Jean, 230

Smith, Malcolm, 98, 219

Smoler, Fredric, 230

Smyrl, Marc, 230

Sofaer, Abraham, 23, 29–30, 230

Solarz, Stephen, 108, 173

Somalia, 108–9, 169–71, 174, 178–79

Sorensen, Theodore, 29, 230

Southeast Asia, 91–92, 94

Southeast Asia Collective Defense Treaty, 52, 54, 79, 80–83, 94, 171. *See also* SEATO

Soviet Missles, 22

Stennis, John, 82, 84, 96

Stevenson, Adlai, 230

Stewart v. Kahn, 70, 74

Strasser, Fred, 230

Stueck, William, Jr., 230

Summers, Harry, Jr., 7, 93, 230

Sundquist, James, 59, 230

Supreme Court, 22, 23, 25, 32, 37, 38, 69, 172

Syrett, Harold, 28, 30, 40, 230

Szulc, Tad, 231

Taft, William Howard, 17, 18, 20, 28, 57, 231

Take care clause, 16, 32, 39, 46, 49

Talbot v. Seeman, 25, 39

Threat to national security/peace, 121

Thurmond, Strom, xviii

Tomain, Joseph, 231

Towell, Pat, 231

Treaty, 14, 40, 45, 47, 48, 51, 52, 56, 58, 61, 69–70

Treverton, Gregory, 110, 231

Trigger, 66, 71, 90, 102, 107–8, 173

Truman, Harry S, 1, 2, 10, 36, 41, 50, 51, 59, 177, 231

Truman, Margaret, 8, 231

Tucker v. Alexandroff, 33, 40

Tugwell, Rexford, 40, 231

Tullis, Jeffrey, 9, 27, 216

Turner, Robert F., 9, 30, 97, 102, 110–12, 163, 231

Turnsill, Charles, 231

Undeclared War, 23, 40, 108–9, 128, 177

United Nations, 3, 7, 15, 18, 54, 63–64, 66; Chapter VII, 66–68, 72, 124–25, 130–31, 134–35, 144, 148–49, 177–78; Charter, 6, 53, 63, 65–66, 69, 72, 82–83, 88, 148; Participation Act, 127–28; Security Council, 2, 5, 6, 56, 63, 66–68, 70, 101, 103, 122, 124–26, 131, 136, 139–41, 147, 150, 152, 156

United Nations Resolutions, 63, 65, 67, 70, 83, 125, 128–29, 131–132, 134, 138, 146–47, 154; *No. 660*, 122, 124–26, 128–29, 131–32, 135–37, 139, 144, 149–50, 156, 160; *No. 661*, 124, 126–29, 131–32, 134–37, 139, 149, 156, 160; *No. 662*, 125–26, 128–33, 135–37, 139, 149, 156, 160; *No. 664*, 129, 131–32, 135–37, 139, 145, 149, 156, 160; *No. 665*, 131, 135, 137, 139, 145, 149, 156, 160; *No. 666*, 134–35, 137, 139, 149, 156, 160; *No. 667*, 135, 137, 139, 149, 156, 160; *No. 669*, 136, 139, 149, 156,

160; *No. 670*, 136, 139, 149, 156, 160; *No. 674*, 140, 149, 156, 160; *No. 677*, 141, 149, 156, 160; *No. 678*, 142, 148–50, 152–158, 160, 163; *No. 794*, 170
United States v. Anderson, 70, 74
United States v. Curtis-Wright Export Corp., 37, 39, 40–41, 70
United States v. Sweeny, 39
Use all necessary means, 3, 24, 53, 81, 83, 125, 133, 137, 147, 150, 152–53, 156–57, 169
Use of force, 18, 24, 90, 93, 128, 133, 161–63, 168, 172, 178–79
Use of military Force, 51, 86–88, 90, 92, 101, 103, 112, 142, 156–58, 160
U.S.S. Stark, 107, 114

Vance, Cyrus R., 102, 107, 110, 173, 179, 235
Vandiver, Frank, 8, 235
Vienna Convention, 135–36, 140
Vietnam, 2, 4, 5, 7, 8, 9, 22, 27, 39, 51, 53–54, 60, 74, 79–81, 85, 93, 95, 98, 138, 168, 176, 178
Vyzhutovich, Valery, 235

Wait-and-see, 137
War-making, 5, 19, 30, 40, 46, 57, 60, 74, 85, 94, 97
Warner, John, 111
War Power(s), xvi, 9, 15, 17, 18, 20, 25, 26, 30, 40, 58–59, 70–71, 73, 84, 92, 94–95, 98, 101–2, 104, 106, 108–10, 120, 127, 143; Reporting, 86–87; Resolution, xvii,

1, 2, 4, 5, 9, 10, 13, 61, 85, 91, 93, 107, 111–13, 121, 140, 142, 148, 151, 155, 157, 160, 163, 167–68, 170, 173, 175–76, 179
Warren, Charles, 236
Washington, George, 47, 48, 58
Watergate, 176
Watts v. United States, 33
Weeks, Douglas, 74, 236
Weicker, Lowell, 111, 236
Weinberger, Caspar, 236
Weisband, Edward, 222
Westerfield, Donald, 219
Westin, Alan, 41, 236
Westmoreland, William, 7, 236
Weston, Burns, 72, 93, 236
Wilcox, Francis, 57, 236
Wildavsky, Aaron, 40, 236
Will, George, 236
Wilson, Woodrow, 57
Withdraw unconditionally, 122, 126, 139, 147, 154, 156
Woodward, Bob, 10, 236
World War I, 168
World War II, 35, 36, 57, 168
Wormouth, Francis, 7, 9, 74, 236
Wright, Jim, 107, 114, 167, 177

Yemen, 122, 124, 132, 149
Younger, Irving, 110, 236
Youngstown Sheet & Tube Co. v. Sawyer, 37, 41
Yugoslavia, 109, 171

Zablocki, Clement, 106
Zurhellen, Owen, 105

About the Author

DR. DONALD L. WESTERFIELD is a professor in the Graduate School of Webster University. He has written three books for Praeger Publishers: *Mandated Health Care: Issues and Strategies* (1991); *Congressional Intent* (with Thomas Curtis) (1992); and *National Health Care: Law, Policy, Strategy* (1993). He has authored over one hundred published articles and research and professional papers. He is a reviewer/referee for two scholarly journals and a former Director of Webster University in London, England. He has been a Visiting Professor in Geneva, Switzerland; Leiden, Holland; and Vienna, Austria.

ISBN 0-275-94701-7

EAN

9 780275 947019

HARDCOVER BAR CODE